Building a Digital Home Entertainment Network

Multimedia in Every Room

TERRY ULICK

800 East 96th Street,
Indianapolis, Indiana 46240

Building a Digital Home Entertainment Network: Multimedia in Every Room

Copyright © 2006 by Que Publishing

International Standard Book Number: 0-7897-3318-8

Library of Congress Catalog Card Number: 2004111340

Printed in the United States of America

First Printing: August 2005

08   07   06   05   4   3   2   1

Trademarks

Warning and Disclaimer

Bulk Sales

Que Publishing offers excellent discounts on this book when ordered in quantity for bulk purchases or special sales. For more information, please contact

U.S. Corporate and Government Sales
1-800-382-3419
corpsales@pearsontechgroup.com

For sales outside of the U.S., please contact

International Sales
international@pearsoned.com

ASSOCIATE PUBLISHER
Greg Wiegand

ACQUISITIONS EDITOR
Todd Green

DEVELOPMENT EDITOR
Kevin Howard

MANAGING EDITOR
Charlotte Clapp

PROJECT EDITOR
Seth Kerney

COPY EDITORS
Kris Simmons
Rhonda Tinch-Mize

INDEXER
Ken Johnson

PROOFREADER
Juli Cook

TECHNICAL EDITOR
Eric Griffiths

PUBLISHING COORDINATOR
Sharry Lee Gregory

MULTIMEDIA DEVELOPER
Dan Scherf

DESIGNER
Anne Jones

PAGE LAYOUT
Eric S. Miller

Contents at a Glance

Table of Contents

II INSTALLING THE NETWORK

vii

III MANAGING A HOME ENTERTAINMENT NETWORK

About the Author

Terry Ulick is the president and co-founder of Good Time Networks, a next-generation TV network designed to deliver all-original TV shows via broadband delivery on home entertainment networks that blend TVs and PCs. Good Time Networks shows include *Good Time Wine*, *Camp U.S.*, *First Resorts*, *Snacks*, and *At Home with Tech*. His mission is to have people use their PCs to power their media experience in their homes.

Terry has extensive experience chronicling the revolutions in PCs and producing TV and new media. He has written extensively on PC use since the late 70s and was a columnist for *PC Magazine* in its earliest days. He went on to publish the first magazine on desktop publishing, *Personal Publishing*, in the mid-1980s and to write three of the first books on desktop publishing. In 1995, he co-founded the first online digital photo service for America Online, PicturePlace, an AOL Greenhouse Venture.

The combination of his editorial experience, his inside knowledge of the planning and delivery of entertainment-based content to PC/TV devices, and experience in creating a TV network makes him uniquely qualified to write this book.

Dedication

To my love, Lisa.

Acknowledgments

I would like to thank: Everyone at Que Books for their help in getting this book in good shape, including Todd Green and Kevin Howard. All of the manufacturers who provided information, products, and support with special thanks for Melody Chalaban at Belkin Corporation who went above the call of duty every step of the way, Michael Chin at Bite Communications for showing me what's coming next, Mark Mohammadpour at Weber Shandwick, and Darek Connole at D-Link Systems. To Jack Lydon for his generosity and support. Finally, ongoing and total respect and appreciation to David Fugate for being a super agent.

We Want to Hear from You!

As the reader of this book, *you* are our most important critic and commentator. We value your opinion and want to know what we're doing right, what we could do better, what areas you'd like to see us publish in, and any other words of wisdom you're willing to pass our way.

As an associate publisher for Que Publishing, I welcome your comments. You can email or write me directly to let me know what you did or didn't like about this book—as well as what we can do to make our books better.

Please note that I cannot help you with technical problems related to the topic of this book. We do have a User Services group, however, where I will forward specific technical questions related to the book.

When you write, please be sure to include this book's title and author as well as your name, email address, and phone number. I will carefully review your comments and share them with the author and editors who worked on the book.

Email: feedback@quepublishing.com

Mail: Greg Wiegand
            Associate Publisher
            Que Publishing
            800 East 96th Street
            Indianapolis, IN 46240 USA

For more information about this book or another Que title, visit our website at www.quepublishing.com. Type the ISBN (excluding hyphens) or the title of a book in the Search field to find the page you're looking for.

Introduction

Power Your Home with an Entertainment Network

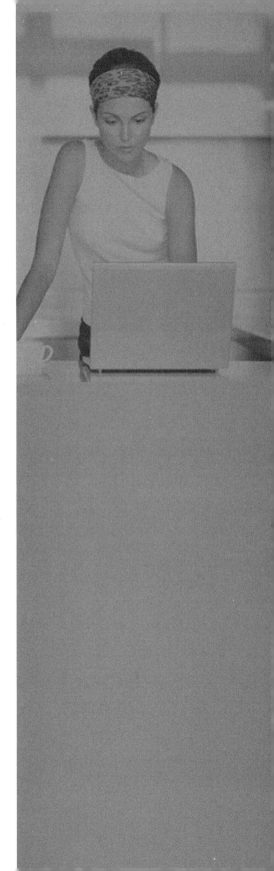

One of the most exciting uses for a personal computer is as an entertainment device. Most PCs being sold today are fully capable of being the hub of a whole-house entertainment center. Current home PCs can

- Play and record DVDs
- Play and record music
- Play and record TV, including HDTV
- Play and edit home videos
- Play music and videos from the Internet
- Play and record audio CDs and MP3s
- Play games both locally and online

In fact, properly configured, your PC is one of the most powerful entertainment devices you can find at any price. Even better, when you examine the cost of using your PC as your home entertainment center, you realize it is the lowest cost solution—after considering how much it would cost to buy dedicated consumer electronic devices that do all of the preceding tasks.

As you will discover in this book, you can create a home network of your PCs, TVs, stereos, and other entertainment devices. Once put together in a home entertainment network, those devices will become your new home entertainment center. It will be powered by your PC, and it will take full advantage of content from the Internet. With a home entertainment network in place, you can do the following:

- Use one PC to act as your entertainment "server" that will provide media content to other PCs and network devices throughout your home
- Share one Internet connection with other PCs and devices on the home network

- Bring all your entertainment devices, such as TVs and home stereos, together as a part of the home network

This book is about how you bring all those devices together to work with each other. If you are like most people, you probably have never thought of your TVs or stereos as devices that can work with your PC—but they can. In fact, you will learn that for a very low price, such devices become "extensions" of your PC and allow you full access to all the media content on your PC—and broadcast, cable, or satellite services, too.

Building with What You Have

One of the nicest things about building a home entertainment network using your PC as the "hub" is that you can put all the devices you currently own and use to work in the network.

If you have a fairly current PC (such as a Pentium PC with Windows XP), some TVs, and home stereos, you already have most of the key devices you need. A home entertainment network most often consists of the following:

- **Hub PC**—One main PC acts as the entertainment "server" and hosts media files for other devices to share.

- **Additional PCs**—If you have a laptop or other PCs in your home, they can all be part of the entertainment network.

- **TVs**—Your existing TVs find new life as "clients" in your entertainment network, getting content from the main hub PC.

- **Stereos**—Your stereos can play music from files on the hub PC, and they can also provide quality audio for TV viewing.

- **Portable devices**—If you have a Pocket PC or other portable media player device, you can use it to access content from your home entertainment network.

All the preceding devices can be put to work in your home entertainment network. You need to add a few items to allow this equipment to become a part of a networked home.

Adding Networking Hardware to Your Current Devices

PC-based home networking not only allows you to network PCs, but it also allows you to add TVs and stereos.

Your PCs need a network interface card (NIC) to become a networked device. Most current PCs come equipped with an Ethernet port, but if yours doesn't, it's easy to add one. Once PCs are equipped with Ethernet ports, you can connect them wired or wirelessly to a home entertainment network.

Just as a PC needs a network card, TVs and stereos need a way to become a part of the network. Unlike PCs, which are, of course, computers, TVs and stereos need network adapters that add a small amount of computing power. Called *media extenders*, the network devices that connect to your TV or stereo are small computers that pull audio or video from the hub PC and play them on TVs or stereos they are connected to.

As you will learn in this book, media extenders are an important part of a home entertainment network. Where you traditionally need a PC for playing media, you now can use a media extender. The device is ideal for the purpose, and it costs far less than a PC.

Putting Them All Together

When you take your PCs, add a home network, and add media extenders to your TVs and stereos, you have something totally new: a home entertainment network.

It brings the amazing media creation, storage, and media playing abilities of your PC to every TV, stereo, or portable media playing device in your home. You can access all the media content on your PC anywhere you like, using the devices that are easiest to use: TVs, remote controls, stereos, and even radios.

By bringing your entertainment devices together with your PC, you can also get at media content from the Internet on devices that have never been able to play such media before. Your home stereo can play streaming audio from Internet radio stations. You can watch videos of all types from the Internet on your TV. This setup gives your TV and stereo access to more content than any broadcast, cable, or satellite service can offer.

This book is your guide on how to put your computer devices and your entertainment devices together into a home entertainment network.

Who This Book Is for

You will definitely fit into one of the following categories:

- **Computer users of any skill level**—This book is for anyone who is comfortable using a computer. You do not need to be technically inclined. Home PC networking has become so easy that with a little patience, you can network your PCs and entertainment devices together.

- **People who use their PCs for media**—The book is also for people who love TV and music and love viewing their home videos and pictures on their PCs. You can take that experience and put it where it belongs: on your TVs and stereos.

- **People who love TV and music**—If you love TV viewing, this book is also going to show you how you can use your PC to record TV programs digitally and can change the way you think about watching TV. With TV shows recorded on your hub PC, you can watch them when it's best for you—and skip past commercials, if you choose.

It's also okay if you are a highly experienced, know-how-to-do-it computer user! A lot of the ideas in this book are about how to change the way you use media—not just how to hook up devices and configure your PCs.

What You Need to Use This Book

Users of this book should have at least one PC, a high-speed connection to the Internet (although dial-up will do if a high-speed connection is not available), and a TV source such as cable, satellite, or antenna near the computer. You also need some basic home networking equipment such as a wired or wireless router and network adapters for devices on the network. You can use your existing TVs and audio devices.

Icons Used in This Book

The following is a brief description of the icons used to highlight certain types of material in this book.

TIP OR STRATEGY
Each tip gives you additional information that adds to the topic under discussion. The information typically springs from something in the immediately preceding paragraph and provides a succinct suggestion that you might want to follow up while working through the chapter. In effect, a tip says, "You should try this as well."

NOTE
A note is just that: a note. Usually, a note provides information related to the topic under discussion but not essential to it for the purposes of working through that topic. A note says, essentially, "Here's an interesting point about the topic or something you might want to keep in mind."

CROSS-REFERENCE
The Cross-Reference icon refers you to other chapters that cover a point just mentioned in the text in more detail. You'll also sometimes find cross-references in parentheses.

How This Book Is Organized

I've divided this book into four main sections. After introducing you to the basic concept of a home entertainment network in this Introduction, it starts with planning your home entertainment network and then looks at installing it, managing it, and how to get the most out of it. The following sections describe briefly how the book is organized.

Part I: Planning Your Home Entertainment Network

This part will help you create a strategy and plan for your home entertainment network. It will identify all the places you can add PCs and entertainment devices in your home and identify the networking hardware and media extender devices you need to create your home entertainment network.

Part II: Installing the Network

This section will take you through the steps required to install all the hardware and devices for your home entertainment network. It will also guide you through creating the network using Windows XP and its networking tools and wizards.

Part III: Managing a Home Entertainment Network

With all your PCs and entertainment devices connected in your home entertainment network, this section will show you how to manage and administer it. It will cover how to share media files, record content, and establish viewing rights.

Part IV: Going Beyond the "PC" Network

Although a home entertainment network is built on PC-based equipment, you will be able to stop thinking of it as a computer-based activity. This section talks about how to leave the "PC" out of the home entertainment network and focus on media creation and playing.

Part V: Appendixes

A list of networking vendors plus third-party hardware and software that you can use in a home entertainment network appears in the appendixes.

Planning Your Home Entertainment Network

Part I

Planning the Right Home Entertainment Network for Your Home

To create a home entertainment network, you first need to create a wired or wireless PC home network. The speed and performance of PC-based home networks have reached a point where they can handle large media files in addition to sharing Internet connections and basic computer files such as spreadsheets. With a properly configured home network, you can make your PC the hub of your home entertainment system. It will be able to share videos, music, pictures, and media content from the Internet.

Regardless of what type of dwelling you live in, you can create a home entertainment network that allows you to access and share media files from your PCs and the Internet from just about any room. Using just about any combination of wired or wireless networks and Windows XP's networking wizards, home networking has never been easier—or more reliable.

To build a successful home entertainment network, good planning is essential. Unlike more traditional PC networking where desktop PCs and laptop computers might be connected for sharing data files, an entertainment network can include multiple PCs, TVs, media extender devices, portable computing devices (such as PDAs), and even stereos. The goal is to connect all those devices together to allow you to access media content such as recorded TV, video files, DVDs, music, and photos from anywhere in your home.

The most exciting development in networking the home is the addition of TVs and stereos to the network. It is possible to use one PC as an entertainment server that can be accessed by a stereo or TV connected to extender devices so you can play media files virtually anywhere in your home. The chapters that follow will explain how such connections are made, but for now, it is good to think of TVs and stereos as a part of the home entertainment network.

The first step in creating such a network is to make a plan that diagrams your home, identifies all the locations where you will have networked devices, and indicates what type of network connections you will use to bring them all together.

Making a Plan

It's a good practice to diagram your home network on paper (or using a diagramming program if you have one on your PC).

The first step is to create a drawing of your home layout. You will want to identify the following items:

• The overall layout and arrangement of your rooms

• Walls

• Location of phone jacks

• Location of cable or satellite jacks for TV services

• Location of cable modem or DSL connections

• Existing placement of TVs and stereos

• Existing locations of PCs

Figure 1.1 shows a typical three-bedroom home layout that has been diagrammed. It shows the key PC and entertainment device locations and where cable and phone/DSL jacks are located.

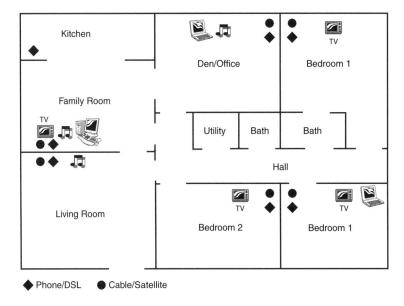

Figure 1.1

Example of the initial home diagram.

The initial diagram should show how your home is currently configured with your PCs and entertainment devices. What you are looking for are simple ways to connect the devices using a wired network when possible and locations where only a wireless connection makes sense.

The diagram will also help you in planning where you will want to expand your entertainment network. It might be attractive to add rooms such as the kitchen into your network or add new devices to bring PC-based media to locations where you might have had a TV but never thought of having a PC, such as a bedroom.

The most important items to identify on the plan are the following:

- **Internet access**—Access points to the Internet such as phone jacks or cable connections that are used for high-speed Internet connection.

- **Phone jacks**—Phone lines that can be used to access the Internet or possibly be used for some networking connections.

- **TV signal sources**—Jacks for satellite, cable, or antenna.

- **Primary PC**—Location of your primary PC—the one that is used to connect to the Internet.

It is entirely possible to build a home entertainment connection without being connected to the Internet, but that would limit your access to media content—and information about media content. More and more media content (such as movie rentals and TV shows and also music in both purchased and streaming forms) will be made available to you online, so connecting to the Internet is an important part of the network.

With a simple diagram pointing out the items listed here, you can begin crafting the plan for your home entertainment network. At this time, it is good to understand two basic types of networks that can be used: wired or wireless. The chapters that follow will explain each type in greater detail, but for now, it's good to simply know the key benefits of each:

- **Wired network**—A wired network uses a high-speed data cable to connect your devices. Wired networks are extremely reliable, fast, and inexpensive.

- **Wireless networks**—Wireless networks use adapters connected to your devices that send data using radio frequency signals much in the same way as cordless phones. They allow connection of devices where wired solutions are not practical and also allow portability. They are generally fast enough, and reliable enough, for media content.

Wherever possible, a wired network is attractive because it is highly reliable and very inexpensive. It also limits where devices can be located, and depending on your home layout, it might not be possible in all locations.

> **STRATEGY**
>
> Think of your home as a place where you should be able to access media content from any room or even your backyard or patio. By networking all your devices (PCs, TVs, and stereos) using a mix of wired and wireless networks, you can view or listen to media content wherever you are in your home.

Wireless connections help address any locations that cannot be wired and also create a great deal of flexibility in the network plan. Although wireless devices cost more than wired connections and are subject to interference and network slowdowns at times, current wireless standards are now good enough for media content in the home.

The good news is that you can mix and match both wired and wireless connections in your network. With that in mind, the next step in the process is to identify where, whenever possible, you can create wired connections in your plan.

Wired Networking: Running into Walls

With your diagram in hand, the next step is to examine if, and where, you can create a wired network. To do this, it is good to know the essential elements of a wired network connection.

Wired Network Basics

Wired networks are the best option for your home network. They are low-cost, fast, and reliable and provide a high level of security.

A wired network in your home requires the following basic components:

- **Router**—A router is a device that connects your PCs to each other and manages the network connections and flow of data. It also connects to your Internet connection and allows several PC devices to access that connection. You could purchase a simple hub or switch to make a connection between PCs, but a router offers the benefit of combining all your network management—your home network and the Internet—with one device.

- **Cables**—In a wired network, high-speed Ethernet cables are used to connect a network device such as a PC to the router. The cables can be quite long, and for most home uses, cable length should not be a concern.

- **Adapters**—Most newer computers come with an Ethernet adapter that will allow it to be connected to your wired network or router. If you have an older PC without an Ethernet adapter, you can add one as an expansion card (or PC card if it is a laptop). If needed, you can also purchase an adapter that will use a USB port for this purpose. Other devices such as printers, media extenders that allow you to connect a TV to view media from your PC, and even digital video recorders such as TiVo or ReplayTV also use adapters for connection to the network.

The primary wired network is a router connected to your main PC and the Internet and other devices connected to the router using adapters and cables.

Figure 1.2 shows a simple diagram of a wired network. Refer to this diagram when thinking of where you can build the wired portion of your home entertainment network: It will help you identify where your network "hub" should be located. The network hub is where your primary PC, router, and connection to the Internet are located.

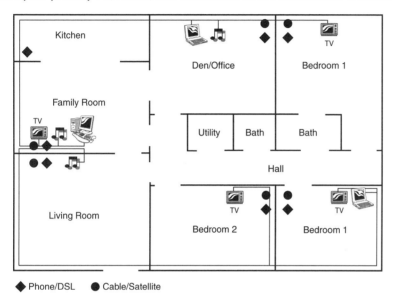

♦ Phone/DSL ● Cable/Satellite

Figure 1.2

Basic wired network diagram.

The main PC is used to configure the network and most often to manage it. For this reason, it is the "server" in your network. If you have been using a PC for a while, most likely you already have a primary location where your PC is located and you connect it to the Internet. This location might be the correct placement for the server PC in your home entertainment network, and the diagram will help prove whether it is the best location.

Benefits of a Wired Network

Wired networks have three main benefits in a home entertainment network:

- **Signal**—Because you use a cable running from the router to the networked device, the signal is fast and dedicated to connecting the devices. In general, it is not subject to interference and is the most reliable type of network connection.

- **Security**—Because the connection between your router and devices is wired, unlike wireless signals which can sometimes be tapped into by people nearby using the same type of wireless network, wired connections offer the least amount of security issues.

- **Cost**—When connecting devices that have Ethernet connections, the cost of networking is the price of the cables used between the devices. You can purchase even long networking cables, such as 50-foot, for under $30.

TIP

Wireless routers include ports for wired devices. This allows you to have a wireless router managing your wired network.

The security and signal benefits of a wired network make it an attractive option for a home entertainment network. Even better, because you can add a wireless router at any time and use its "wired" switched ports for your existing wired devices, it will work in a wireless configuration too.

Running Cables

Figure 1.3 shows cables and connectors that are used for a simple wired network. The cables can be purchased with connectors, or you can purchase the cable in bulk and add connectors yourself, allowing the creation of custom length cables. Chapter 4, "Getting the Right Networking Gear," will provide all the details about which cables you should purchase.

For most people, cables with connectors in set lengths work for most applications. The cables come in lengths from 6 to 100 feet, and you can also use couplers to connect two cables together to form a longer cable.

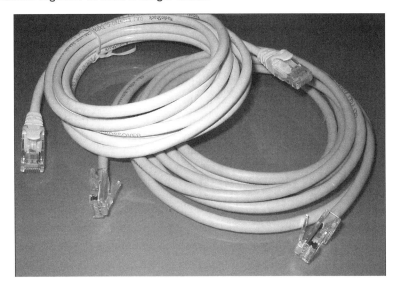

Figure 1.3

Basic wired network cables and connectors.

For larger homes, you probably need to buy cable in bulk and add connectors. This plan works best for long cable runs and where excess cable is not desired.

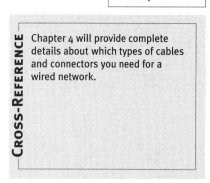

CROSS-REFERENCE

Chapter 4 will provide complete details about which types of cables and connectors you need for a wired network.

Dealing with Walls

One of the greatest challenges of a wired network in the home is appearance and running cable through walls. Many new homes are being built prewired for Ethernet. Each room has an Ethernet jack, and there is a central location for a router in the home where all the cables run to. If you are going to wire your existing dwelling, it is not that easy.

Each location in your home where you will have a computer or networked device will need a cable running from that location to your router. That means that you can run the cables around baseboards, over doorways, and through walls—but it is clunky and unsightly.

The best solution is to run the cables behind walls, if that is possible. It's a lot of work, and often studs and obstacles make it impractical.

If you have wall-to-wall carpeting, it is often possible to run cable around the baseboard and hide the cable between the carpet and the wall. It is still visible and can easily be displaced when cleaning or bumping it with your feet.

A practical solution to this problem exists if your home has a basement or an attic.

By running cable up to the attic, or down into a basement from the proper location in each room, you can wire your home without cables being visible. A typical wiring example appears in Figure 1.4.

If you have a single-level dwelling with a basement or attic, you should be able to run many of the cables for the wired network as shown in Figure 1.4. If you have a two-story home, it might still be possible to run wires behind walls, but the jump to the second story can be tricky.

Often, two-story homes have laundry shoots, heating vents, and other open paths between the levels where you can run cables. If that is the case, a good solution is to run the cables from the basement all the way up to the attic and then run the cables down into the second-story rooms.

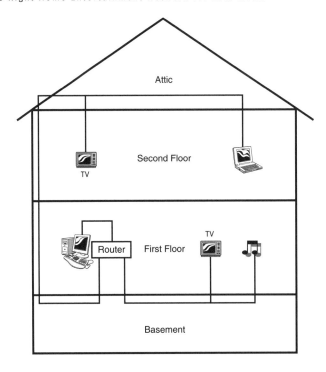

Figure 1.4

Running wires using a basement or attic.

FINDING PROS TO WIRE YOUR HOME

If a wired network is best for you and you aren't comfortable fishing wires up through walls around your home, another option is to hire a service to do the job for you. Telephone installers, network installation specialists, and home theater installers are all service providers you can turn to for help with running wires in your home.

When planning a wired network, you might encounter a situation where you can't run wires. Luckily, you can augment the wired network with wireless access points.

Wireless Networking: Homes Without Walls

Wireless networks allow the greatest ease of installation in most any dwelling—but there are specific drawbacks, as discussed earlier in this chapter. Security and network speed are each crucial issues to your home entertainment network. Although wired networks are the preferred solution for a stable and secure home entertainment network, there will be situations where a wireless network might be the best or only solution.

Wireless Network Basics

Wireless networking equipment is similar in nature to a wired network, but it uses radio frequencies to distribute data rather than cables. To add devices such as PCs, TVs, and stereos, you must attach a wireless adapter to them so that they can receive and send wireless signals.

The following items represent the basic equipment in a wireless home entertainment network:

- **Wireless router**—A wireless router is a device that connects directly to your hub PC and allows both wired and wireless connections to other PCs and devices. It connects directly to your Internet connection and allows other PCs and devices to access that connection. It uses radio frequencies to make wireless connections to other devices, making it the access point for the wireless network.

- **Wireless adapters**—Because the router uses radio frequencies to send and manage data, the PCs and devices must also have compatible wireless networking adapters connected to them to be a part of the wireless network. The adapters must match the same standard used for the router. Adapters can be PC cards that go in an available card slot inside a tower or desktop PC, a PC card slot for laptops, or a Universal Serial Bus (USB) adapter that attaches to a USB port on any PC, laptop, or device that has a USB port.

- **Cables**—Wireless routers include ports for wired connections to PCs and other devices. For wired connections, you need to use high-speed Ethernet cables to connect network devices to the router.

- **Standards**—Wireless network equipment such as routers and adapters are offered in a variety of industry standards. The standards assure compatibility and define the speed and performance of the wireless network. Although there are a number of standards, for a wireless home entertainment network, you need to work with the most recent standard, 802.11g. This standard is fast, reliable, and good for viewing video and music on the network. Chapter 4 covers wireless network standards in greater detail.

When making your home entertainment network plan, you should be thinking about where your devices will be located, how many there are, what type of adapter they will need, and also how far they are from your wireless router.

Benefits of a Wireless Network

Wireless networks offer amazing benefits in a home entertainment network:

- **Easy addition of devices**—Because there is no wiring required, it is easy to add a wireless device anywhere in the home. All that is required is that the device have a built-in wireless network adapter or that you add a wireless adapter to it.

- **Portability**—With a wireless networked device, it's not tethered to the location of a cable so you can easily move it and rearrange its location in the room or in the house.

- **Flexibility**—Wireless networks are flexible and can even allow the easy addition of visiting devices such as a friend's laptop or PDA, if they're equipped with a wireless adapter. The ability to move devices, easily add devices, and rearrange their locations makes a wireless network the most flexible solution for a home entertainment network.

Figure 1.5 looks at the sample home network, only this time using a wireless network.

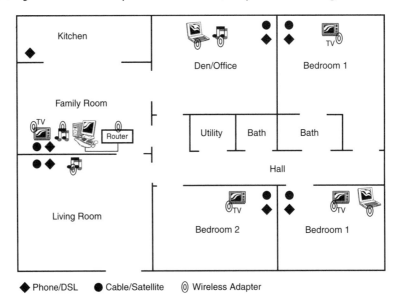

Figure 1.5

Wireless home network diagram.

As you will learn later in this book, you need to take some special measures to keep your home entertainment connection "secure" from outside signals or even people who can tap into your network with their wireless devices. Although security is an important issue, it can be managed and should not limit your incorporation of wireless networking.

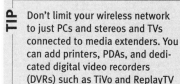

TIP
Don't limit your wireless network to just PCs and stereos and TVs connected to media extenders. You can add printers, PDAs, and dedicated digital video recorders (DVRs) such as TiVo and ReplayTV to your wireless network plan.

Dealing with Signal Strength

Wireless networks are fantastic because they eliminate all the wiring that is so hard to install in existing homes. The problem is that as with any wireless device, the signal strength can vary and even drop out occasionally. Think of the performance of other wireless devices you use, such as cordless phones and cell phones. As handy as they are, the quality of the signal sometimes degrades.

If all you were moving over the wireless networks was data such a word processor files or viewing websites, the performance issue would be easy to deal with. It would just take longer to access a file or a website, and such files are actually pretty small and don't take too long to send or receive.

In a home entertainment network, the wireless network is sending music files, video files, and streaming media. Not only are those huge files, but when you are listening to music or viewing a video, network slowdowns and dropouts are a big deal. It means the music or video stops!

Media player software such as Windows Media Player help with this a great deal by "buffering" media as you watch it. It grabs a bunch of video or music data and stores it in a buffer so that if there are dropouts, it uses the data stored in the buffer to keep playing without interruption. As good as that is, it's not going to overcome a really slow wireless connection or a complete dropout of signal.

In creating your home plan, here are some thoughts on locations that create possible signal problems:

- **Long distances**—Like any radio frequency device, a wireless network has a "range" where it works best. The devices list the ranges on their specifications. If you will be using a device that is on the edge of that range or outside of it, you might not have a strong signal.

- **Interference from structures**—Other radio frequency devices such as cordless phones, electrical panels, large metal structures, and even walls with metal studs all can block or interfere with wireless signals. Your home plan should identify such possible obstacles, and you should take them into account when deciding whether a wireless device will work well.

Overcoming Signal Problems

The good news is that with a plan, you can identify the devices that are too far away, or ones that might be prone to electrical or structural interference, and do something about it.

One way to get a better signal for a wireless device is to add or replace the antenna. If you are using a wireless device that has a removable antenna and you can replace it with a better one, this move might help you get a better signal.

Most wireless network brands offer "signal boosters" that you can locate in your home to overcome signal strength problems. These simple devices receive the signal from the wireless router or device and boost the signal to help it reach the other device. As range extenders, they do a great job, and although they do add to the cost of the network, they allow you to have a wireless network in tricky locations.

Another, very simple, technique is harder to plan but should be kept in mind. Sometimes, finding a better signal is simply a matter of moving the router or networked device around the room to see whether the signal gets better. This trick only works after you have the device and are using it, but it's something to keep in mind.

When all else fails, one of the great things about wireless routers is that they do allow you to add wired devices. They come with ports for wired connections and that might be the best answer for poor reception locations.

Mixing Wired and Wireless Networks

As we've seen, there might be no perfect way to create either an all-wired or all-wireless network.

Wired networks are reliable, secure, and low-cost—but they are hard to install in most existing dwellings.

Wireless networks allow the addition of network devices anywhere in your dwelling, but security, signal slowdowns, and reliability when playing media files are issues to be considered.

An excellent solution is to mix both wired and wireless together into one network solution. Figure 1.6 takes a look at the sample home diagram, this time using a mix of wired and wireless networking.

The rules of a mixed network are pretty simple:

- Whenever possible, for devices that remain stationary and can be wired practically, use a wired network connection.

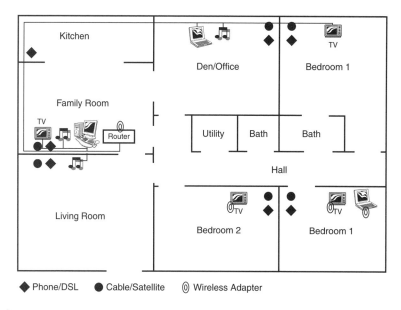

◆ Phone/DSL   ● Cable/Satellite   ⦿ Wireless Adapter

Figure 1.6

Home entertainment network using both wired and wireless networking connections.

- For locations that cannot easily be reached using a wired connection, use wireless adapters.

- For devices that require portability, such as a laptop computer, use wireless adapters.

Mixed Network Plan

In creating the plan for your home entertainment network, it might be tempting to go with all-wireless and endure some network slowdowns occasionally. Although an all-wireless network might work well, it is a good idea to develop your plan using a mix. That way, if the wireless performance is not ideal, you can fall back to wired runs where needed.

Because video, more than anything other data type, requires high bandwidth and a reliable signal, it is good to identify which devices in your plan will play video and make that a strong consideration for a wired connection.

Locations that primarily play music or view photos are much better suited for wireless connections. Music and photos require less bandwidth and are more forgiving in general.

STRATEGY

Try wireless networking first. Because you most likely need to use wireless for parts of your dwelling, you will start with a wireless router. If signal strength and performance are satisfactory, you might want to go with wireless throughout. If the quality of signal strength is not adequate, use the wired ports on the wireless router to connect your devices with a wired connection.

Now, look at the plan, as shown in Figure 1.7, with locations that are best served by a wired connection. Any location that connects to a TV or a PC playing video are now identified as wired. Locations that are easy to wire can be wired but can also be connected wirelessly if you choose.

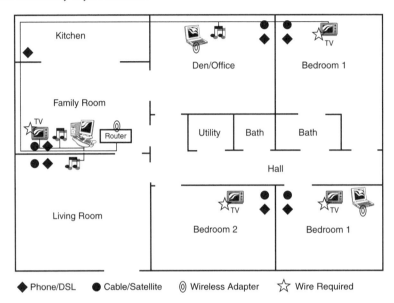

Figure 1.7

Plan modified to identify "wired-only" locations.

At this point, you have developed your plan to meet the realities of your dwelling and identified the uses of each device in the network, what type of connection is best suited for both the location, and for the type of media that will be viewed at that location.

The final consideration for your plan is understanding how demanding TV and video can be in a home entertainment network.

Making Sure the Network Can Handle Media

As mentioned in this chapter, one of the most important requirements of a home entertainment network is its ability to handle video files.

Throughout this book, you will learn that you can record and share TV shows and home videos and access streaming video content from the Internet. In a home entertainment configuration, you want to store video files such as recorded TV shows on your main computer and allow other devices on your network to view them.

Wired networks, using Ethernet connectors and cables, are capable of moving data at 100mps (megabits per second). That is great for video file sharing.

Wireless networking standards are now fast enough to distribute video and rich media. The "g" standard, 802.11g, operates at speeds up to 54mps. This is just about the minimum speed for handling rich media files such as video. Considering that wireless networks do slow down due to conditions in your home, using an even faster wireless solution is desirable.

Recently, many manufacturers have begun offering "turbo speed" mode wireless network devices under the 802.11g standard that can increase data transmission speeds by about 35%, meaning rates close to that of a wired network. That makes them close, in concept, to a wired network.

The faster data transfer rate helps overall, and even if the wireless network has a slow-down, it still is moving data pretty fast.

By combining a wired network at 100mps and a wireless high-speed mode network that can operate at 54mps or faster, you will have a home entertainment network that can handle video—and all the other media files such as music and photos that you will be using.

Summary

You can create a home entertainment network capable of sharing music, video, photographs, recorded TV shows, and other rich media using wired or wireless networking equipment or a combination of both. Operating at data transfer rates of up to 100mps, wired networks are reliable and low in cost. Wireless networking equipment using the 802.11g standard can move data at speeds of 54mps or even higher when using high-speed mode equipment. Making a good plan of your dwelling prior to purchasing networking equipment allows you to identify all the locations that can work with a wired network and those that need a wireless networking solution.

Configuring Your PC As an Entertainment Server

Personal computers have come a long way since their inception. Originally used as, well, computers, they have become so capable and powerful that they are being used for everything from special effects for motion pictures to navigation systems for NASA space flights.

PCs are especially well suited for music, video, and graphics. As an entertainment device, they are well on their way to making stereos, photo albums, CD players, DVD players, and even TVs obsolete. Figure 2.1 shows a new generation of PCs dedicated to being "media centers" for your home.

Think of how PCs have changed music. You can "rip" your CDs and then burn your own custom mix CDs for your car or home. Rather than go to the store to buy a CD, you can buy just the songs you want online and then burn them using your own CD-R drive. And if you are like many people, you listen to music directly from your PC using a good set of powered speakers connected to it, and your stereo is getting dusty.

With the release of Media Center Edition PCs (using Microsoft's exciting Media Center operating system), PCs are being used as TVs. You connect your TV to your PC, and you can watch and record TV programs.

The PC is one of the best digital video recorders you can get. PCs are changing how we watch TV, just the way it did in how we buy and listen to music.

You don't have to purchase a Media Center Edition PC to get all those benefits. You can upgrade your existing PC with a TV tuner card, a video card that allows you to use a regular TV as a monitor, and upgrade your sound card for surround sound. Those upgrades will turn your PC into a media center for your home.

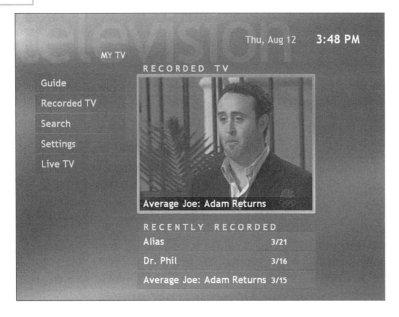

FIGURE 2.1

TV finding a new home on PCs, as shown here with Media Center PCs.

STRATEGY

Planning on purchasing a new PC? Consider a Media Center PC using Microsoft Media Center as the operating system. It comes configured, out of the box, as a full-blown media PC capable of viewing and recording TV, playing all media with a simple TV-based user interface, and you can connect it to a TV, a computer monitor, or both. Even better, it makes a great entertainment server for your home.

With its amazing media playing and recording capabilities, a PC is the next entertainment center in the home. But who wants to sit in front of a PC to watch TV or listen to music? And wouldn't it be great if you could take all the media on the PC and use it anywhere in the house?

That's where a home entertainment network comes in. It allows you to use the media content stored on one main computer with other PCs and even TVs and stereos located anywhere in your home. The network distributes the files for other devices to use, and the main PC connected to the router essentially becomes an entertainment "server."

This chapter looks at the requirements for an entertainment server and helps you know whether your current PC is up to the task.

Making Sure That Your PC Can Network

After making your home entertainment network plan, the next step is to take a hard look at your PC and make sure it has what it takes to be a network entertainment server.

The first requirement for successful networking is to have Windows XP Home Edition or Windows XP Professional installed on your PC. Windows XP is essential for a number of reasons. It was designed to be a networked product, it offers networking security, and it has a number of wizards and tools that make setting up a home network easier than with any previous version of Windows.

If your PC is running a previous version of Windows such as Windows Me, Windows 95, or Windows NT/2000, you should upgrade to Windows XP and take advantage of all its networking and file sharing features. This book will assume that your PC has Windows XP installed.

Windows XP requires the following as the minimum equipment to run the operating system:

- PC with 300MHz or higher processor recommended; 233MHz minimum required. Intel Pentium/Celeron family, AMD K6/Athlon/Duron family, or compatible processor recommended.

- 128MB RAM or higher recommended (64MB minimum supported; might limit performance and some features).

- Super VGA (800×600) or higher resolution video adapter and monitor.

- CD-ROM or DVD drive.

- Keyboard and Microsoft Mouse or compatible pointing device.

The preceding requirements allow Windows XP to operate, and it might be possible that your computer is at or near those specifications. Playing media files, functioning as a media server, and running a network all require a more powerfully configured PC. You will want to consider the following as essential for a home entertainment networked PC:

- **Processor**—Most PCs being sold today have processors in the 2.0GHz or greater range. If you are buying a new computer, it is good to purchase one with an Intel Pentium processor of at least 2.4GHz or greater. If you are working with an existing PC with a slower processor, you will probably be okay if it is in the 1GHz or higher range.

- **RAM**—The rule here is simple: You can't have too much RAM. Even more important than processor speed, RAM helps with the complex multitasking networking and media playing your PC will be performing. If you can, have at least 512MB of RAM as your starting point.

- **Hard drive**—Media files take up a tremendous amount of hard drive space. A typical uncompressed video file can be as large as 1GB for each minute of video! When combining photo files, music files, and video files, even a large hard drive fills up fast. A good hard drive size for your hub PC is 120GB or greater. In addition to a large hard drive, it is good to have a fast drive. Older hard drives spin at 5400rpm, but you should only consider 7200rpm drives if you are buying a new computer or upgrading your existing hard drive. Faster spin times and a larger drive cache (8MB or better) help serve glitch-free video to more than one PC or TV.

- **Display card**—For your primary PC, you should have a display card that is capable of sending a video signal to both a computer monitor and a TV. The card should have a video graphics adapter (VGA) or digital visual interface (DVI) connector for a computer monitor and an S-Video connector for TVs. Because display cards are essentially small computers with their own processors, they also have RAM on them. Look for at least 64KB of video RAM, with 128KB being ideal for dealing with video and support of both a TV and a computer monitor at the same time.

- **CD-ROM and DVD drives**—The cost of CD and DVD burners is now so low that there is no reason not to have a DVD burner. You can get a DVD+/- RW 8X speed DVD burner for around $100, and it will allow you to burn CDs and DVDs in both the + and – formats and play CDs, video CDs, and DVDs. In a ideal configuration, you have two of these drives if your computer has two open bays.

- **Keyboard and mouse**—Because you are using your PC as an entertainment device, the last thing you want is a cord between your PC and you from the couch! Purchase a cordless keyboard and mouse.

- **Network connection**—Newer PCs come equipped with an Ethernet port. This is required for a wired network or a wireless network. Routers connect to your PC using an Ethernet port. If your computer does not have one, you need to add a 10/100 Ethernet card. If you have a desktop or tower PC, you can add one in an existing card slot. Laptops can use a PC card version.

If you take an existing PC and add RAM, a large and fast hard drive, a network card, and a display card that supports TV output; and it is operating with Windows XP—it will be capable of supporting your home entertainment network.

The preceding configuration makes your computer capable of running a network, but you also want to think about what will make it good at playing and working with media.

Adding TV and FM Tuner Cards

Figure 2.1 from earlier in this chapter shows a PC playing TV. That means that you need to get TV signals into your PC. A TV tuner card is the device that allows you to bring TV signals into your computer. With it, you can watch TV and record TV programs to your hard drive.

As its name implies, a TV tuner card "tunes" TV stations in the exact same way as your TV does. The TV tuner card connects to an antenna, cable, satellite box, or even a video source such as a VCR or analog port of a camcorder.

The standard TV tuner card takes the analog TV signal and converts it to a digital signal that can be used by your PC. If you have HDTV, you can purchase an HDTV TV tuner card, which brings the digital HDTV signal into your PC.

To view that signal, most TV tuner cards come with TV viewing software that essentially turns your PC into a TV, displaying the TV signal on a computer monitor or a TV connected to your PC display card. Many TV tuner cards come with remote controls and you can channel surf the channels just as you would any TV.

So the big question: Why not just watch a regular TV?

When you use your PC as your TV, you gain all the benefits of digital video recording. Those benefits will forever change the way you think of TV viewing. They include the following:

- **Time shifting**—As a digital stream of data that is actually being stored and buffered on your hard drive, the TV signal that you are viewing can be paused, rewound, fast-forwarded, and returned to live TV. Called "time shifting," it allows you to control your TV viewing at all times. If the phone rings, you can pause the program you are watching and then start playing at that point when the call is over. If you see something that you want to view again, you can rewind the program. You can start watching a program and walk away, and in about 15 minutes, you can come back, begin watching from the beginning, zip through the commercials, and regain about 15 minutes of your life for more important activities.

- **Recording**—With a large hard drive, you can record a lot of TV programs. After they are recorded, you can view them with all the benefits of time shifting listed and have the benefit of watching shows when you want rather than when they are on. Even better, after a show is recorded, you can save the show to a DVD using your DVD burner. This frees up space on your hard drive and allows you to archive your favorite shows.

- **Watching one show while recording another**—You can watch a recorded show while a live show is recording. Because your shows are recorded as files on your PC, it also means you can watch recorded shows from other PCs and devices on your home entertainment network.

- **Scheduling recordings**—TV tuner cards often come with electronic program guides (EPGs) that allow quick and easy scheduling of shows. You can find shows by time and date but also do searches on show titles, names of actors or characters, and types of shows and genres. It is even possible to schedule recordings from a remote location. Using the Internet, you can schedule recordings on your home PC while you are away, such as on a vacation or at work. Neat!

TV tuner cards are a key part of building a home entertainment network PC. Recording TV, time shifting, and sharing programs will be a big part of your configuration.

If you have a standard desktop or tower PC, you want to get a TV tuner card that fits into a Peripheral Component Interconnect (PCI) card slot in your PC. As shown in Figure 2.2, the TV tuner card has a set of connectors almost identical to those found on the back of your TVs. Connectors include the following:

- **Antenna in**—This connector is a coaxial cable connection. You can connect a standard antenna to it or use the coaxial TV-out connector from your cable or satellite box. This is a standard connection found on most all set-top boxes from cable or satellite services. This connection carries both TV signal and sound to your PC. For HDTV cards, you connect an HDTV antenna.

- **S-Video in**—You can obtain a better signal using the S-Video connector if your cable or satellite set-top box has one. This connection only carries a video signal, and it separates the color information from the brightness information and delivers a cleaner picture. Depending on the TV tuner card, the audio-out from the set-top box connects directly to audio-in connectors on the TV tuner card or to the audio-in connector on your PC's sound card.

FIGURE 2.2

TV tuner card showing antenna and S-Video and audio connections.

After you install the TV tuner card in your PC and make the appropriate connections to your antenna, cable, or cable/satellite set-top box, you can start watching and recording TV on your PC—that is, after you install the TV viewing/recording software that came with the card. You need to use the Settings menu in the software to identify your TV source (antenna, S-Video, or component connections).

If you are using a set-top box as the TV source, you also need to make appropriate connections for changing the channels on the set-top box. High-end TV tuner cards come with a remote device that you place in front of the set-top box. It acts the same way as a remote control and changes the channels from the TV viewing/recording software.

TV Tuners for Laptops

If you are using laptops, you need to get an external TV tuner. A number of USB TV tuner cards, as shown in Figure 2.3, allow you to have all the benefits described earlier.

The USB TV tuner simply connects to a USB port on your laptop. You connect your TV source in the same way and use the same type of TV tuning and recording software. One key difference is that most USB TV tuners do not offer the remote control found with many card-type TV tuner cards.

FIGURE 2.3

The USB TV tuner, ideal for laptops.

FM Tuners

High-end TV tuner cards often offer FM radio tuning in addition to TV tuning. The card has an extra coaxial connector for FM signals. When you connect a simple FM radio antenna to this connection, you can listen to FM radio broadcasts on your PC. Just as with TV, you can time-shift radio broadcasts. Being able to pause and replay radio is a great feature.

The TV/FM tuner card comes with software that allows you to tune to FM stations, set presets, and time-shift. Although it is possible to record FM radio, for legal reasons (meaning copyright laws and pressure from the music industry), recording FM broadcasts is generally not a feature that is included.

DVR Software

After you install a TV tuner for computers, the next step is to install the software that allows you to watch and record TV. The software for recording is often referred to as DVR (digital video recording) or PVR (personal video recording) software.

CROSS-REFERENCE

Chapter 12, "Managing Media Content Across the Network," contains more information on viewing TV on your PC and scheduling recordings.

After you install the TV tuner card, you can use the software that came with your device. You can also find other DVR software and electronic program guides that will schedule recordings on your PC using your TV tuner device.

One example of such a source is Titan TV (www.titantv.com). This website contains TV listings for broadcast stations, and each show contains a red "record" button, as shown in Figure 2.4. When you click on the button, it schedules a recording of the show using your PC's TV tuner card and DVR software.

Having a choice of TV recording software and electronic program guides is a good thing. Electronic program guides are only as good as the accuracy of their show times and descriptions. A site like Titan TV uses real-time schedule information from broadcasters, so it's very accurate. Description of shows, ways to find programs using searches, and ease of use are also key factors.

Chapter 12 will cover scheduling and recording shows in greater detail.

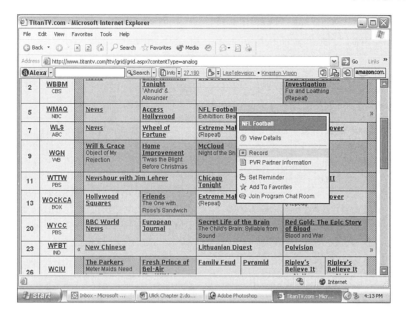

FIGURE 2.4

Scheduling TV recordings on Titan TV.

Having Enough Storage

Even when the files are compressed, digital video still is a "hog" when it comes to eating up hard drive space. With the ability to record TV shows, create vast music libraries, and store your entire photo library (now and pictures yet to be taken) on your hard drive, be sure you have enough storage.

The good news is that hard drives are really inexpensive and it's easy to upgrade your drive with either internal or external hard drives.

There are three main considerations when adding or upgrading your PC storage:

- **Cost per GB**—Drives are available from a number of manufacturers, and today's drives are extremely reliable—even from manufacturers that you might not be familiar with. At the end of the evaluation process, it comes down to cost per gigabyte of storage. As a rule, you do not want to spend more than $1 per GB for an internal hard drive. With sales, rebates, and smart shopping, you should be able to find a great drive for well under that price. External hard drives allow you to expand storage if there is no bay open for adding an internal drive, but they cost more. You can find a good external hard drive, with rebates, for as low as $1.20 per GB.

- **Drive speed and cache**—For your home entertainment PC, you should only purchase a hard drive that is 7200rpm or better. (Don't get one of the older 5400rpm drives, as attractive as the price and claims might be.) It should also have a "cache" of 8MB or greater. The cache is the area that keeps the data while the drive is searching and recording and reading at the same time. (Remember how you can watch and record a show at the same time? The cache helps with that.)

- **Internal or external**—If you have a USB 2.0 port or a Firewire (IEEE 1394) port, you can add external hard drives. This is an attractive way to expand your storage because you can keep the hard drive that is currently in your PC. You can add as many external drives as needed, and they can be easily moved from one PC to another (such as taking the drive with you for use with your laptop away from home). External drives cost more than internal drives, but you should be able to find one on sale or with a rebate for around the $120 per GB goal.

Choosing Drive Size

When working with video files and media files, get the largest drive you can. Most computers are sold with relatively small hard drives, such as 60GB or 80GB. When you consider that just the operating system, temporary file allocations, and a basic set of programs occupy around 10GB in most PCs, you need to make sure that you have room left for media files.

> **STRATEGY**
>
> A good strategy for storage is to dedicate the main C drive in your PC to just the operating system, program files, and temporary Internet files. For all data and media files, use a second drive or an external drive. This arrangement increases ease of file management, media files never encounter lack of space used by a temporary file allocation, and you get better performance overall because the media files are not competing with the operating system or program functions on the main drive.

In a networked configuration, your main "hub" PC also stores files from other PCs in your home. It is good to put all your media files on one main drive for all other PCs and devices to access. This adds to the space required on your main PC that acts as the server.

When adding a drive, start with 120GB as the minimum and look to find a good deal on a 160GB or preferably a 250GB drive. The larger the drive, the better the cost per GB in most instances. Shy away from the largest sizes. They are usually the newest arrivals and carry a premium price. For example, you might be able to find a 250GB drive for about $200, but a 500GB drive is $550. Remember, if you are using external drives, you can add several drives to your PC so it might be better to add two 250GB drives than one 500GB drive from a cost perspective.

Choosing Internal or External Drives

There are a number of things to consider when it comes to choosing an internal or external drive.

If you have a good internal drive (such as a 80GB 7200rpm 8MB cache drive), it makes sense to keep it in place and use it. Because the primary C drive will be used for the operating system, programs, and temporary files, you would benefit by keeping it as your primary C drive. It probably has been partitioned to have a D drive, and you can use that as a storage area if you choose.

If you replace it, you lose the value of a perfectly good hard drive. The cost of the new drive is not just its cost; it's the cost of the storage you are losing on the existing hard drive.

A better solution is to add a second hard drive if your PC has a bay and a connector for it. Most desktop and tower PCs have an open bay and connectors for a second hard drive. If that is the case, keep your current hard drive and add a second drive.

Figure 2.5 shows the connectors on an internal hard drive. Adding the drive is a simple process, where you connect a cable to the hard drive, connect the power cable to it (there will be extra power connectors in your PC), and set one jumper pin following the instructions that came with the drive.

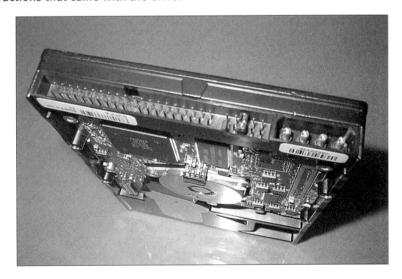

FIGURE 2.5

Connections for data cable and power connectors on an internal hard drive.

Most all hard drives come preformatted, so after you connect the hard drive, it is ready to use. If your main hard drive is still being used, because it is most likely partitioned as C and D drives, your additional hard drive appears as the next available drive letter, such as E.

Hard drives come with formatting and partitioning utilities that allow you to reformat the drive and to create multiple partitions, such as a 150GB E drive and a 100GB F drive when using a 250GB hard drive.

TIP

As an easy add-on solution for storage, external hard drives are great, but they do add "clutter" to your PC. If you are using your PC in a living room or family room, adding little boxes might not be the most attractive solution. You can tuck additional hard drives away in a cabinet or behind other devices by having a longer cable—but be sure to read the maximum cable length instructions that come with your drive.

Partitioning takes one hard drive and divides it into multiple partitions. From your My Computer folder, it appears that each drive is a standalone hard drive, but each is actually a partition on one physical drive.

You might do best with leaving the additional hard drive as one large partition when dealing with media files. Regardless of your preference, if you do plan to partition the drive, do so prior to storing data on it—partitioning deletes files.

If your PC doesn't have an extra drive bay, or if you simply want to add more storage in an easier way, external drives are a great solution.

Figure 2.6 shows an external hard drive. It's small and easy to connect and can be placed on or near the PC. If you add more than one drive, they stack easily.

FIGURE 2.6

Placing external hard drives just about anywhere.

Current external hard drives come as USB 2.0 drives, Firewire IEEE 1394 drives, or configured as both. To use the drive, your computer must have one of these types of connections. USB 2.0 is becoming standard on all new PCs, and you can add a USB 2.0 connector to an older PC or laptop running Windows XP. The same is true for Firewire. If your PC or laptop doesn't have a Firewire connection, you can upgrade it.

Which is better? They are both very fast interfaces that work well for media files. USB 2.0 is a bit more common, but as you will learn later in the book, to work with digital camcorders, you need Firewire connectors on your PC. If you have to make a choice, USB 2.0 is good, and a dual-connector drive with both connections is better.

Figure 2.7 shows a drive with connections for both USB 2.0 and Firewire. Such a drive is easy to use on a number of different PCs. Because USB 2.0 is backwards compatible with USB 1.0, it also works with most any PC, even older ones.

FIGURE 2.7

Firewire and USB connectors on an external hard drive.

Just as with internal hard drives being sold today, external hard drives come preformatted and ready to use. They also come with utilities for reformatting and creating partitions. Again, if you plan to reformat or partition your drive, do it before using it for data storage because those processes erase files.

Backing Up Important Media Files

With all hard drives, it is a good practice to regularly back up your data. Media files pose a challenge for backups. The files are large—usually too large for backups to CDs or DVDs. Imagine a 250GB drive full of media files. Where do you back up such large files?

> **TIP**
>
> Many external Firewire drives can be used by Macintosh computers and Windows PCs. Depending on the brand, they might come formatted for Macintosh with a utility disk for changing the format to Windows. If you add your drive and Windows does not recognize it, it might be formatted for Macs. If that is the case, simply run the formatting and portioning utility, and you'll be all set.

About the only good answer is to add an external hard drive of the same size for backups. Although there are tape drives and all sorts of backup programs for CDs and DVDs, they are just too small in format or too clunky for media file backups.

This solution might seem expensive, but consider this: Media files are in many ways the equivalent of a photo album. Would you risk losing all your digital photos? Your music library? Home videos? Probably not. Media files are often some of the most important ones you have.

That might not be true for TV programs. You can always move TV shows to a DVD, and in most cases, they are not "precious memories" in the same way as digital photos.

If you organize your media drive correctly and put photos, videos, and music in one main folder and other media such as TV shows in a separate folder, you can create a strategy for just backing up important files such as photos. This strategy might be possible to implement with DVD data disk backups or a smaller external hard drive such has an 80GB drive that you can find at a great price.

> **STRATEGY**
> Use your D drive to make regular backups of your important media files using a backup utility program. On a regular basis, at least once a month, back up all your important media files to an external hard drive or to DVD data disks that you can store in a fire safe, another location, or a safety deposit box.

By managing your file folders, backing up data is easy. Although you could (and should) back up your important media files to your primary drive's D partition (remember that you have a lot of space on the D drive in most configurations), you still run a risk of losing the files if the D drive crashes or your computer is stolen or faces damage of any sort.

The advantage of an external hard drive for important media files is that you can place the backup drive in another room or even in a safety deposit box or fire safe. This is a good practice, one to strongly consider if you value your media files.

Summary

Your main PC must be capable of running Windows XP and have enough processing power, RAM, and hard drive space to act as the network "hub" and as an entertainment server. By upgrading your existing PC or purchasing a new PC equipped for media networking and media serving, you can store, play, record, and share media for all devices connected on your home entertainment network. Display cards that connect to TVs, TV tuner cards that allow viewing and recording TV shows, and large hard drives are all essential components in a home entertainment network PC.

Using PCs and TVs As Clients in Your Network

If you have ever worked in an office or used computers that were a part of a large network, you've seen how one large computer acts as a "server" to provide data and even programs for a number of "clients" connected to it through a network.

You can create many different types of networks when you combine computers and share data. Although this book is using a straightforward approach without trying to complicate things with a lot of tech terms, you should know some basic networking terms. As an example, your home entertainment network can be configured as one of the following:

- **Peer-to-peer**—Often referred to as P2P or ad hoc, peer-to-peer is a simple approach to networking where you connect any number of PCs together on a network, and each is an independent device with its own files and programs. Each computer can share files and devices with other computers on the network, and you can establish which files and devices are shared by each computer. You can think of a peer-to-peer network as a "file sharing" configuration.

- **Client/server**—In a client/server configuration, one main computer is dedicated as a server. The server contains most all data, and the other devices on the network, clients, access and use data from the server. The server can also be the primary device connected to the Internet with client devices sharing that Internet connection. Used most often in business and workplaces, this type of network allows easy management of files and access to data.

Each of these network strategies works well in a home network. At home, if you have two computers and you network them together, a peer-to-peer network is a simple solution when sharing files and a printer or accessing the Internet is the goal.

A client/server network is a good choice when a home network is configured for entertainment. As you will learn throughout this book, you can have essentially non–computer devices such as TVs and stereos playing media files from a computer on a network. Because such devices do not have their own storage and have simple computers that power them, they become clients that require a server.

Because media files can be very large and you want to be able to access them from any device in your home, it makes sense to put all your media files on one main storage device—the server.

In a client/server network, you can put most of your investment in the main server and use relatively inexpensive devices as clients. If all you want to do is listen to music from your main PC in your bedroom, rather than buy another computer and place it in your bedroom, you can simply buy a wireless media player and put it in the bedroom connected to a TV or a home stereo or set of powered speakers. It is a "client" device and it doesn't need its own hard drive or computer display.

Let's take a look at how each type of network works in a home entertainment network.

Using a File Sharing Configuration

A P2P configuration (referred to here as simply file sharing) works perfectly in a home entertainment network. If you have a number of PCs, this might be a good solution. Each PC has its own hard drive that can store media, and you can configure the network in a way that each computer can share the media files from other computers in the network.

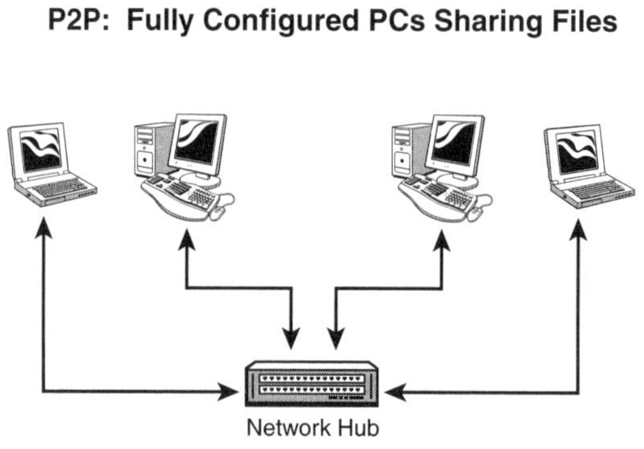

P2P: Fully Configured PCs Sharing Files

Network Hub

FIGURE 3.1

In a file sharing network, fully equipped PCs each share data and devices such as printers or connections to the Internet with each other.

P2P or file sharing networks, as shown in Figure 3.1, work essentially as a file sharing solution. A number of PCs in one local area network (LAN) operate as self-standing PCs.

When needed, the PCs in the P2P network can share files and even devices that are connected to them, such as printers.

When creating a file sharing network, you can still use the strategy of making one PC on the network the primary location for storing media files. Although there are multiple PCs on the network, each with its own hard drive, it is still a good practice to use one main drive for storing shared media files.

File sharing networks work best when all the devices in the network have a true "peer" status: They are fully independent computing devices that can function without a network present. In a home entertainment network, new types of devices on the network are essentially media players without data storage or even an operating system that require a host computer to act as a server to them.

A client/server network is appropriate when you use media player devices.

Understanding Client/Server Networks

When you have media players and media extenders on a network, they require a server where they get media content files to play. This setup creates a more traditional client/server network, as shown in Figure 3.2.

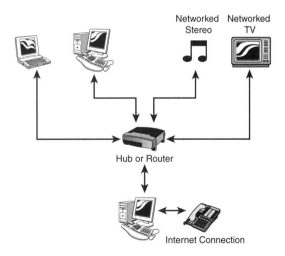

Client/Server: One Main PC serving Data to other PCs and Networked Devices

Networked Stereo   Networked TV

Hub or Router

Internet Connection

FIGURE 3.2

A client/server network has a main PC acting as a data server to both PCs and media player devices such as TVs and stereos connected to media extenders.

As shown in Figure 3.2, the primary PC that is used as the media server is connected directly to a router. It acts as the network hub and controls access to files from the other PCs and devices on the network. It also controls access to an Internet connection and other PCs and devices in the network access the Internet through its connection. With media extender devices or even other PCs, they can all use the security and firewall of the hub computer.

To understand this configuration better, a look at media extender devices is required.

Using Media Extenders in a Client/Server Network

Media extenders are relatively new devices, and they are essential additions to any home entertainment network. Here's why.

It really doesn't make sense to buy a full-powered PC that is capable of connecting to a TV, stereo, or powered speakers when all you use it for is viewing media files. And in many ways, a computer is a little too complex for the task: It requires keyboards and a mouse, and it's big, clunky, and expensive.

A better solution is a small device that can connect directly to a TV or stereo and allow you to view video or photos or play music anywhere on the network.

Such devices, called *media extenders*, are now available at most major electronics stores, and they are changing the makeup of a home entertainment network. Selling for about $100 to $250, it's a small computing device designed to work on a Windows XP home network. Each media extender contains its own simple user interface and TV and audio connectors; you connect it to a TV and a stereo. Using a supplied remote control, you can easily find and play a media file from your server PC.

Figure 3.3 shows a typical media extender and its connections for networking and attaching to a TV or stereo.

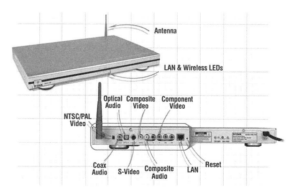

FIGURE 3.3

Media extenders connect to your network and play media files on TVs or stereos.

The media extender uses media player software that installs on a PC to play media located on that PC via the extender. It is essentially a client to a PC acting as a server. The media extender has the ability to interact with the media player software on the server and pull media files through the network and play them.

CROSS-REFERENCE Chapter 9, "Adding TV and Media Extenders to the Network," shows how media extenders work and how you add media extenders to your home entertainment network.

Media extenders are client/server networked devices. When you have several media extenders in your home, you find that the strategy of a client/server network works well for the media extenders and also for other PCs (although they do not require any special media serving software). The other PCs can simply use Windows Media Player or other media playing software accessing files shared from the main server PC.

Using PCs on a Client/Server Network

One of the advantages of a client/server network is that you can use PCs as clients. When acting as a client, you can use a PC that has a minimal configuration. You do not need client PCs to have large hard drives, DVD burners, or much of the power that the server PC has.

It's okay if the client PCs are fully powered and as well equipped as the main server PC, but it's okay if they're not. As long as they meet the minimum requirements for running Windows XP (detailed in Chapter 2, "Configuring Your PC As an Entertainment Server") and are equipped with a network connection, either wired or wireless, you can access media files from your main server.

For a PC in a home entertainment network, even though you don't need some of the large storage and processing power that the server PC has, you need the following to use the client PC as a media playing device:

- **TV-out display card**—Your display card should have a TV-out connector so that you can view video, recorded TV, and pictures on a TV connected to the PC. You can use a TV rather than a computer monitor to view media. If you have a large enough computer monitor and it is used in a smaller room, you might find a computer monitor connected to a client PC adequate for most media viewing.

- **Powered speakers or connection to a stereo**—Whether you are listening to music files or viewing video on your client PC, you want a good sound system connected to it. Your client PC is essentially becoming your home stereo device, and even TV viewing is enhanced with a good sound system.

- **Wireless keyboard and mouse**—As with any PC used as a media player, you want the freedom and flexibility of a wireless keyboard and mouse when using your client PC.

With the preceding equipment, just about any PC functions well as a client PC. In addition to the benefits of playing media content from the main server PC, the client PC continues to function as a traditional PC in your home, making it a great multitasker.

Putting the Right Device in the Right Place

If you are mixing both PCs and media extenders in a client/server home entertainment network, it is important to put the right device in the right place.

By understanding what type of activity you do in each room, you can easily determine what type of device is best for each location.

Because you are creating a home entertainment network, it's a given that you should be able to access all your entertainment content from any device located in your network. A bigger question is how you experience that content. The type of display you use, the size of the display, the basic ergonomics of your room, the sound system—these are all key factors in having a great media experience.

> **TIP**
> Just because you are building a home network doesn't mean you need multiple PCs. You can have just one PC that acts as the entertainment server to TVs and stereos connected to media extenders throughout your home.

With a mix of PCs and media extenders, the same is true for a great computing experience. When you are surfing the Web, reading and writing emails, word processing, and using creative programs for photo editing and music management, you need a good computing work space.

A PC using a TV as its display is perfect for watching TV and videos, but you do not want to do much traditional computing with such a display. TVs are extremely low-resolution and can be fuzzy for computing work. Also, if you've set up your room for media watching, you'll probably be sitting pretty far back from the display and on a comfortable chair rather than an office chair.

The reverse is true for media playing. If you've set your client PC in an office setting, it's great for computing but won't be comfortable for watching a long movie or listening to music for any length of time.

This whole "TV versus computing dilemma" is termed the 10-inch/10-foot experience. Using it as a rule helps you plan which type of device configuration is best for a room based on whether you will be primarily doing computing or playing media. Figure 3.4 shows the computer viewing experience, and Figure 3.5 shows the TV viewing experience:

- **Ten-inch**—General and office computing tasks are best done at least 10 inches from a display, as shown in Figure 3.4. You also should use a high-quality, high-resolution computer monitor for computing.

- **Ten-foot**—Watching TV, watching picture slideshows, and listening to music is best done about 10 feet from a display, and that display should be a good TV.

FIGURE 3.4

General computing is best done with a computer monitor as a "10-inch" experience.

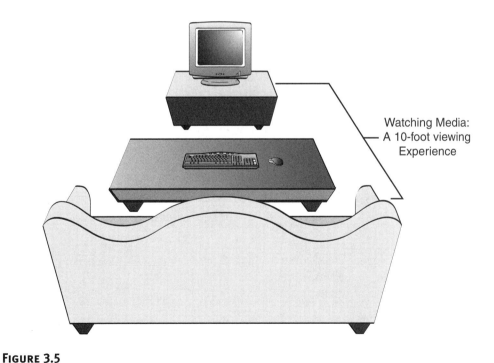

FIGURE 3.5

Watching media is best done with a TV as a "10-foot" experience.

Of course, the preceding rules could be 6-inch/6-feet or even 12-inch/12-feet, depending on your displays and what is comfortable for you.

There will be locations where you plan to do both media viewing/playing and computing. One solution is to use a PC and take advantage of the display card's ability to connect both a computer monitor and a TV to the PC at the same time.

When you are using the PC for general computing, sit at a table or desk in the room and locate the computer monitor there for a 10-inch experience. When you want to kick back and play some media, take the wireless keyboard and mouse over to the couch and have a 10-foot experience watching media files on the TV.

Using PCs When Computing Power Is Needed

Even when watching media, sometimes a PC is the best device if you want to mix your media experience with content and information from the Internet.

Media extenders are essentially media playing devices that are limited to playing media files but have little or no computing power. They are not designed to surf the Web or do any traditional computing functions.

If you want to find more information about shows you are watching, play along with interactive TV shows from their websites, order a CD when you are listening to a song playing from a streaming music channel, or take a quick break to check your email, you might want to use a PC rather than a media extender—at least in that location.

Currently, PCs still have an edge over media extenders because they do allow you to mix content from the Internet with the media you are playing. When needed, you can always use them as PCs for email and getting news, sports, and weather.

Table 3.1 is a simple guide to which type of client is best suited for any location.

TABLE 3.1 SELECTING A PC OR MEDIA EXTENDER CLIENT

Activity	PC	Media Extender
Watching TV	•	•
Viewing photos	•	•
Listening to music	•	•
Ripping CDs	•	
Viewing enhanced TV	•	
Surfing the Web	•	
Editing video	•	
Email	•	

As you can see, PCs are capable of all activities, but they cost more than a media extender. Many of the activities in Table 3.1 can be done on one single PC, and you might find that a full PC is not needed in many locations if they are primarily used for media viewing and playing.

Using TVs for Media Playing

Just as PCs are best suited for detail work such as general computing, TVs are best for media playing for a number of reasons and some surprising new ones.

On the most basic level, you probably have at least one good TV, perhaps several, that you can put to work as displays connected directly to your PCs' display cards or to media extenders. This keeps the cost of your home entertainment network down because you are using equipment you already have—in a brand new way.

Lowest Cost Media Viewing Solution

PC monitors, especially flat panel LCDs, are still pretty expensive when compared to TVs. A 20-inch computer LCD monitor is at least $1000 compared to at 20-inch TV, which can be purchased for as little as $100.

Traditional TVs, which are cathode ray tube (CRT) displays, have a very low resolution of 320×240 pixels and are not good when used as a display for general computing. Figure 3.6 shows the difference between the same website viewed on a TV (left) and a standard computer monitor (right).

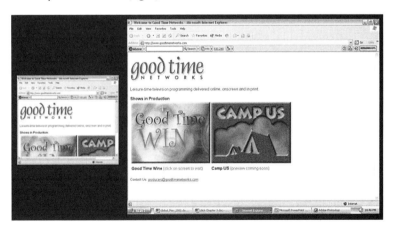

FIGURE 3.6

The same website displays differently on a TV (left) and a computer monitor (right).

The TV image is small (320×240 pixels), and also the image is blurry and hard to read. The computer image has a much higher resolution (for example, 1024×768 pixels, and often much higher depending on your video card and monitor) and is extremely sharp. TV displays were never intended for computing applications, and because standard TV images are so low in resolution, regardless of which display they are viewed on, TV images are low quality by their very nature.

That applies to TV as we have known it for the last 50 years. Recent changes to TV broadcasting and display technology are changing all of that. Digital TV broadcasts in high definition are changing the quality of TV images and TV monitors. If you are using an HDTV tuner card, and if you plan to use a computer monitor for viewing HDTV, you need a video card and a computer monitor that can display the full HDTV resolution of 1920×1080 or better.

If you've been to just about any electronics store lately, you've no doubt been dazzled by a whole new generation of high-resolution flat panel TVs that come in plasma and LCD varieties. Flat panel screens are the future of TV, and the great news is that not only are they incredible TVs, but they also make great computer monitors. Figure 3.7 shows one of the new flat panel plasma TVs in action.

FIGURE 3.7

A Gateway flat panel plasma TV works great for viewing TV or computer applications.

Plasma and LCD TVs are essentially the same technology as LCD computer monitors. Many on the market today can function either as a TV or as a computer monitor. Even when one is functioning as a TV hooked to the TV-out connector of your computer's display card, it has such a high quality image that it can be used to view computer applications.

In a home with plasma or LCD flat panel TVs, you can freely mix both media viewing and computer applications on the same display. Remember to use a screen saver (most media extenders and DVD players feature them) because plasma and LCD TVs are subject to "burn in" if you keep the same image on the screen for long periods of time.

Listening to Music with TVs

A TV can also be a good device for listening to music. Because TVs have their own speakers, it might be good enough for music, but chances are it's not.

If you are using a TV connected to a media extender, you might want to consider connecting the audio-out connectors on the media extender to a set of powered speakers (or a home stereo if you prefer). Connect the video-out connector to the TV. This setup provides you with a perfect combination of picture and sound.

Some TVs have audio-out connections of their own, which allow you to connect the TV's audio directly to a set of powered speakers or a home stereo. If this is the case, you can use those connectors. Connect the audio-out from the media extender to the audio-in of the TV. Then, connect the audio-out connectors on the TV to the speakers or stereo.

> **TIP**
> Media extenders that you attach to your TV have a set of audio jacks that can be connected to a stereo or set of powered speakers. If the sound from your TV isn't that great, you can add a set of powered speakers to the media extender and have great sound using your TV as your onscreen guide to your music.

In a home entertainment network configuration, you select music and control it using either a TV or computer monitor, so it's good to begin thinking of music as something you control with a visual interface.

Summary

Whether you configure your home entertainment network as a peer-to-peer or client/server network, you mix PCs and media extenders connected to TVs, powered speakers, or home stereos. Media extender devices allow a low-cost solution where existing TVs can be used as displays connected to a media extender client playing media from a main server PC. TVs are good for playing video and displaying simple media menus but are not high enough quality for computing applications. A new generation of flat panel plasma and LCD TVs are capable of functioning both as TVs and computer displays.

Getting the Right Networking Gear

When it comes time to go out and purchase networking gear, you will be glad you took the time to create your home entertainment network plan. This chapter looks at the networking equipment choices you have and helps you understand what each piece of equipment does.

Home networking equipment has evolved into low-cost devices that are sold just about everywhere—from high-end computer consultants all the way to Wal-Mart. A key strategy is to shop, shop, and shop for the best deals. At any moment in time, you can pay full manufacturer's suggested retail price (MSRP) for a router or adapter or get the same item down the street on sale and with a rebate. Table 4.1 shows an example.

TABLE 4.1   MSRP VERSUS SALE AND REBATE PRICING

Item	Store A	Store B
Wireless router	$129	$30 instant savings
		$40 rebate
Final price	$129	$59

When a particular brand of networking equipment is on sale, usually just about all of the items you need are on sale at the same time, such as the router and adapters. Even extenders will all be on sale together.

Although devices such as routers and adapters are on sale or rebates are being offered, the same might not be true for cables. In fact, cables are a premium profit item for many retailers, and you can pay as much for a long Ethernet cable as you do for a router. Again, careful shopping is essential. You can find a 25-foot Ethernet cable at a major office supply chain for $29 and then go down the street to Wal-Mart and find the exact same cable (same brand) for half the price.

A good practice for cables is to shop online, using one of the many "best price" shopping services. Simply list the standard of cable you want and the length and then see what results are returned to you. There is no need to pay major office-supply or home electronics stores a premium price for a commodity item.

As mentioned earlier, networking equipment is easy to find, and you have a choice of brands. Each of the major brands sells complete lines of networking equipment that most often include the following:

- Router

- Hub

- Notebook card adapter

- Peripheral Component Interconnect (PCI) card adapter

- Signal booster

> **STRATEGY**
>
> Knowing that you can mix and match equipment from various manufacturers, identify the devices you need and make sure that they meet the networking standard you will be using. Then, shop both retail and online for the best sales prices and be on the lookout for rebates. Don't pay full MSRP price for any equipment or cables.

Although you can purchase all the equipment from one manufacturer, you can also mix and match equipment from different manufacturers. Because both wired and wireless networking equipment conform to industry standards (standards are covered later in this chapter), devices from various manufacturers work with each other.

Identifying the Gear That Fits Your Plan

With your plan in hand, you should start making a shopping list of the networking gear you will shop for. It's easy to overlay the equipment needed at each location on your plan.

Prior to that process, you need to decide whether you will be using a router or a hub as your primary networking device. Here's a simple set of rules that will help you make that decision.

Hubs

Hubs are most often used for a file sharing (peer-to-peer) network. In such a network, the hub is simply the device that allows you to connect more than two PCs to each other. If all you are using are two PCs in a peer-to-peer network, you could simply use one Ethernet cross-over cable connecting the two PCs. A hub allows you to connect several PCs together and make the same connection between multiple PCs as a cable connecting each one directly.

Routers

If you are sharing an Internet connection between PCs and devices, a router is the correct network device to use. In the most basic sense, a router manages the flow of information between two separate networks. In a home network, it manages bringing two networks together: the network of devices in your home and the Internet, which is really just one giant network.

Routers perform all the actions of a hub and add the benefit of an Internet connection directly to the router for sharing between the devices. Routers are ideal for client/ server networks because the router is directly providing Internet access to devices on the network. When you are sharing Internet access between devices or building a wireless network, choose a router.

For most home entertainment networks, a router is the best choice because it provides both the practicality of a hub and the client/server solution of sharing an Internet connection.

Let's take a look at the original home layout used in Chapter 1, "Planning the Right Home Entertainment Network for Your Home," and identify the devices that are needed at each location in the plan. Figure 4.1 shows devices added to the plan.

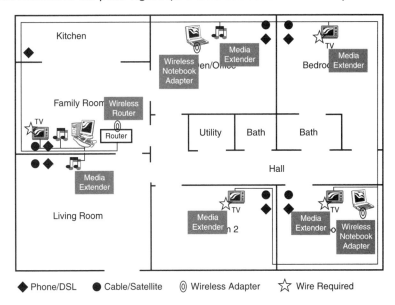

Figure 4.1

Networking devices identified for each location on the home entertainment network plan.

Note that in the plan, the TV and the stereo located next to the main hub PC do not have media extenders. They can connect directly to the main PC and do not require a network connection. The main PC will use the TV to play media and use its powered speakers to play music and sound from TV and video.

The plan has done a good job of creating a shopping list. In this sample plan, you need to shop for the following:

- One wireless router

- Two wireless notebook adapters

- Four audio/video media extenders

- One audio media extender

- An Ethernet cable to reach wired devices

- Audio and video cables for connecting TVs and audio devices to PCs and media extenders.

Note that even though one of the bedrooms has a stereo located next to a laptop, it still has its own media extender device. Because the laptop is portable and can be used in other locations, such a configuration keeps the laptop free of wired connections.

The router and hub/server PC are located next to both a TV signal source and an Internet connection. The plan looks great, and the next job is getting familiar with the different types of network devices, standards, and options that will be used in your home entertainment network.

Understanding Network Types

There are a variety of networks designed for home use, and it is good to understand them. Some can work in a home entertainment network; some should be avoided. When shopping for network devices, you will encounter the following basic types of home networking types.

Wired Ethernet Network

This book refers to a wired Ethernet network simply as a "wired" network. In a wired network, each computer or device is attached to the network with a high-speed Ethernet cable. Although you can attach two computers together with one cable, when you want to network more than two computers, you use either an Ethernet hub or router. The hub or router has a number of Ethernet connections that allow you to connect each PC or wired device to each other through the hub or router.

Figure 4.2 shows the connection panel of a small four-port Ethernet router. There are four ports for connecting up to four PCs or Ethernet devices and one port for connecting to an Internet connection, such as a cable modem or DSL modem.

Figure 4.2

Connections on the back of a wired Ethernet router.

Wired Ethernet routers sometimes are called Ethernet broadband routers because they are used to share a high-speed Internet connection between several computers.

You can build a complete home entertainment network with a wired Ethernet hub or router—if you can run cables between locations.

Whenever possible, a wired network is your best solution in terms of data transfer speed, network security, and cost. A wired network is also best for dealing with the high-bandwidth demands of video files on a network.

Wireless Networks

A wireless network is actually part of a wired Ethernet network to some degree; at a minimum, the wireless router is connected with an Ethernet cable to a main/server PC and to an active Internet connection. With those wired connections, you can provide access to your home entertainment network server wirelessly to other PCs and devices that have wireless adapters.

A wireless router uses radio frequencies to send and receive data, most often in the 2.4GHz range that cordless phones operate on. Other PCs and devices on the network use adapters that allow them to be a part of the wireless network, turning each PC or device into access points in the network.

Figure 4.3 shows the back panel connections found on most wireless routers, which include ports for wired connections and a wired connection to an Internet source such as a broadband or DSL modem.

Figure 4.3

Connections on a wireless router.

Wireless routers have either one or two antennas for sending and receiving signals, and those are also attached most often to the back panel.

The front panel of a wireless router most often contains a series of small indicator lights that show network status and connections in use, as shown in Figure 4.4.

In addition to the main router, wireless adapters are required for other PCs and devices on the wireless network. They are easily added to a PC or other media device and allow that PC or device to communicate with the network. Wireless networks have reached a level of performance and network security where they are suitable for a home entertainment network. As good as they are, wireless networks are subject to radio interference in any dwelling, and that can slow data transfer rates. It will not be an issue for most music and picture viewing on the network, but it can stop or pause the playback of video files such as recorded TV shows.

Power Line Ethernet Networks

As you shop for home network equipment, you will see a number of "power line" network devices. Using the electrical wiring in your home rather than Ethernet cable, power line network adapters help deal with the difficulty of running a wired network in an existing home.

Figure 4.4

Front panel status lights on a wireless router.

Because virtually all homes have electrical wiring, power line networks take advantage of the wiring by sending data through them to PCs and devices attached to the power line network. As you can imagine, because you are attaching a PC or other media device to a power outlet, a very special network adapter is required to make sure you don't send 110 volts of electricity into your PC's Ethernet port.

Belkin Powerline Ethernet Adapters were tested for this book, and they work extremely well—although they are a bit too slow for most video. The devices work at roughly 14Mbps as opposed to the 100Mbps of wired Ethernet using Fast Ethernet cables.

To use the power line adapters, you simply plug one adapter into an electrical outlet by your main computer and router and plug in another power line adapter by the PC or device you want to add to your network. Each adapter has an Ethernet port, which you attach to the router and other PC/device with a supplied Ethernet cable. To your router and network, the added PC or device is viewed as an Ethernet connection.

Unlike an Ethernet network where each device is wired to a router or hub, a power line network uses power lines, which run as one loop or various branches from that loop without dedicated lines to each power outlet. The power line Ethernet adapter has a

TIP

When a wireless signal is a problem and you have a location that is too hard to wire, use a power line adapter—but not for video. The slow data transfer rate of power line adapters might not be adequate for high-bandwidth video files.

unique address to locate the adapter in the power line network as if it were a dedicated cable in an Ethernet network configuration.

Due to the slow data transfer rates, it is not recommended that you use power line adapters in most applications of the home entertainment network, but the data transfer rate is certainly good enough for music, pictures, and non–video files. If you need a wired connection where it's too hard to run Ethernet cable and you are using a device that doesn't require high-speed data transfer, power line adapters can be a practical solution.

Figure 4.5 shows a Belkin Powerline Ethernet Adapter and the simplicity of its connections.

Figure 4.5

The Belkin Powerline Ethernet Adapter running a wired network connection using electrical wiring.

Using Other Network Solutions

You will see a number of other network solutions when shopping for networking equipment. Most are designed for simpler peer-to-peer networks and are essentially converters or adapters that take relatively standard wiring, such as home phone lines or phone line cables, or use Firewire or Universal Serial Bus (USB) ports and cables to create network connections.

Although it is entirely possible to use phone lines, Firewire, or USB cables to communicate and send files between computers, there is more to a home network than simple communications between machines.

Home entertainment networks require high-speed data transfer and phone line connections generally operate at about 1/10th of the transfer rate of Ethernet. In addition, new home entertainment devices such as media extenders are designed to work with industry-standard wireless networks or with an Ethernet connection.

Considering that most computers now come equipped with an Ethernet port, and that most routers and wireless routers are designed to transfer data at a high speed through Ethernet ports, it makes sense to use Ethernet connections and shy away from alternative connections such as phone line networks.

Most phone line and even power line network devices are attractive because they overcome the wiring problems people experience with existing homes. Because these networks generally only operate at 10Mbps, it makes more sense to use a wireless network operating at speeds of up to 54Mbps.

Understanding Wired Ethernet Networking Hardware

When shopping for a wired Ethernet network, you will want to look at the following devices.

Router

Wired routers connect to an Internet connection via an Ethernet cable and use Ethernet cables to connect to PCs attached to Ethernet ports on the router and manage the flow of data between networks (the Internet and your home network). The number of ports is the important consideration. Wired routers come with at least 4 ports and can have as many as 12 ports. Figure 4.6 shows the front panel of a wired router, which contains lights indicating connected devices in use and connection to the Internet.

Figure 4.6

Wired Ethernet router front panel.

Hub

A hub is the simplest of networking devices. It allows you to connect several computers to each other via the hub rather than have a direct connection between each computer or device. A good example is four computers on a home network. If you want to share data from computer A with computers B, C, and D, you have to make three separate connections to each of the three computers. With a hub, each computer makes a connection to the hub and each computer can communicate with any computer connected to the hub.

Switch

A network switch is similar in nature to a hub in the sense that it allows you to connect several computers or networked devices to it and it allows data to flow from any computer to any other computer. Unlike a hub, which allows the flow of data from one device to be made available to all other devices on the network, a switch controls the flow of information from one device to another device at a fixed rate of transfer speed. It manages the flow of data between devices by managing bandwidth and allocating bandwidth for each device connected to the switch.

In a larger network, or one where a lot of data is flowing simultaneously, switches ensure the overall performance of the network by managing connections and by dedicating fixed bandwidth for each connection.

For most home entertainment networks, a switch is not required but it might be a better choice than a simple hub in a peer-to-peer home entertainment network. Figure 4.7 shows the front panel of a 5-port switch.

Figure 4.7

Front panel of an Ethernet network 5-port switch.

Cables

For home networks using Ethernet routers, hubs, or switches, you need to use Ethernet Category 5e cables, often referred to as CAT-5e cables. Figure 4.8 shows a CAT-5e cable with two male connectors on each end. CAT-5e cables come in various lengths (most often sold in 6, 12, 25, 50, and 100-foot lengths). For longer runs, you should consider using bulk cable and adding your own connectors or using couplers to join fixed-length cables.

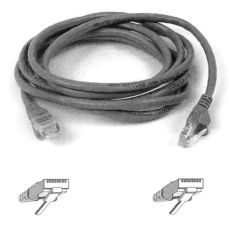

Figure 4.8

Ethernet CAT-5e cable showing males connectors at each end.

Understanding Wireless Networking Hardware

Before exploring each of the different types of hardware in a wireless network, it is good to understand that the primary type of wireless networking hardware you want for your home entertainment network meets an industry standard called 802.11g.

Although there are other wireless network standards, such as 802.11b, currently the "g" standard is the best one for dealing with media files on your network.

The industry standard makes sure that your wireless devices operate correctly with each other and that you can be sure they perform in an expected manner regarding network speed, performance, and data management.

TIP

As wireless standards progress, you might discover new wireless standards on the latest wireless devices on the market (such as the emerging "n" standard). With any wireless standard, you need to make sure that the new standard is backwards-compatible with previous standards. It means that you can use older equipment that is supported by the wireless network. A good example is that the "g" standard supports "b" standard devices.

Table 4.2 shows the current industry standards for wireless home networking devices.

TABLE 4.2   WIRELESS STANDARDS

Wireless Standard	Area of Coverage	Speed
802.11b	150–300 feet	Up to 11Mbps
802.11a	50–100 feet	Up to 54Mbps
802.11g	150–300 feet	Up to 54Mbps
Bluetooth	30–60 feet	Up to 1Mbps

As you can see from Table 4.2, 802.11g offers the best combination of area of coverage and speed. If you have some existing wireless hardware, 802.11g devices are also backwards compatible with 802.11b wireless devices. Also, it's good to understand that because any wireless network signal is subject to slowdowns and might be supplying data to multiple devices, it will seldom reach its full speed of data transfer in real-world use.

You might discover that many media extender devices, particularly audio-only media extenders, use the 802.11b standard. They were some of the first media extender devices on the market, and they are being replaced by newer 802.11g models. Although they might be good deals pricewise, you should seriously debate the small savings they offer versus the better performance of 802.11g devices. With media files, higher wireless network speed is an important consideration.

Another name that you will see relating to 802.11 devices is "Wi-Fi." Wi-Fi is a brand name that indicates devices that meet the 802.11 standard of interoperability and that can work with one another. For this reason, if your device is Wi-Fi, it communicates with other Wi-Fi devices and works on a Wi-Fi network.

Many technical specifications within the 802.11 standard indicate how data is packed for transmission and what frequencies it sends and receives. Rather than read pages of the specifications, for the purposes of a home entertainment network what is most important is that you use compatible Wi-Fi standard devices that meet the 802.11 specification. If you do, you will have a solid wireless network that will work well and be easy to establish and use.

When shopping for wireless network equipment meeting the 802.11g (or higher, as newer devices enter the market) standard, here are the devices you need, depending on the PCs and media extender devices in your plan.

Wireless Router

Wireless routers connect to an Internet connection via an Ethernet cable and use an Ethernet cable to connect to a main PC. In addition, wireless routers have Ethernet ports that allow wired connections to PCs and other devices.

The wireless router manages the flow of data between the two networks you will be using—the Internet and your home network of wired and wireless devices.

The wireless router has either one or two antennas used to transmit and receive data. The front panel of the router, as shown in Figure 4.9, has status lights showing the connection status of wired devices and that the Internet connection is active.

Wireless routers should be located in a central location if possible. Because a wireless router has a potential range of 300 feet, a central location is important for overall reception and interaction with other wireless devices—and this is important if you have a large dwelling. If you have devices located at distances greater than its practical range, you can add signal boosters, as described later in this section.

If you are using a standard wired router, you can also add a wireless access point—a device that allows you to connect a wireless device to a port on the router.

Figure 4.9

Wireless router front panel indicator lights.

Desktop Wireless Network Card

Beyond your main hub/server PC that connects to the wireless router, if you are using other desktop or tower PCs, you can use a desktop wireless network card, as shown in Figure 4.10, to give them access to the wireless network.

You place the desktop wireless network card in an open PCI slot inside of the desktop or tower PC. The card has a small antenna that receives and transmits data. If needed, you can also add an external extension antenna if reception is a problem.

Figure 4.10

A desktop wireless network card allowing desktop and tower PCs to join a wireless network.

Wireless Notebook Adapter Card

Your laptop might or might not need a wireless notebook card. If you are using a recently purchased laptop computer that has built-in wireless networking (such as one with an Intel Centrino processor), you can use its internal wireless adapter to connect to your wireless network. If the laptop uses a slower 802.11b internal network adapter, you can always add a wireless notebook adapter card, as shown in Figure 4.11.

The card fits into the standard PC card slot on your laptop, and the part that protrudes from the card slot is the antenna that also has activity lights showing a signal is present and a status light which blinks to show network activity.

Wireless USB Network Adapter

Another option that works with media extender devices, laptops, desktops, and tower PCs is a wireless USB adapter. This small adapter connects to a USB port on any computer or device and adds wireless network connectivity. Figure 4.12 shows a wireless USB network adapter.

The USB adapter is especially useful for devices that do not have an Ethernet port but do have a USB port, laptops that have another adapter in the PC card slot, or desktop/tower PCs that do not have an open PCI card slot.

Figure 4.11

The wireless notebook adapter card, which fits into the PC card slot of your laptop computer.

The USB network adapter can fit directly into a USB slot, or it can rest in a stand that connects it to a USB port with a provided USB cable. The device has a light to show activity and connection to the network.

Figure 4.12

A wireless USB network adapter.

Desktop Antenna for Desktop Network Cards

As mentioned earlier, depending on the location of your desktop or tower PC, you might want to use an extension antenna to gain better reception. A desktop antenna, as shown in Figure 4.13, is easy to add. A cable runs from a connector on the desktop card to the extension antenna, and you can then position it for the best reception.

Figure 4.13

Desktop antenna for desktop network cards, helping provide a better signal when needed.

Signal Booster

For very large dwellings, or when signal reception is less than ideal, you can also add a signal booster to your wireless network. Placed between the router and wireless devices that are too far for normal reception or are having problems with reception, a signal booster receives the signal from the router and then resends it from that point. This effectively extends the range of your signals in your home. You can add more than one signal booster if needed.

There are other wireless network devices such as wireless media extenders, wireless print servers, and wireless music players. I cover these devices later in the book in various chapters. For now, the devices in this chapter are the essential wireless devices for your home entertainment network.

Putting the Plan into Action

With your plan, and the understanding of what wired or wireless networking devices you need for your home entertainment network, you are ready to purchase your equipment.

The next chapter will look at starting to build your network by adding a router to your main PC.

Summary

Using your home entertainment plan, you should identify what type of network device is required for each PC or media device in the network. Using a wired network, wireless network, or combination of both, you begin to assemble the equipment needed to build your home entertainment network.

Installing the Network

Part II

Adding a Network Router to Your Main PC

This chapter will look at taking the plan you created for your home entertainment network and implementing it. The first task is adding a network router to your main PC. A router provides two essential functions in the home entertainment network:

- Managing your Internet connection for all the devices attached to the router either with a wired or wireless connection

- Allowing all devices connected to the router to share data and media files

Connecting PCs, your Internet connection, media extenders, and TVs and audio equipment creates a whole-house entertainment system, but it all begins with the PC's ability to network the devices together. A home entertainment network is built with standard PC-based home network equipment, so it is important to know the equipment involved and how the equipment empowers your network.

To begin, you need your router (which can be either a wired broadband router or a wireless broadband router) and the installation software that came with it. After the router is installed, your other home entertainment network devices need the following:

- An Ethernet port for wired connections to your router

- Wireless adapters that are compatible with the wireless standard your router uses (if you have chosen to use a wireless router)

- Ethernet cables for wired connections.

With the plan and equipment in hand, the next job is to begin installing the hardware.

Getting Ready for Router Installation

After you purchase your wired or wireless router, you need to take a look at your PC and the devices you will be using on your home entertainment network to make sure you have all the connections, adapters, and cables you need to successfully install and begin using your router.

The PC you are connecting your router to must have the following:

- An Ethernet port on the PC you will connect your router to

- Installation software that came with your router and the instruction manual for the router

- "Start-up" documents that your Internet service provider (ISP) provided for installing your cable or DSL modem

If you have all these items, you are ready to begin installing your router.

Identifying Your PC's Ethernet Connection

The first step in installing your router is to identify whether your PC has a built-in Ethernet connector. You need to install an add-on Ethernet card if it does not have one built in.

You take two steps to make sure that your PC has an Ethernet connector: Inspect the connectors on the PC to identify whether it has an Ethernet connector, and then check your system control panel to make sure that the system recognizes the Ethernet port and it is operating properly.

Finding an Ethernet Port on a Desktop PC

Figure 5.1 shows a typical Ethernet port on the back of a desktop PC. This port might be part of a series of standard connections that are on the panel of the PC, along with keyboard and mouse connectors, or it might be located on a expansion card. In either case, it is labeled "network" or "Ethernet" or is simply represented by a network of computer symbols, as shown in Figure 5.1.

If your computer does not have a network/Ethernet port, you need to add a network interface card (NIC) to your PC. You can purchase an 10/100BASE-T Fast Ethernet network interface card as shown in Figure 5.2, open your PC, and install it in an open Peripheral Component Interconnect (PCI) slot.

You want to be sure to get an Ethernet card that conforms to the following standard: 10/100BASE-T Fast Ethernet and 32-bit. Most NIC cards sold in major office, electronics, and computer stores meet this specification. You should also make sure the card is Plug-and-Play compatible (PnP) by looking for symbols on the package stating that the card is designed to work with Windows XP and is PnP-compliant. Figure 5.2 shows a typical Ethernet NIC for installation in a PCI slot.

FIGURE 5.1

Ethernet connector on the back panel of a desktop PC.

Use the following steps in the order listed to add an internal Ethernet card to an open PCI slot in your PC:

1. Turn off the power to your PC and disconnect the power cable.

2. Following the instructions that came with your PC, remove the side panel of the casing that covers the PC. This gives you access to the expansion slots for PCI cards.

3. Remove the screw that holds a metal plate over the expansion slot on the back panel of your PC, being sure to save the screw and the metal plate.

4. Touch any metal part of the PC so that you dissipate any static electricity that might be present before you open the packaging of the actual Ethernet card.

5. Remove the Ethernet card from its antistatic bag, and avoid laying it down on any other surfaces prior to installation to prevent static electrical build-up.

6. Carefully position the card in an open PCI slot in the PC, making sure that the connector faces the outside of the PC, that the connector plate fits gently into the open back panel, and that the connectors are positioned over the PCI connector inside the PC.

7. After the back panel and connector are in the correct position, gently press the connector into the PCI slot until it fits snugly and securely in place.

8. Check the back panel of the connector from the outside of the PC, making sure that the fit is proper, that there are no gaps, and that it is not loose in any way.

9. With the card securely in place, use the screw that you removed from the metal plate covering the back panel slot to secure the card to the slot.

10. Reattach the side panel of computer casing.

11. Reattach the power cord to your PC.

12. Turn the power on to your PC.

13. Save the metal plate that originally covered the back panel slot on the PC by keeping it either in the box for the Ethernet card or in another location for PC parts. If you ever remove the card, you will want to cover the open slot with the metal plate.

FIGURE 5.2

10/100BASE-T Fast Ethernet NIC for installation in the PCI expansion slot of a desktop PC.

After you power up your PC, you should check that the system recognizes the new NIC. When you use a PnP card, Windows XP recognizes that new hardware was installed and adds the card to the system. After an onscreen prompt indicates that the system recognizes the new hardware, it also presents a pop-up message: New Hardware Has Been Installed and Is Ready for Use.

If for some reason the system does not recognize the hardware or it needs a special driver that is not in the Windows XP driver directory, it asks you to insert the driver disc that came with the card. Then, it completes the installation using the drivers provided by the manufacturer. In this case, simply follow the wizard to complete the installation.

To check that the Ethernet card is now a part of the system and is recognized by Windows XP, follow these steps in this order:

1. Choose Start, Control Panel, System.

2. Select the Hardware tab.

3. Select Device Manager.

4. You see a list of all the hardware attached to your PC, organized by type of hardware. Choose and click on Network Adapters.

5. Your new PCI Ethernet adapter should be listed. You can click on it to see its Properties menu, find information on the drivers it uses, and note whether it is working properly.

If your new card's icon has a round yellow symbol with an exclamation mark next to it, it is not working or it was installed improperly. You can use the device's Properties menu to troubleshoot and resolve any driver or device conflicts.

Understanding Network Interfaces on a Laptop

The need for a NIC on a laptop is different from that of a desktop PC.

You can encounter three common types of network connections when using a laptop:

- An Ethernet port built in to the laptop.

- A PC card slot that can accept an Ethernet notebook adapter card if your laptop does not have one built in and you need to use a wired connection. The same PC card slot can also accept a wireless network adapter card if you are using a wireless connection.

- A built-in wireless adapter. Many newer laptops, such as those that come with Intel Centrino technology, include a wireless adapter built in. These newer laptops most often include a built-in Ethernet port for wired connections. Be sure to check the speed and standard (such as 802.11) of the built-in wireless adapter.

The following is for laptops that do not have a built-in wireless network adapter.

If you are going to be using a wireless card with your laptop, it does not require an Ethernet port. The wireless adapter for the laptop is a NIC. It works well in a wireless application, but if you will be connecting your laptop to a wired home entertainment network, you need to be sure that you have, or add, a standard Ethernet network interface for your laptop.

Laptop PC card slots can be single or dual—allowing you to add one card or two cards at the same time. With many slim laptops, there is only a single slot for a notebook adapter card. To expand your laptop, with only one slot you must use either a wireless network card or an Ethernet NIC. You can't do both at once. Figure 5.3 shows a wireless adapter in the PC card slot of a laptop. Figure 5.4 shows an Ethernet card with a cable attached.

FIGURE 5.3

Wireless network adapter in the PC card expansion slot of a laptop.

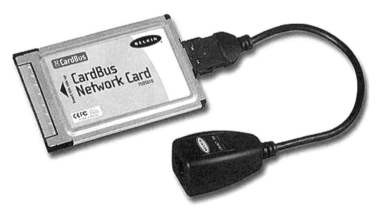

FIGURE 5.4

Ethernet NIC in the PC card expansion slot of a laptop.

There are some good solutions to this problem. First, it is possible to switch cards when needed. When you are wireless, insert the wireless adapter. When you connect with a cable for a wired connection, switch to the Ethernet card.

If your laptop does not have a built-in Ethernet port and you need an Ethernet card for a wired solution but still want to use wireless, too, you can use a Universal Serial Bus (USB) wireless network adapter rather than a PC card wireless adapter.

TIP Even though the wireless network card for a laptop functions as a network interface and does not require an Ethernet port, it's still a good practice to have an Ethernet port on your laptop for making wired connections to a router when needed.

Figure 5.5 shows a USB wireless network adapter attached to a laptop that has an Ethernet NIC installed. This gives you the option of using both a wired and wireless interface to gain access to the network, but it is a bit clumsy for laptop use.

FIGURE 5.5

Ethernet NIC in the PC card expansion slot of a laptop and a wireless USB adapter connected to the USB port.

In most instances, you want to use one solution almost all the time. It is good to know that if you do switch from wired to wireless occasionally, you can have both options.

If your PC or laptop has a built-in Ethernet port, you are all set. If you add a network expansion card, the next action is to make sure that you have the correct "drivers" installed on your PC.

Installing Drivers for Your NIC

When you purchase a NIC, it comes with a set of drivers. The drivers are for installation as a network adapter device. If it is a PnP device, Windows will most likely recognize it and use its own driver database for the network adapter card functions.

It also requires drivers to allow it to function as part of the wireless network and to work with the router. Those drivers are provided by the manufacturer and will not necessarily be part of the Windows driver database.

When you add new hardware, Windows presents a pop-up window to take you through the installation process, as shown in Figure 5.6. You have the choice of letting Windows automatically install the drivers or indicating a location where the drivers are located (such as a floppy or CD-ROM).

FIGURE 5.6

Helping you through the installation of drivers for a new NIC.

If your card came with a driver disk, place it in your computer. The Add New Hardware Wizard asks whether you want to search the Internet for the latest drivers. Choose no, and select the option to use the driver that came with your hardware. The next screen prompts you to either let Windows search for the driver or choose a specific location. The best option is to have Windows search for the driver. It looks both at the drivers that came with your hardware and at the drivers that Windows has in its own driver directory, allowing Windows to choose the most current one.

After you finish the installation process, Windows notifies you that your new hardware is installed and ready for use.

If Windows is not able to identify any driver, or your hardware did not come with a driver disk, be sure to visit the website for the hardware. Download a driver for your NIC and then go launch the Add New Hardware Wizard again.

Using either the Ethernet port that came with your computer or the add-on card that you installed if it was not equipped with one, you are ready to connect your PC to a variety of networking devices and cables.

Just as with a desktop PC, after you install a network adapter card or USB network adapter or use a built-in wireless adapter for your laptop, you should check that it is part of your system and functioning properly by following these steps in this order:

1. Choose Start, Control Panel, System.

2. Select the Hardware tab.

3. Select Device Manager.

4. You see a list of all the hardware attached to your PC organized by type of hardware. Click on Network Adapters.

5. Your new PCI Ethernet adapter should be listed. You can click on it to see its Properties menu to find information on the drivers it uses and to check whether it is working properly.

If your new card's icon has a round yellow symbol with an exclamation mark next to it, it is not working or it is installed improperly. You can use the device's Properties menu to troubleshoot and resolve any driver or device conflicts.

Choosing Ethernet Cables

Wired networks and even wireless routers use Ethernet ports to connect to your PCs and to make wired connections between devices. Although the devices you purchase might come with the appropriate cables to make connections, it is good to understand which type of Ethernet cable you need to use and to understand the different varieties of cables.

You want to use an Ethernet cable that is labeled RJ-45 CAT-5E patch cable. Although they come in a variety of colors, the cable has two RJ-45 connectors at each end, and it is designed to work on 10/100BASE-T Fast Ethernet networking equipment. Figure 5.7 shows the connectors at each end of a CAT-5E patch cable. In case you are unsure of the cable, the type of cable is often printed on the wire part of the cable.

You use the CAT-5E patch cable for almost all the wired connections in your Ethernet-based home entertainment network. You might need another type of CAT-5E cable when connecting to a DSL or cable modem or when making a direct connection between two computers without a switch or router. It is called a *cross-over* cable. Two main wires used for data transfer are "crossed" to allow direct communication between PCs and other devices that require a cross-over.

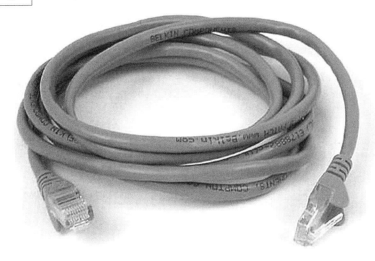

FIGURE 5.7

A Ethernet CAT-5E patch cable with RJ-45 male connectors at each end.

A cable or DSL modem comes with the appropriate cable for connecting it to your PC. The cable and connection might be a standard cable or a special cross-over cable. (It will probably be the only time you need a cross-over cable.) Generally, cross-over cables are used to connect two PCs together without the use of a router or hub, and some cable or DSL modems do use them.

> **TIP**
> Wiring your home is something you can tackle yourself. Although you can hire a professional to run cables, with a bit of practice (and a willingness to patch and repaint walls in many cases), you can do it yourself with the right tools. Using bulk CAT-5E cable and RJ-45 wall jacks, you can run cable from your router's location to other rooms in your home. To make long cables, you can use couplers to join fixed-length cables together.

When you connect your cable or DSL modem to your router, you should use the exact cable provided with the modem to connect it to your PC—except that now you use the cable to connect the modem to your router. If for some reason you need a longer cross-over cable, look for an Ethernet CAT-5E cross-over cable. Usually they are yellow in color and well marked as a special cable.

You can purchase CAT-5E cables in fixed lengths complete with RJ-45 connectors at each end, or for longer cable runs, you can purchase bulk cable and attach your own RJ-45 connectors to the ends. This task requires investing in a crimping tool to attach the connectors.

Although the thought of attaching the connectors can be intimidating, the crimping tools are actually easy to use (after a few tries!).

If you are running cables through walls, an easier method is to use RJ-45 wall jacks. They have simple connectors in which you connect wires in the cable to screw-on connectors, and they are easier to use than RJ-45 connectors. Wall jacks also provide a finished appearance for your home. You can purchase RJ-45 wall jacks at any major electronics store such as Radio Shack for well under $10 each.

If you are not ready to try attaching your own connectors to bulk cable but you need long cable runs, you can purchase fixed-length cables with connectors at each end and connect them using a simple coupler. A coupler is a small device that allows you to join two cables by attaching the male connectors from the cable to the two female connections on the coupler.

There is a limit on the length of cable you can use in an Ethernet connection. With the Fast Ethernet 10/100 standard, a single connection can be about 328 feet. This length is more than adequate for just about any home installation. If by some chance you need a cable run longer than that, you can add devices called repeaters, but it is unlikely you will need such equipment in a home setting.

Connecting a Router for the First Time

Having an Ethernet connection on your main PC allows you to start on the first task in building your home entertainment network—adding a router.

A router is the most important device in a home entertainment network. It manages and shares your Internet connection between all your PCs and media devices. It also manages the sharing of media files and data between PCs and devices.

Because a large part of a home entertainment network is getting content from the Internet (Internet radio, streaming videos, and other entertainment content), the router allows you to use one high-speed Internet connection from a cable or DSL modem for all PCs and devices. It does this by

- Establishing the Internet connection, including a username and password for your access to an Internet service provider, and sharing it with other devices without the need for each device to log on to the ISP

- Providing network security by using its own "firewall," which is an important safeguard against invasion of your home entertainment network from outside sources attempting to install programs, view your files, or infect your networked devices with spam or viruses

- Managing Internet access across the devices on your home entertainment network

In addition to managing your Internet connection, it also allows you to network your home PCs and devices as a separate network and manages both networks. As the main device in creating a home network, it performs the following:

- Networks all devices on your home entertainment network. The network it creates and manages allows you to share files and devices such as printers.

- Manages the home network. A wireless router allows both wired and wireless connections between PCs and devices and manages the wireless connections using industry-standard wireless protocols and security features.

The router's main job is to manage and connect two separate networks; in your home entertainment network, it manages the Internet network and your local area network (LAN), which is the network of devices in your home.

Using an Installation Wizard

Whether you are using a wired or wireless router, the process of connecting your router to your Internet connection and to your main PC is essentially the same. Most routers come with two ways to install your router: a manual process where you make all the needed settings or an installation wizard or setup routine that gets your router working with your PC and Internet connection.

The installation wizard or setup routine is basic. It only connects the router to your PC and to the Internet, and it requires the following steps in this order:

1. Disconnect your Internet connection (DSL or cable modem) from your PC by turning off your PC and then removing the Ethernet cable that runs from the modem to the Ethernet port on your PC.

2. Restart your PC and use the installation procedure and software that came with the router. This step involves running setup software and then following onscreen prompts to reconnect your Internet source such as a cable or DSL modem.

3. Following the specific instructions from the installation routine or installation wizard your router came with, you connect your Internet modem to the wide area network (WAN) or Internet port on your router and connect the router to the Ethernet port on your PC.

4. The installation software or wizard attempts to make an Internet connection, and once it does, it verifies that your router has been installed correctly. You might be asked to enter your username and password for your ISP during this point in the process. Enter them, if requested, to allow the router to make your Internet connection.

At this point, it is a good practice to launch your web browser and visit any website. If the router has been connected correctly and has made an Internet connection, you can use your web browser or email client in the same way you did when the modem was connected directly to your PC's Ethernet port.

Figure 5.8 shows a typical installation routine using a wizard provided by the manufacturer that takes you through the installation routine.

FIGURE 5.8

First step in the Belkin wireless router installation wizard.

Web-Based Control Router Installation

If your router does not come with an installation wizard or you want to gain more control over the installation routine, you access your router's main control panel by launching a web browser and entering the IP address of the router. The IP address appears in the manual that comes with your router. Figure 5.9 shows the web-based controls for installing and managing the router.

The web-based setup routine offers you total control of all settings for the router, and you need to follow the instructions that come with your router for disconnecting your Internet connection, connecting the router, and reconnecting your Internet connection.

Features in a web-based router interface include the following:

- **Login/logout**—Allows you to log in to or out of the router.
- **Internet status**—Shows the status of your current Internet connection.
- **LAN settings**—LAN settings for the IP address of your router, DHCP server function and the local domain name for your home network.
- **Internet settings**—Allows you to change your ISP or change your username and password.

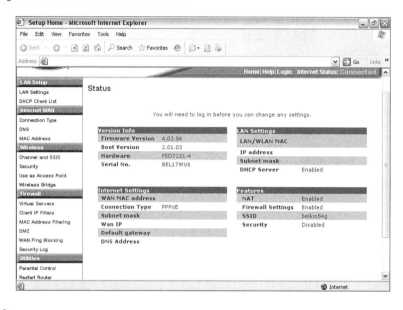

FIGURE 5.9

Web-based installation controls for a Belkin wireless router.

Routers and home networks use a variety of network protocols, IP addresses, and security measures. To enable a number of devices to work with each other, and to optimize your home entertainment network's security, you often need to manually control the network and router settings—but not during the basic installation routine.

Routers come configured to use default settings that allow the router to work with most devices, including the main PC, without your making any special settings. These settings assume that you will be using devices mostly from the same manufacturer and meeting the same network standards and settings as used on the router.

When you use the web-based controls for installation, you need to make settings on both your PC and the router, following the steps outlined next.

Step 1: Connect the Router

When using the web-based controls, you first need to connect the router to your main PC using an Ethernet CAT-5E cable.

Connect the cable from the Ethernet port on your PC to one of the device ports on the back of the router, as shown in Figure 5.10. (Usually there are at least four ports, and they are numbered: You can use any of the ports.)

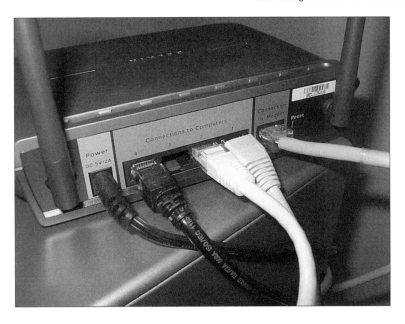

FIGURE 5.10

Connecting a cable from the network port of a PC to the connected devices port on the router.

In addition to making the connection between the PC and your router, you need to connect your DSL or cable modem to the router. The router has a separate connection labeled WAN for this purpose. This port might be labeled Internet on some routers. Be sure to use the same cable that came with your DSL/cable modem to make the connection from the modem to the router. Because some modems use a crossover cable, you also need to be sure that you do not confuse cables when you are setting up the router.

Finally, you need to connect the power supply to the router and make sure that the modem powers up.

Once connected and turned on, the router has a series of lights on the top or front panel that begin to flash. These status lights provide you with visual indication of what is connected and whether your router is functioning properly.

Each device that is connected, including your modem, has its own status light. If the light is on, it means that a device is connected to that port. If the light is flashing, it most likely means that there is activity. Your router manual will have a chart detailing what the flashing, and color, of the status lights indicate.

Step 2: Configuring Your PC to Work with the Router

After connecting your router to the PC, you must configure your PC to work with the router. Change your PC's settings using the following steps in the following order:

1. Choose Start, Control Panel, Network. You see icons for your network adapters, so right-click on the adapter for your Local Area Network connection. You see the Properties menu for the network adapter.

2. On the General tab is a list of items that the adapter uses. Highlight Internet Protocol (TCP/IP) and then click on the Properties button underneath the list.

3. From the General tab of the Internet Protocol properties menu that appears, you can select to either obtain an IP address automatically or enter an IP address. Choose to obtain the IP address automatically.

Internet Protocol (IP) addresses are numbers that identify a specific device in a network, including Internet network connections. Your router has an IP address, and you can choose to enter that address if you want, but at this point in the process, it is best to automatically assign IP addresses in your home entertainment network.

When you choose to automatically assign addresses, your PC is in a DHCP mode. DHCP stands for Dynamic Host Configuration Protocol, which is used to assign IP addresses in network. This is the easiest way for you to work with all the devices on your home entertainment network.

Step 3: Configuring the Router

After making the preceding settings, use your web browser to access your router's settings and controls. Find the default IP address of the router in the manual that came with it, and enter just the number into the address bar of the web browser. You do not need to enter a www or http prefix, just the number as shown in the manual (such as 198.162.1.1).

Because you can reach your router by typing the IP address using a web browser, you should think about using a password to access your router's controls. A button on the screen allows you to log in to the router. It allows you to assign a password or, if you choose to not use a password, leave the password field blank.

Whether you use a password or not, you first need to log in to the router to make any changes. If you chose to not use a password, leave the password box empty and press the Submit button to log on to the router.

Figure 5.9, shown earlier in this section, shows the web-based controls for a router. Depending on your manufacturer, the page might have a different appearance, but it does allow you to access all settings for the router in a similar manner described here.

The settings range from the basic identification of your router's IP address to security settings, firewall controls, and other utilities such as parental controls. I cover these topics in upcoming chapters, but for now, you want to complete the installation of your router by entering the correct settings to allow it to manage your Internet connection.

Step 4: Connecting to the Internet

Your router will manage your Internet connection, but it needs to know what type of Internet protocols your ISP uses. It is a good idea to have your "startup" package from your ISP handy during this part of the setup process. Your ISP should have provided you with all the information you need to make a connection.

If you do not have this information, you should contact your ISP and obtain it.

The list of menu items from your router's control page will have a section for Internet. It might also be labeled as Internet/WAN. Click on the menu button for Connection Type.

This menu allows you to choose the type of Internet connection that will work with your ISP. Several are listed, and they should include the following:

- **Dynamic**—This type is the most common form of connection type and is most often used for cable modems. If you have a cable modem or you are not sure of your connection type, choose this connection setting.

- **Static**—Some ISPs require that you use a static IP address to connect with their service. Although this method is not common, if your ISP requires a static connection, it will provide you with the IP address, and you should choose this setting.

- **PPPoE**—This terms stands for Point-to-Point Protocol over Ethernet, which is most often used for DSL service. If you use DSL and your provider gave you a username and password, choose this setting.

- **PPTP**—This term stands for Point-to-Point Tunneling Protocol, which is used mainly in European countries. If your ISP does happen to use this standard, choose this connection type.

- **Telstra BigPond**—You should use this Australian standard only if your ISP requires it.

Based on the information provided to you by your ISP, select the connection type that best matches the connection type the ISP uses. Each connection type on the menu allows you to make further settings for the connection.

The following section details the information or selections you need to provide for the three main connection types—dynamic, static, and PPPoE.

Settings for Dynamic Connections

If you use a cable modem, chances are that the dynamic setting is the right choice for you. After you make this selection, the next screen asks you for a host name. In most cases, simply choosing this setting is enough to make the connection to the Internet through your ISP. In some cases, you might need to enter the name that identifies the ISP (hostname); it should have been provided to you by your ISP. Enter the host name and submit it.

If you have connected your PC to the Internet without a router, your connection might require the existing Media Access Control (MAC) address. If it is required, you will have an option to change the MAC address and clone the one from the prior use of the ISP with your PC. This process is automatic, and you do not need to manually enter the MAC address. Every device connected to your home network will have an individual MAC address. The router represents the entire LAN to your ISP as one address even though your LAN will be made up of several individual devices.

If all you need to do is change to the Dynamic Connection setting, the Connected to the Internet light on your router lights up. If it doesn't, add the host name and then clone the MAC address, if needed.

Settings for Static Connections

Static connections are not common in cable modem and DSL broadband services. However, if your ISP does use a static IP address, the original paperwork should have its IP address, subnet mask, and ISP gateway address. After you select Static as the connection type and click next, you need to enter the three items on the menu. After you enter them and submit the information, the Internet Connection light on your router should light up to confirm that you have an Internet connection.

If your ISP uses multiple static addresses, it should have provided a list of the IP addresses. Choose the option for My ISP Uses Multiple IP Addresses and enter the IP addresses. This task allows the connection to use any of the addresses to establish and maintain a fast Internet connection.

Settings for PPPoE Connections

If you use DSL, chances are that you need to use the PPPoE connection settings. The following things indicate that you need to use this setting:

- Your ISP gave you a username and a password to access the service.

- Your ISP provided you with a special program to launch your Internet service each time you turn on your PC.

- You need to launch your Internet service from an icon on your desktop or your Start menu.

From the PPPoE connection menu, enter the username and password provided to you by your ISP. There will be a space for the service name. If you don't know it, or it was not provided, leave this field blank. After you submit the information, the Connected light on your router should light to indicate that the Internet connection has been established.

Completing the Installation

After making the physical connection between your router, your cable or DSL modem, and your PC—and after using the web-based router controls to identify your Internet connection type—you should have a connection to the Internet.

To check it, simply launch a web browser, enter any Internet address, and make sure that you have an active Internet connection. You can also visually confirm the connection because your router has a Connected indicator that shows an active connection to the Internet.

This section completes the installation of the router and provides an introduction to the router's control settings, which you will also use for the firewall and security settings covered in future chapters.

Working with Dial-up Internet Connections

If you will only be using a dial-up ISP, you need to indicate that you don't have an active Internet connection when installing the router.

Routers are primarily designed to be used with a broadband connection. With dial-up service, you use the network to share your dial-up connection from a PC that allows that connection to be shared on the network. This will be managed by the router in the same way it manages an always-on broadband connection. If you are not going to be using a wireless network and you will only use dial-up for your Internet connection, you could use a less expensive network hub rather than a router. The router's main job is to manage the flow of information between two networks—the Internet and your home network. Without an active full-time connection to the Internet, the router is essentially acting as a network hub, and your dial-up Internet connection will be shared through your home network.

A router is a much better choice for sharing an Internet connection. Once you connect to the Internet using your dial-up connection, the router will manage your connection between all of the devices on the home network that need to share it.

Adding Other PCs to the Router

After the initial setup of your router, you will be ready to add other PCs to the network. If your additional PCs will be sharing only an Internet connection, there is little to do except make a wired or wireless connection to the router. If you will be sharing files and media content, you need to make network connections between the computers and devices.

Chapter 8, "Adding Additional PCs to the Router," covers both simple Internet access and full file sharing by PCs on a home entertainment network.

Summary

After creating a home entertainment network plan, and deciding on a wired, wireless, or combination network, the next step is installing a router. After making sure that your PC has a 10/100BASE-T Fast Ethernet port and that you have the appropriate Ethernet CAT-5E cables, you disconnect your Internet connection from your PC, install the software for your router, connect the router to your main PC, and reconnect the Internet connection to the router directly.

Once connected, you use the router's installation wizard or web-based controls to establish and maintain an Internet connection.

Securing Your PCs

Because a home entertainment network relies upon standard PC-based home networking equipment and includes an active connection to the Internet, it is equally vulnerable to security threats from the Internet such as viruses and spyware.

It is essential that you treat your home entertainment network with the same caution as you would a standard PC home network. You need to secure the PCs and the entire network from outside attacks from the Internet and even from people near your home who have wireless networks that can possibly allow their computers to read your files.

This chapter looks at the importance of securing any PC on your home entertainment network—even before you connect it.

Securing Your PCs

After installing a router with an active, full-time connection to the Internet, you should take some simple steps to secure all the PCs that will be connected to the router.

Security has become such an important issue that Microsoft recently release Windows XP Service Pack 2 (SP2) specifically to address PC security.

Threats to your PC most often come to your PC through the Internet. Although viruses can come as emails or attachments to emails, it is also possible to face harm when visiting websites or when downloading documents or media files. About all you can do is make sure that your PC has as many safeguards as possible and that you defend it from any unwanted spying or viruses.

Types of Security Threats

Security threats are constantly changing and adapting to countermeasures to prevent them. Although security threats will change, the most basic way to deal with them is to not allow them to ever gain entry to your PCs. For this reason, it is important to begin your home entertainment network security measures before adding any additional PCs to your router—either wired or wirelessly.

There are two types of security on a home entertainment network:

- **Network level**—Network-level security prevents threats from the Internet that arrive through the Internet connection managed by your router. It also prevents people outside your home from using your network with their own wireless devices or gaining access to your PCs and devices through a wireless router (if you are using a wireless system).

- **PC level**—Each PC on your network needs its own security measures. Some threats from the Internet and from sharing files cannot be prevented by network-level security measures. Examples are viruses, spam, and spyware.

This section is specific to securing your PC. It is a good practice because your network-level security cannot protect your PCs from every threat.

To understand how to prevent unwanted entry to your PC, you need to know the basic types of threats and what you can do to stop them.

Viruses

Viruses are so threatening to computers that when a major virus surfaces, it is reported on the news. You will often be notified via email by your Internet service provider (ISP). Viruses can cause minor harm to files and to the operating system of your computer, but they are also capable of flooding your Internet connection and account with email, harming your personal files, and even erasing or renaming important files on your PC.

If you do not connect to the Internet, use your PC for emails, or make any other form of contact with users and information outside of the PC, then you are not likely to get a virus. If you use your PC for interaction through the Internet, you *will* encounter them. Viruses are a fact of life in the online world, and the first time you install and run a virus checker on your PC, you almost always find that files on your PC have some type of virus that you didn't know was there.

Most viruses come in the form of email attachments and are small, hard-to-detect, executable applications that launch when you open them, thinking that they are a legitimate document or file. They can also lay dormant on your PC, waiting for a time to activate or for you to open them. In general, viruses have made it hard to trust most emails or files from all but the most reliable sources, but even then, the person sending you something might have a virus without knowing it and pass it along to you.

The best tool in dealing with virus prevention is to install an antivirus program and make sure that you allow it to update its list of known viruses on a regular basis. The antivirus program actively scans the files on your PC along with all new emails and documents and detects any known virus. If it finds one, it alerts you and quarantines or destroys the file.

You can find excellent antivirus programs in almost all stores that sell computer software, and you can purchase and download them from the providers on their websites. Some popular and respected antivirus software available for online purchase and automatic updates include the following:

- McAfee VirusScan

- Symantec's Norton AntiVirus

- Trend Micro PC-cillin

Each of the products listed here offer full-time antivirus monitoring and keep their database of known and new viruses up-to-date and available for automatic updates whenever your PC is connected to the Internet. Although it is possible to find freeware programs, be sure that any antivirus software you use offers updates.

You might also be able to take advantage of free antivirus software provided by your ISP. Most all major ISPs scan all email for viruses and also offer some type of antivirus software to load onto your PC as an additional measure. Do not rely only on the virus scanning preformed by your ISP on email: use an antivirus program installed on each PC.

Using free antivirus software, such as AVG Anti-Virus 7.0 or later (available at http://free.grisoft.com), is also an option. With any freeware program, be sure to check user ratings and feedback to see what other users think. Most free download sites offer user ratings and reviews, so be sure to consider those and also how long the program has been in use and how often updates are made available.

Installing antivirus software is simple; it follows the general steps described here:

1. Install the antivirus software. During the installation procedure, you are asked which files you want scanned and how often to scan them.

2. Before you run the virus check, use the update feature of the program to get the latest set of virus definitions. This will bring your program up-to-date before you run the check.

3. After installation, be sure to run a full check of all files on all drives and boot sectors and all files on your PC.

4. After performing a full file scan, set your antivirus software to check emails, attachments, and all the incoming files from any drive. Also schedule full checks on a regular basis such as once a week.

5. Turn on automatic updates. This step updates your software with the latest known virus scans on a virtual real-time basis.

TIP

There are two things you should do to protect your PC from virus activity. First, install antivirus software and update it on a regular basis. Next, if your ISP offers virus scanning of emails and attachments, be sure that you turn on those features using the controls and settings of your ISP hosting service.

The leading antivirus programs are pretty good; they are your best defense for detection, and when updated, they keep you protected against new threats. As good as they are, a big part of dealing with virus protection is up to you.

You should, as it is now so widely publicized, be cautious of any documents, especially in emails, that come from people or sources you are not sure of. If you don't know the sender and there is an attachment, don't open it! Delete the file. It's as simple as that.

Appendix A, "Resources," features a list of companies that offer antivirus software for your PC.

Spyware

If viruses weren't bad enough, a more sinister type of threat exists with spyware.

When you visit websites or even download shareware or freeware from the Internet, it is possible for the website to install a program that appears to be a cookie used by your web browser or an ActiveX control used by the web browser. This process is common for many websites, and it can happen without your even knowing it. In most instances, they add functionality to your web experience, but they can be used to install privacy-invading programs.

As its name implies, spyware is a program that collects information from your keystrokes or a list of websites that you visit and information that you send to them. The collected information can include checking and credit-card account numbers and passwords. It can also include a lot of private information, such as the phone numbers, addresses, and supportive information you use with a checking or credit-card account. Nice.

In addition to spyware, browser hijacking has become a related threat. Using Internet Explorer's ability to be changed remotely, an outside party can go in and change allowed and disallowed pages, change your home page and make changes to your browser's security settings and preferences. Good spyware prevents the installation of the small programs and ActiveX scripts that allow browser hijacking to occur.

The threat of spyware is very real, especially if you visit a lot of websites, download a lot of programs from unknown sources, and use the Web for transactions of any sort. You can take a number of actions to prevent spyware and detect it.

First, there are spyware detection programs that will scan your computer's hard drives, looking for spyware-type programs. They list the program and its source and ask you whether you want to disable it. Here's a good way to think of it: If you didn't ask for it to be on your computer, disable the file using the features of the spyware detection program. There will be controls to ignore, disable, or even delete the file. Because you might not be sure if the file is actually harmful (or even know what the file is), disabling is the best step. If it's needed for a legitimate website in the future, it will install it again for you.

Spyware protection programs are available as programs you can purchase online to download, and they are also being offered by more ISPs. Be sure to check whether your ISP offers a downloadable program. America Online, for example, has made its own spyware protection software available to its users at no extra cost. Most vendors who offer antivirus software are now also offering spyware detection software, so check whether "package" deals combine the two products at one lower price.

Spyware detection programs, like antivirus programs, run a full check of all your files on the first use and then run in background mode to monitor any attempts made to install suspect spyware on your PC. If you download or purchase spyware detection software, follow these steps:

1. Install the spyware detection software using the installation routine, and if prompted, be sure to turn on real-time monitoring.

2. Run a full scan of your PC's hard drives and files to detect any suspect programs that might be spyware.

3. If the programs the spyware detection software identifies are from an unknown source or are known as a threat, disable them. Disabling does not delete the file; it keeps it from running and possibly acting as spyware.

4. Turn on automatic updating. As with viruses, the list of known spyware program types grows daily, and you must update the software to be fully protected.

> **TIP**
> There are two things you should do to protect your PC from spyware. First, install spyware protection software and update it on a regular basis. Next, be sure to upgrade Windows XP to SP2 and use the Internet Options Security setting to prevent any applications from being installed on your PC without your permission.

The second action you should take is setting controls for program installations from websites. The good news is that you actually have pretty strong controls in the latest release of Windows XP SP2 and Internet Explorer. You can turn off the ability for a website to install any type of application to your computer using the Security options in Internet Explorer's Internet Option menu.

Figure 6.1 shows the Security settings from the Internet Explorer Internet Options menu. As you will learn, you can block all installations of applications or ask to be prompted first so that you will be aware of who is attempting to add an application and decide whether they are a trusted source.

FIGURE 6.1

Security options from the Internet Options menu of Internet Explorer.

If you set all the types of programs that can be installed to a disable or prompt level, you will find that visiting and using your favorite websites is an endless session of saying "okay" to prompts. Today's websites use of a lot of temporary applications, and even some permanent ones, to make the web experience better. So you are faced with a problem: have a good web experience and run the risk of spyware or eliminate the risk and spend your days answering prompts or disabling key features in websites.

You can control settings for "trusted sites" that allow them to download needed applications. On the same Security menu in Internet Options is a button for Trusted Sites. When you select it, you can add a list of the URLs for websites you trust and use often and then modify the security settings for just those sites. It is a bit of work, but it's a good practice.

Appendix A features a list of companies that offer spyware detection software for your PC.

Computer Invasion

Another type of threat happens when you have a full-time connection to the Internet. In the same way that you can network your computers and devices together and allow them to share data, that open connection to the Internet can also make it possible for someone to use the Internet to view, copy, delete, or modify files on your PC.

As with all of the Internet, what makes it good also makes it bad. The ability to use your computer from a remote location (such as work), called remote sharing, is a great feature—and Internet hacks have learned to use it to invade your PC without your knowing it. As scary as that sounds, it's something that you can prevent.

The simplest thing is to not connect to the Internet, but that defeats the whole purpose of having an Internet connection. Assuming that you want to use the Internet, you need to use the "firewall" feature of Windows XP. A *firewall* essentially sets up a barrier between your PC and any access to its data or system—except when you allow it.

There are two places where you want a firewall: on your router (which is covered in Chapter 7, "Securing Your Home Entertainment Network") and your PC.

The firewall for your router is hardware-based and the firewall is a part of the router's firmware. Your Windows XP PC uses a software-based firewall that became a standard feature with Windows XP.

You can control the settings for the Windows firewall by going to Start, Control Panel, Windows Firewall. Figure 6.2 shows the first Windows Firewall menu indicating that the firewall is active.

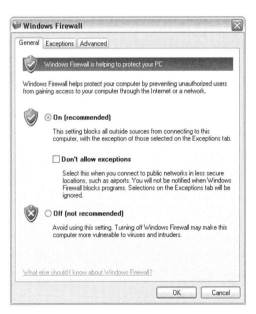

FIGURE 6.2

Windows XP Firewall control panel menu.

There are two main settings:

- **On**—This is the recommended setting, and Windows XP uses a software firewall to protect any Internet connections that you have installed. There is an additional setting to not allow any "exceptions." Exceptions are the Internet connections that you have installed and that you want to have open through the firewall. They include your ISP, special services such as iTunes, and a remote desktop, if you are using that feature. You can select to turn off any exceptions. This choice is appropriate for instances such as using a laptop at a hotspot like a coffee house or airport.

- **Off**—You can choose to disable the firewall, and there might be times in your home entertainment network where you can let your router perform the firewall function, but this is not a good practice. Even though your router has a firewall, it is still better to use the Windows XP firewall.

As mentioned earlier, you can control the outside sources that you allow to come through your firewall to create a network connection. Figure 6.3 shows the exception list from the Windows Firewall menu.

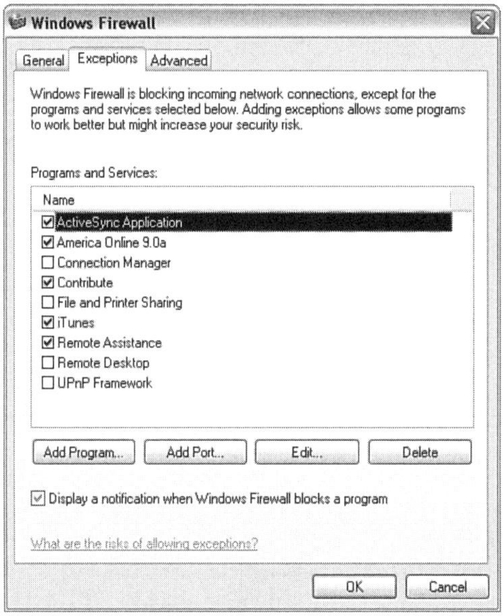

FIGURE 6.3

The Windows XP Firewall menu for exceptions, where you can decide which network connections to allow access to your PC.

Many of these settings happen when you agree to install a program or use a service. If the firewall is blocking a service that you are using, such as an online movie or music service, you can go to the Exceptions menu and add, delete, edit, and turn exceptions on or off.

You find the next set of firewall controls by clicking on the Advanced tab; you see the menu in Figure 6.4.

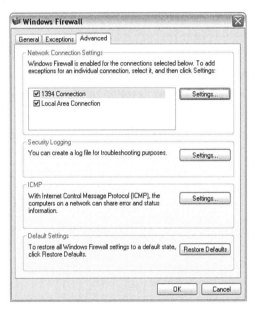

FIGURE 6.4

Windows XP Firewall Advanced settings menu.

The advanced settings allow specific control over the basic Internet connections (primarily the ports that are used to make your Internet connection, such as the Ethernet port). The other settings allow you to "log" information about security on your PC. You might need this logging if you are experiencing security breaches and you want to locate where you should make changes to the firewall. You can send the logs to Microsoft Technical Support, for example.

> **TIP**
> Windows XP includes a strong firewall as part of the operating system. Be sure to protect your PC from viruses and invasion through your Internet connection by turning on the Windows Firewall.

There is also a logging setting (ICMP, Internet Control Message Protocol) that allows computers in your home network to share log information and to return all settings to the default Windows XP settings.

Understanding What the Firewall Can't Do

The Windows firewall blocks any attempt from an outside, Internet-based entity to make a network connection with your PC and read, copy, or delete files on your computer. It also blocks any attempt to control your computer.

It does not look for viruses, spyware, or other harmful files. It also doesn't keep you from opening emails with applications or viruses attached. You need antivirus and spyware programs in addition to a firewall.

Adding Firewalls

It is possible to add other software-based firewall programs to your PC and not use the Windows firewall. Commercial firewall software offers a number of features that do not appear in the Windows XP SP2 firewall, such as the following:

- Being able to turn the firewall off for a short duration when needed. The firewall program automatically turns itself back on after a specified period so you don't have to remember to do it.

- Program control, which only allows programs you choose to make Internet connections. This feature keeps programs such as spyware from accessing the Internet.

- Hiding your PC from any outside source. Effectively, your PC is invisible to anyone on the Internet.

- Information blocking features that keep items such as account names or passwords from being sent without your knowledge.

Firewall software adds control to your PC's firewall, and it is available from many of the same manufacturers of antivirus software listed earlier in this chapter. As with spyware detection software, you might find "bundle" deals that keep the cost of a package containing antivirus, spyware detection, and firewall software close to the price of one single program.

With the release of Windows XP SP2, the firewall is now a part of the operating system, and you should examine whether there is any benefit to using an additional firewall program—even if it is a part of an antivirus or spyware program or utility. Make sure that the program you are using is not causing a conflict with the Windows firewall.

Using Common-Sense Security Measures

With all the possible threats to your PC, you need to become an active part of your PC's defense system. As you have seen in this chapter, you need to do the following:

- **Protect your PC**—Use a firewall on your PC to only allow Internet connections that you choose—and keep all other Internet connections to your PC blocked.

- **Protect your data**—Use antivirus software to keep viruses off your computer. Use spyware detection programs to keep outside parties from finding out your Internet usage and keeping track of your passwords, credit-card numbers, and keystrokes.

You are the first and last line of defense in keeping your computer secure. To make sure that your computer is as protected as possible, you should do the following:

- **Update regularly**—Antivirus software, spyware detection software, firewall protection programs, and Windows XP all need to be updated on a regular basis. Once a week is a good setting for all of these updates. Each of them has an "automatic update" setting that should be active. Be sure to find this setting in each application, turn it on, and choose how often the program should search for updates. Many programs have a routine where they automatically update when an update is available. This is the best setting to use for antivirus and spyware detection programs.

- **Use caution**—When you install programs, especially if they are applications on web pages, you should use caution and only accept programs from extremely trustworthy sources.

- **Use ISP controls**—Chances are your ISP has antivirus, spam filtering, and other security measures that you can use. Be sure to turn those settings on from the control panel or settings menu that your ISP provides. Many computer threats come in the form of spam and unwanted email, and your ISP can help you filter such threats before they ever reach your PC.

- **Don't share your passwords**—We are all creatures of habit. For any security settings on your PC that need a password (such as your ISP, remote access, and network administrator), do not use the same passwords that you use for online transactions, music buying, or any place on the Internet where you have a username and password. Using one common password might make it possible for an outside source to attempt to break your security measures by using remote access features built into Windows XP to hack into your PC.

In addition to following these rules, use common sense. Turning off security settings, allowing more than one person to make security setting changes in your home, and not updating your security applications are all ways to put your PC at risk.

Don't share your settings or passwords or open unknown programs or files!

Summary

Your PC is at risk from viruses in outside emails or files from unknown sources. It is also possible for outside sources to track data and usage on your PC to invade your privacy. When unprotected, your PC is subject to outside parties using your Internet connection to gain some control over your PC and the files on it.

Chapter 6	Securing Your PCs

By installing and regularly updating antivirus and spyware detection programs, you can protect your computer from the threats. By using the Windows XP firewall (or a stand-alone firewall program, if you prefer), you can secure your computer from any entity outside your network.

Securing Your Home Entertainment Network

Using a DSL or cable modem and broadband router presents two unique security challenges: keeping outside parties from gaining access to your computers through your router and keeping others with wireless devices from using your network if you are using a wireless router.

Just as with your own PCs in your home entertainment network, other people who have a wireless network card and are close enough to your router can potentially gain access to your PCs and devices. You might have heard of "hot spots" in public places where you can bring your laptop and connect to the Internet if you have a wireless network adapter. Your home network is similar in nature, and you need to secure your wireless home entertainment network.

This chapter will look first at how to keep hackers out of your network by making sure that your DSL or cable modem and your broadband router have firewalls and then at how to prevent access to a wireless network from outside parties.

Understanding Hardware-Based Firewalls

The purpose of a firewall is to create a barrier against unwanted information or interaction with unwanted hosts from the Internet. It also keeps outside hackers or hosts from interacting with your PCs as if they were trusted sources.

For example, you connect with your Internet service provider (ISP), a trusted source, to send and receive emails that are stored on your computers, to connect to websites, and to download files. Your ISP has established itself as a "port" on your network. Your PCs and your ISP's servers can talk to one another and exchange data.

Hackers attempt to disguise themselves as a legitimate port, a trusted source, and gain the same level of access to your network and all the devices on it. That allows hackers to gain access to your files, place harmful files on your PCs, and even destroy or harm your files.

A firewall maintains a list of certain "ports" that it will allow access to your PCs and devices. Typically, these ports include the following:

- Simple Mail Transfer Protocol (SMTP) mail servers

- Post Office Protocol 3 (POP3) mail servers

- File Transfer Protocol (FTP) servers

- Transmission Control Protocol/Internet Protocol (TCP/IP)

These ports are essential to effectively use the Internet. They allow email to move between mail servers from your ISP or mail servers you select, they allow the transfer of files between your computer and trusted sites, and they let you connect with web-sites.

If a firewall blocked all ports or connections to outside sources from the Internet, you would not be able to use the Internet at all. The firewall opens "ports" to essential servers that you connect to through the Internet and uses a number of filters to block unwanted or suspect data and ports from the ports it does allow.

Each firewall—whether the software firewall from Windows XP, a third-party firewall that you install, or the hardware-based firewalls on your broadband router or DSL or cable modem—has a set of filters that allow interaction with reliable and trusted ports. Through your own settings or through ongoing "permission" to access content and sites from the Internet as you are online, you control additional ports and permissions to create a network connection between your network and a remote network.

The next sections take a look at firewalls that protect your entire home entertainment network, as opposed to just one single PC, as covered in Chapter 6, "Securing Your PCs."

Firewall on Your DSL or Cable Modem

You should contact your ISP to learn whether the modem it provides comes with a built-in firewall or whether they provide firewall software. Most do, but you should check to be sure.

Because the DSL or cable modem is the first point of entry to your home entertainment network, it is the first line of defense against access to your network and PCs you have on the network.

Because your DSL or cable modem is generally provided to you from your ISP (or is one that you purchase at a retailer that is designed to work for a specific ISP), it might have a built-in firewall that the ISP installed for your protection. This point is most often true for modems that also provide wireless access or have a router built in.

Simpler modems that do not have a router or wireless networking feature generally do not have a built-in firewall, and you need to use a software firewall provided by the ISP.

Hardware-based firewalls have ports established to make the correct connection to the ISP's network server, and you also benefit from the firewall the ISP has in place to protect both its network and yours.

There are few controls over the ISP firewall, and it is designed to keep outside hackers from gaining access to your home network. It also keeps your (and the ISP's) network safe from spam, mass emails, and outside sources gaining control of your PC.

If you learn that your DSL or cable modem does not have a built-in firewall, your ISP most likely offers free firewall software that you may download. The software-based download offers protection on a specific PC but does not offer the same first-tier level of protection as a firewall built into the actual modem.

Figure 7.1 shows a firewall program that can be added from an ISP.

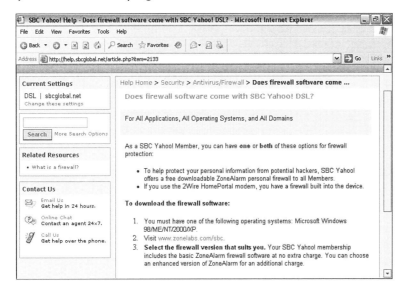

FIGURE 7.1

Example of an ISP that offers a free software-based firewall when using modems that do not have a hardware-based firewall.

Installing a software-based firewall requires the following steps:

1. Download the firewall software from your ISP's site. It is a good practice to choose "save" rather than "run" when starting the download process. This choice allows you to save the program for installation on other computers at another time or to easily re-install the program if needed in the future.

2. Run the installation program. After the program is downloaded, you are asked whether you want to open the folder where the file was stored. Open the folder, click on the setup program, and follow the menu prompts for installation.

3. Set any preferences during the installation process. Preferences might include enabling or disabling ports or Internet sources and services and filtering types of programs and mail sources.

4. Set automatic updating, if available.

Firewalls on Your Broadband Router

Just as it's essential to use a software-based firewall for each PC on your home entertainment network, you also need to use the firewall that is installed on your broadband router.

Most broadband routers sold today, both wired and wireless, have a built-in firewall. The first thing you need to do is check the owner's manual that came with the router to make sure it includes firewall protection. If it doesn't, you would be wise to upgrade to a broadband router that has a built-in firewall. The router's firewall is your first line of defense against a variety of attacks on your PC and privacy through your Internet connection.

Figure 7.2 shows the position your broadband router has in your home entertainment network and why it is the most important place to have a firewall.

The firewall installed on the router is hardware-based. It works all the time, and it is designed to keep your network protected before any threats can reach a PC. The software-based firewall that Windows XP includes protects only the PC it is on and only after the PC is fully booted and running: It does not protect the PC during the start-up process.

The firewall on the router also protects non-PC devices that do not have their own forms of firewall protection, such as networked TVs and stereos and other networked devices you might connect such as a TiVo or Xbox.

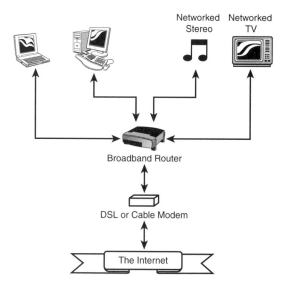

FIGURE 7.2

The most important location for a firewall: the router that is positioned between your Internet connection and all your PCs and networked devices.

The firewall that comes with your router will protect your network from a large number of possible threats, including the following:

- **Remote access**—Using an Internet connection and learning your IP address, outside parties can attempt to connect to your computer and control it. Once they gain access to your computer, they can attempt to view, access, or modify your files and install and run harmful programs on your computer. They can also gain access to your saved passwords.

- **SMTP session hijacking**—SMTP is the most common method of sending email over the Internet. Hacking your PC allows attackers to get a list of email addresses and send unsolicited email to email addresses to which you have sent mail.

- **Email bombs**—An email bomb is where someone sends you one email hundreds or thousands of times. It fills your mailbox to the point where it can't accept any more legitimate emails.

- **Viruses**—Everyone is pretty familiar with viruses, which are programs that can install themselves on your PC and cause a variety of damages, including destroying data on your PC or starting processes that can slow your system down.

- **Source routing**—Data that you access from the Internet comes from specific sources, and your firewall determines whether they are legitimate and trusted sources.

Hackers can attempt to make usage data appear to come from a trusted source by altering the source routing data for the information. Firewalls disable source routing.

Although the firewall on your broadband router attempts to filter as many threats and unauthorized access to your network as it can, it is virtually impossible for any firewall to be totally effective. For this reason, in addition to the firewall on your broadband router that attempts to prevent hacking into your system and prevent spam, viruses, and other access to your files, you should install additional protection on each PC, including the following:

- **A PC-based software firewall**—Use the Windows Firewall that is now a part of Windows XP, and make sure you have auto update for Windows turned on to keep it current.

- **Antivirus software**—Every PC should use antivirus software to protect the system from viruses attached to files that are downloaded or copied from CD-ROMs and floppies. A firewall cannot protect you from a file copied from a CD-ROM or floppy disk.

- **Spyware software**—Spyware programs are virtually impossible for a firewall to detect. You allow them to be added to your system when you let websites add small programs to enhance the web experience. As explained in Chapter 6, it is essential that you install spyware detection software to protect you from this threat.

- **Password protection**—None of the protections here can fully protect you from easy-to-devise passwords. When choosing a password, using your name, birthday, address, pet name, or other easy-to-remember items might make it easy for hackers who do gain access to some of your files to figure out your system passwords. Use caution and a unique password system—and change passwords on a regular basis.

In addition to offering networkwide protection with its firewall, your broadband router also allows you to control many aspects of what filters and ports you want to have in place.

In a home entertainment network, you will be using non-PC devices to access your network, and the firewall, considering them devices outside of the network, might not want to offer access to the network as a result. It's simply doing its job, and you can manually change the firewall to allow communication with such devices by changing your firewall settings.

Changing Firewall Settings

Sometimes you need to open ports or change settings to your broadband router firewall. Because the firewall establishes which computers outside of your home entertainment network it allows your devices to connect with, the firewall might choose to block new devices you add, such as a media extender.

In addition, you might need to open a port for online media services, such as music and video sites, so you can access their content.

Figure 7.3 shows the web-based firewall settings for a wireless router. The menu allows the addition of ports for specific IP addresses and devices. You can manually add a mail server, a port to a server hosting an online game, an FTP site, or another device from the Internet or your own network such as a media extender.

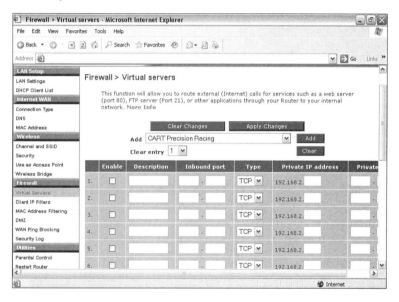

FIGURE 7.3

Initial menu from the web-based controls for a broadband router's firewall settings.

Because you need some knowledge of the IP address or type of connection, the firewall settings on the web-based controls most often contain a list of common ports that you can add. They are widely used mail sites, FTP sites, game servers, data servers, ISPs, and IP addresses for popular services that require an open port to make it through your firewall.

Figure 7.4 shows a pop-up menu showing a variety of popular ports, such as a port to allow MSN Messenger through the firewall.

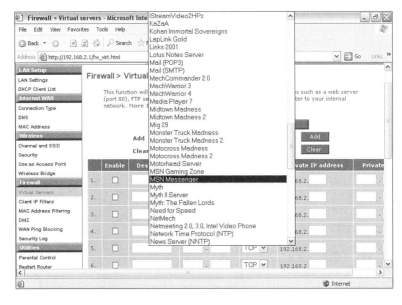

FIGURE 7.4

A pop-up menu of widely used, reliable sources so you can open ports for them.

In addition to using the pop-up list, you can contact a server or find the IP address of a device and manually add it to the list of ports that you allow.

The next option is to create a list of ports or IP addresses that you want to block or filter. You can even choose to restrict what times of the day or days of the week for filtering. This option allows you to block access to a game site, for example, at certain times of the day to keep your children from staying on a game site for too long. Figure 7.5 shows the web-based menu for the filtering process.

Another control you might find useful in settings for your broadband router is allowing one computer on your network to access a "DMZ" area. A DMZ is a demilitarized zone, where many of the rules of firewall protection are forgone to permit the use of complex networks servers such as online video conferences or games where firewalls prevent interaction. A DMZ is a temporary state, and you should handle it with caution because your computer is not protected from hackers in the DMZ.

Figure 7.6 shows the screen for allowing a computer to function in DMZ mode.

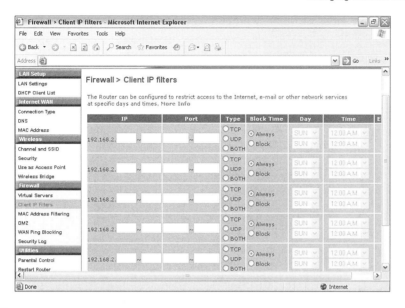

FIGURE 7.5

The pop-up menu of filters for blocking access to ports and network connections.

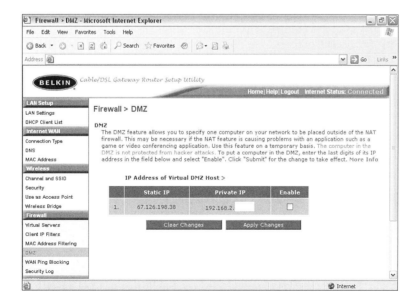

FIGURE 7.6

Temporarily allowing a computer on the network to work without protection from the firewall by allowing it to enter the DMZ.

The final firewall setting that is important in a home entertainment network is one that allows you to add the Media Access Control (MAC) addresses of devices you want to add to your local area network which might not currently be allowed through the firewall. If you are using a device that the firewall is filtering, you can add the MAC number for the device so you can then access it on the network. You will find that you need to add the MAC addresses for a number of home entertainment devices.

As shown in Figure 7.7, the menu allows you to enter the MAC number, and the firewall allows the device to be used on the network.

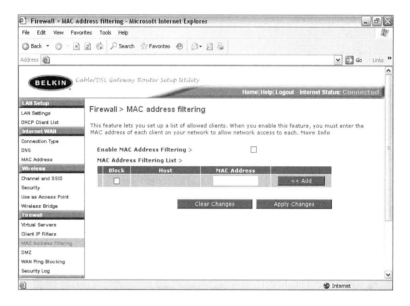

FIGURE 7.7

Adding devices that might not be allowed in the MAC filter menu of your firewall settings.

General Settings for Firewalls

There are a large number of possible settings for your broadband router firewall, DSL or cable modem firewall, or Windows XP firewall. For the most part, most of the settings you should know are listed here.

When you contact another device or web-based service, it will, with your permission, adjust the settings as needed. You do not have to become an expert on firewalls or web-based security to successfully secure your home entertainment network.

If there are times when you are not able to connect to a device or a web-based server or website, the problem might be a firewall setting. Check with the device manufacturer or web service to learn which firewall settings you need to adjust to use them.

Because you have several firewalls, you might have to make adjustments to each one. Always be careful that the changes you make are specific to the desired device or web service, and do not open your firewall to access from outside hackers.

Securing a Wireless Network

After you deal with firewall issues, the next area of your home entertainment network that you need to secure concerns a wireless router. You need to make sure that the only devices that can use your wireless network and your Internet connection are your own PCs and the devices in your home.

Because a wireless router is a radio device, it is sending and receiving signals to other radio devices on the same frequency. It is possible for someone nearby to have the same wireless adapters that you are using and be close enough to tap into your network. That is a scary thought.

Such access allows more than tapping into your Internet connection. If you have file sharing in use on your PCs, it is possible for an intruder to access your files.

This problem does not exist when you use a wired broadband router or a simple wired hub. All the connections between your devices are wired, and there is little or no chance of any outside use of your network.

Wireless routers allow wired connections in addition to wireless connections, so even your wired devices can be accessed when using a wireless broadband router.

The good news is that you can protect your wireless network from outside users and make sure that the only devices that can access your Internet connection and each other are the ones you allow.

As you will learn in Chapter 8, "Adding Additional PCs to the Router," when you add computers to your network, the installation software that comes with your wireless adapters will authenticate them and create a secure connection between the computer and the network.

The first step is to understand how a wireless network creates a secure connection between the computer or device and the wireless network.

Understanding MAC Filtering

Each device on your network has a MAC address. It allows a router to identify a PC or device and give it access to the network.

When you install your network adapter, the broadband router learns the MAC address for the PC or device and gives it access to your network. If you turn on MAC filtering, as shown in Figure 7.7 earlier in this chapter, you are telling the router to only give specific wireless devices access to the network.

If you want virtually any computer or device to be able to access your Internet connection and even share data with other computers on your home entertainment network, you can leave MAC filtering off, and new devices will be able to access your network.

MAC filtering prevents devices not on your network from gaining access through the router. Using it is a good first step to securing your network, but there are other ways that attackers can access your data.

Understanding WEP

Because the data sent between PCs and devices is radio-based in a wireless network, another PC can "read" it as it is transmitted. Data being transmitted is not protected, so a scheme has been devised to encrypt the data, preventing intruders from reading the data during its transmission. The encryption makes is difficult for a hacker to read, and the more complex the encryption, the less likely a hacker will attempt to decode it.

The encryption scheme for wireless networks is called Wired Equivalent Privacy (WEP) or possibly a newer standard called Wi-Fi Protected Access (WPA). Each creates an unique encryption key for your network, and only devices that are on the network and that have the key can code and decode the data.

There are two basic steps to establish WEP or WPA, and you should strongly consider using them:

1. Enable WEP or WPA. From your broadband router's web-based controls, set WEP to "on." If you have a broadband router and network adapters that support WPA, select this option and turn it on because it is a newer standard and offers even more protection. If you use WEP, you have a choice of 64k or 128k encryption. Use the higher level of encryption if all your network adapters support it.

2. Enable your network adapters. Each computer must have its WEP or WPA setting turned on to work with the network after you enable the setting from your router or network access point.

Using encryption makes it hard for anyone who can gain access to your network signals to use or decipher the data, which provides a great deal of security for your data.

If you have a choice between WEP and WPA on your router, the better choice for home entertainment networks is WPA. Your router and other home network devices might refer to this option as WPA-PSK or WPA-Home. WPA is more secure because it actually generates new security keys for the network on a regular basis, making it less easy to hack.

If you have devices that do not support WPA, you can fall back to WEP if needed.

Figure 7.8 shows the menu for selecting the type of data encryption scheme you want to install for your home entertainment network.

FIGURE 7.8

Setting encryption options from the web-based broadband router controls.

If you have a wireless network where you want free and open access to your data from a variety of computers and devices, and security is not a concern, you might also elect to leave encryption off. This choice is not recommended, but it might be appropriate, depending on your location and the nature of the data on your network.

Summary

Using a hardware-based firewall on your DSL or cable modem and your broadband router, and using software-based firewalls on your PCs, you can ward off most attacks from outside hackers and prevent harmful programs from being installed on your PC.

By turning on MAC filtering, you can allow only specific devices on your home entertainment network. Encrypting your data with WEP or WPA keeps data secure while it is transmitted using the radio signals of a wireless network.

Adding Additional PCs to the Router

After you secure your PCs and your home network, you can add any additional PCs you want to your home entertainment network. Because a home entertainment network can have just one PC or as many as you want, chances are you will be using more than one PC, such as a main PC connected to the router and perhaps a laptop.

It is possible to have just one main "server" PC in a home entertainment network powering TVs and stereo devices that use media extenders to play content from the main PC. If that is the case with your home entertainment network, you can jump to Chapter 9, "Adding TV and Media Extenders to the Network," which covers adding non-PC devices—but it would be good to read this chapter to learn how adding PCs works because you might add one in the future or even let a visiting friend or relative log in to your network.

Connecting PCs to the Network

As covered earlier in this book, you need a network port on any PC that you want to add to a wired or wireless network. Even if you only want to connect two PCs together, you do so by connecting them using an Ethernet cross-over cable connected to their Ethernet ports or by using two wireless adapters.

You need to be concerned with two types of network connections:

- **Wired connection**—For a wired network connection (such as connecting a PC to a broadband router using an Ethernet CAT-5E cable), you only need an Ethernet port on your PC. You connect the cable from the Ethernet port of the PC to one of the numbered Ethernet ports on the routers, and your connection is made.

- **Wireless connection**—When you are connecting your PC to the broadband router wirelessly, you need to add a wireless network adapter to your PC, and the wireless adapter makes the network connection without a cable or even an Ethernet port.

You can mix and match wired and wireless connections when using a wireless broadband router, and each has a different type of security that is required for use on the network.

Establishing a Wired Connection

After you connect a PC to a wired port on a broadband router, the PC becomes part of the network and at a minimum can access the Internet because the router is creating a direct connection from the Internet to your PC.

Figure 8.1 shows the appropriate wired connection between a PC and a broadband router. Using an Ethernet CAT-5E patch cable of any length, connect the RJ-45 male connector on one end to the Ethernet port of your PC and the other RJ-45 male connector to any of the numbered ports on your broadband router.

FIGURE 8.1

Connecting each end of an Ethernet CAT-5E cable to the PC and the broadband router.

After you connect your PC to the router using an Ethernet cable, you have full access to the Internet, and it is the beginning step in networking with other PCs on the network if you choose to do so.

Making a simple connection using an Ethernet CAT-5E cable is all you need to do at this time.

Test the connection by opening Internet Explorer and typing in any web address. You should have immediate access to the Internet. In addition, you should also try to access your email server and any other Internet-based services you use, such as AOL or MSN Messenger.

The PC acts essentially the same way as if you connected directly to your DSL or cable modem. You should be able to connect to the Internet and other Internet services without any problem.

If that is not the case, the modem or broadband router's firewalls might be preventing access, and you need to identify which ports to open using your firewall's control program, as discussed in Chapter 7, "Securing Your Home Entertainment Network." You might also need to change your Internet connection settings to use TCP/IP rather than dial-up, if that is what you are currently using.

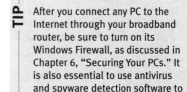

TIP
After you connect any PC to the Internet through your broadband router, be sure to turn on its Windows Firewall, as discussed in Chapter 6, "Securing Your PCs." It is also essential to use antivirus and spyware detection software to protect each PC connected to the broadband router and the Internet connection.

Establishing a Wireless Connection

Although a wireless connection is essentially the same as a wired connection—making a direct connection between a PC and your broadband router—it requires a wireless adapter on the PC to communicate using radio signals rather than a cable.

The wireless broadband router already has a wireless adapter built in, but you need to add a wireless adapter to each PC on the network—including desktop/tower PCs and laptops that you will be using for wireless connectivity. If you plan to use other PCs with a wired connection, there is no need for a wireless adapter on those PCS.

If you are using computers that are in a close proximity to the wireless router (such as a laptop in the same room as the main PC and wireless router), a wired connection might be the best solution for keeping costs low and providing the most reliable connection.

TIP
If you are using a fairly new laptop that features Intel Centrino technology, it has a built-in wireless adapter. If you are using a laptop that does not feature a built-in wireless adapter, you need to add an adapter to it.

Because there are a number of different PC configurations, Table 8.1 lists the appropriate wireless network adapter for each type of PC.

TABLE 8.1 APPROPRIATE WIRELESS NETWORK ADAPTERS FOR PCs

PC Type	Open Port	Wireless Adapter
Tower/desktop PC	PCI	PCI card adapter
Tower/desktop without an open Peripheral Component Interconnect (PCI) port	Universal Serial Bus (USB)	USB network adapter
Laptop with open PC card slot	PC card	Notebook card adapter
Laptop without open PC card slot	USB	USB network adapter

TIP

Be sure to follow the instructions for installing your network adapters. For most all adapters, you must first install the software and drivers—and then the hardware.

The main types of wireless adapters are PCI cards that go into an internal PCI slot of a desktop or tower PC; a notebook card adapter that goes in the PC card slot of a laptop; or, when neither is available on the PC, a USB network adapter that connects to the USB port of a desktop, tower, or laptop.

Each adapter has a process for installation where you first install the software and drivers on the PC and then physically install the network adapter.

Installing Wireless Adapters

To establish a wireless connection between a PC and your wireless router, use the installation procedures described next. Each adapter comes with installation instructions, a CD-ROM containing drivers and installation utilities, and the wireless adapter. This section looks at installing the software and drivers for each network adapter and then installing the hardware.

Installing the Drivers and Software

The first step in installing your wireless adapter is to insert the CD-ROM that came with your wireless adapter and follow the onscreen instructions.

The software takes you through a setup routine where the necessary hardware drivers are installed on your PC, network settings are established, and utilities (either applications or web-based utilities for which you use your web browser to access) are installed.

Figure 8.2 shows the first screen you see. It offers you the option of viewing the manual, and because most manuals today come on the computer rather than in printed books, it's a good time to read how the setup and installation process works.

After reviewing the manual, select Install and you see the screen in Figure 8.3. It is the first in several screens that install drivers and network utilities.

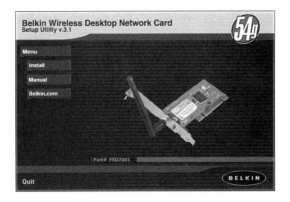

Figure 8.2

Viewing a manual and starting the installation process.

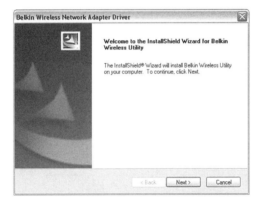

Figure 8.3

Guiding you through the installation to the point where you need to attach the network hardware.

After the installation wizard takes you through the process of installing all needed drivers and network utilities, it instructs you to shut down your computer and install the wireless network hardware. After the hardware is installed and you turn your computer back on, Windows recognizes that it has "found new hardware" and uses the drivers that were installed to complete the installation of your network adapter.

Before that step, let's take a look at how you install each of the different types of network adapters.

Adding a Wireless Adapter to a Desktop or Tower PC

Figure 8.4 shows a typical PCI adapter for a desktop or tower PC that has an open PCI slot. It is an internal card that plugs into the expansion slots of your PC and is fairly easy to install.

FIGURE 8.4

Wireless PCI network adapter for desktop or tower PCs.

The first step you need to take is to check whether there is an open PCI slot, as shown in Figure 8.5.

Follow the instruction manual that came with your PC for opening your PC's case and adding an expansion card. If your manual does not contain this information, the manufacturer's website support area usually has a guide to the process.

After you have the PC open, examine the expansion slots to make sure one is open, as shown in Figure 8.5. If a slot is open, use the following steps to add an internal network adapter card to an open PCI slot in your PC:

1. Turn off the power to your PC, and disconnect the power cable from the PC.

2. Following the instructions that came with your PC, remove the side panel of casing that covers the PC. This step gives you access to the expansion slots for PCI cards.

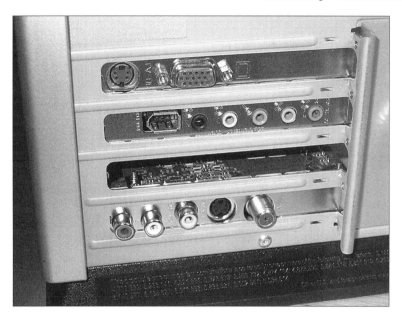

FIGURE 8.5

An open PCI expansion slot in a desktop PC.

3. Remove the screw that holds a metal plate over the expansion slot on the back panel of your PC, being sure to save the screw and the metal plate.

4. Touch any metal part of the PC so that you dissipate any static electricity that might be present before you open the packaging of the actual Ethernet card.

5. Remove the PCI network adapter card from its antistatic bag, and avoid laying it down on any other surfaces prior to installation to prevent static electrical build-up. If the card has a removable antenna, be sure to remove it first before attempting installation.

> **TIP**
>
> Not sure that your PC has an open PCI slot? A simple trick is to look at the back panel of your PC. There are several slots visible that have connectors for audio or video. If there is a blank slot with no connectors, or just a flat panel of metal, it means that there is most likely an open PCI slot. The blank metal panel might be missing, and that is also an indication that the slot is open.

6. Carefully position the card in an open PCI slot in the PC, being sure that the connector faces the read of the PC, the connector plate fits gently into the open back panel, and the connectors are positioned over the PCI connector inside the PC. If your card has an antenna that cannot be removed, be sure to carefully guide the antenna through the open panel on the back of the PC and then attempt general positioning of the card after the antenna has made it through the slot.

7. After the back panel and connector are in the correct position, gently press the connector into the PCI slot until it fits snugly and securely in place.

8. Check the back panel of the connector from the outside of the PC, making sure that the fit is proper, there are no gaps, and the card is not loose in any way.

9. With the card securely in place, use the screw that you removed from the metal plate covering the back panel slot to secure the card to the slot.

10. Reattach the side panel of computer casing.

11. Attach the removable antenna if your card uses that type of antenna.

12. Reattach the power cord to your PC.

13. Turn the power on to your PC.

14. Save the metal plate that originally covered the back panel slot on the PC, either by keeping it in the box for the network adapter card or in another location for PC parts. If you ever remove the card, you will want to cover the open slot with the metal plate.

As shown in Figure 8.6, gently insert the network card into the open slot. This move is a bit tricky because the network adapter card contains a fairly large antenna. You can easily remove the antenna by pulling it out of its connector. Remove the antenna before attempting to install the card.

The card must fit correctly through the open space on the back panel of the PC, and it must also fit snugly into the connector on the PC. After the card is secure in its slot, take the screw and place it in the screw hole and tighten it. Next, look at the back panel of the PC to make sure the network card is correctly seated in the slot and flush against the back panel. Reconnect the antenna, and the card should look like the one in Figure 8.7.

After the card is properly installed, you can turn your PC back on and complete the installation, which is covered a bit later in this chapter.

Adding a Wireless Notebook Adapter to a Laptop PC

Figure 8.8 shows a typical wireless notebook card adapter for a laptop PC that has an open PC card slot. The PC card slot is an expansion slot located most often on the side of laptop, and it can accept a variety of expansion cards for memory, FireWire ports, USB ports, and network adapters. Depending on your laptop, PC card slots can often accommodate one or two PC cards. Be sure to check your owner's manual to see whether you have a single or dual PC card slot.

Figure 8.8 shows a wireless notebook card adapter in front of a PC card slot that is not being used by any other PC card.

FIGURE 8.6

Inserting the wireless network adapter card into the PCI slot.

FIGURE 8.7

PCI wireless network card correctly installed in a PC with wireless antenna attached.

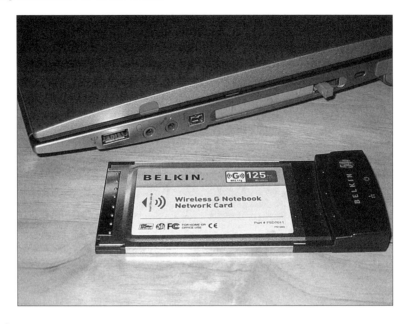

FIGURE 8.8

PC card wireless notebook adapter in front of an open PC card slot of a notebook computer.

Installing a wireless notebook card on your laptop couldn't be simpler. After you have been through the software installation process described earlier using the CD-ROM that came with your wireless notebook adapter, you shut down your laptop, insert the wireless notebook card, and restart your computer. Figure 8.9 shows a wireless notebook card installed in a laptop. The card protrudes slightly because it acts as the antenna.

The notebook card contains two lights. One is for activity, and one shows a connection to the network. Your owner manual indicates what the blinking and the colors used by the lights mean when you are using the network.

The next steps of using the network card are covered later in this chapter.

Adding a Wireless USB Network Adapter to a Laptop or PC

It is best to use a PCI network adapter card for desktop or tower PCs and a notebook card for laptops, but that might not always be possible. Internal PCI network cards are lower in cost than other types of adapters, and most have removable antennas that allow you to add an extension antenna if you are having reception problems. In addition, they do not require other expansion slots such as USB slots and they keep the appearance of your PC neat—an important consideration in home entertainment settings where a lot of wires and devices can add clutter.

FIGURE 8.9

Wireless notebook card adapter correctly installed in the PC card slot of a laptop with the status lights easily visible.

If all your PCI cards are in use on your desktop or tower PC, or if your laptop's PC card slot is in use by another adapter, you might not be able to use those expansion slots for your wireless network adapter.

For such instances, you can use a wireless USB network adapter, as shown in Figure 8.10.

FIGURE 8.10

Using a USB wireless network adapter when no expansion port is available.

Because almost all PCs sold today have USB ports, and because you can use USB hubs that create several USB ports from one available USB port, you will be able to use a USB adapter when no other port is available.

The actual USB wireless network adapter can plug directly into a USB port on the PC. This arrangement is sometimes awkward or unsightly and even prone to damage on a laptop because it literally sticks out about four inches from the USB port. A more elegant solution, as shown in Figure 8.11, is to use an extension cable and stand (provided with the USB network adapter) as shown in Figure 8.12.

FIGURE 8.11

USB wireless notebook adapter connected directly to a USB port on a laptop.

One of the advantages of using an extension cable and stand for a USB adapter is that you can position the adapter where it gets the best possible signal reception. Adapters that are in the PC or laptop don't have this ability to change position.

The installation procedure is simple. Install the software drivers and utilities, turn off the PC or laptop, connect the USB wireless network adapter, and turn on the PC or laptop. Windows recognizes the hardware and uses the drivers to complete the installation of the adapter.

FIGURE 8.12

USB wireless notebook adapter connected to a USB port on a laptop using an extension cable and a stand to hold the adapter.

Completing the Installation

After you physically attach any wireless network adapter to your PC or laptop, Windows recognizes the network adapter as new hardware and launches the New Hardware Found Wizard to complete the installation of the adapter. When this happens, complete the following steps:

1. Using the New Hardware Found Wizard, choose to have the wizard automatically find the software drivers required. They were installed by the setup software you installed prior to adding the card. It is a good practice to have the installation CD in the CD-ROM drive because the wizard might refer to it during the process.

2. After the wizard locates the needed files, click Finish to complete the installation.

3. Observe and confirm after installation that a pop-up menu appears on your desktop to inform you that your new hardware is installed and ready to use.

4. Remove the installation CD and store it for future use.

A number of network utilities were installed during the first phase of the setup program you ran before installing the hardware. The next section looks at those network utilities.

Using the Wireless Network Utilities

With your wireless network adapter installed, you are automatically connected to the wireless network when you turn on your PC and will continue to be connected as long as there is a strong enough signal to make communication with the wireless router.

The network utilities that come with your wireless adapter provide the following features:

- Signal strength meter
- Wireless network utility
- Network selector

Figure 8.13 shows the signal strength indicator that indicates the level of power for the signal connection to your wireless network. In this example, the indicator uses a green symbol for strong signal strength, yellow for weak signal strength, and red when the signal is not adequate and the connection is lost.

FIGURE 8.13

The wireless network signal strength icon.

In this example, the meter is located in the lower-right corner of the Windows toolbar. If you click on the meter, you see a menu that allows you to connect to a network, if you are not automatically connected. In this example, the network has Wired Equivalent Privacy (WEP) protection enabled, and you need to enter a WEP key to connect to the network. Figure 8.14 shows this menu.

FIGURE 8.14

Wireless connection menu showing that the network requires a WEP key to gain access.

Improving Signal Strength

Sometimes the signal being received by PCs using wireless network adapters or other wireless devices is too weak to allow access to the network. A weak signal slows the transfer of data to a point where it is almost useless.

When this occurs, you can do number of things to address the problem. The following are the first things you should try when you have bad reception for wirelessly networked devices in your home entertainment network:

• Move the computer to different locations in a room (and this is easy to do when using a laptop). Often, the location of the device in relationship to the wireless router is a factor in poor reception.

• If you are using a USB wireless network adapter, you can use the provided cable and stand to move the adapter to other locations in the room to obtain a better signal.

• If you are using a PCI network adaptor card with a removable antenna, you can purchase an extension antenna that replaces the one on the card and allows you to move the antenna to a better position, which might help improve the signal.

A good strategy for the wireless router and movable antennas is to place them as high off the floor as possible.

These items are the simplest methods for improving a signal, but they might not always help. Many things in a home interfere with the signal, and you can take other steps to help improve your signal if the preceding actions don't help. Here are some things to consider and possibly change in your home:

- **Interference from wireless phones**—Because wireless networks currently operate on a either a 2.4GHz or 5.2HGHz radio band, cordless telephones that operate on the same band as your wireless router might cause interference with your wireless network. You can change to a 2.4GHz or 5.2GHz phone (or even an older 900MHz model) that does not operate on the same frequency as your wireless network and that might help. A good way to find out whether a phone is the problem is to unplug the cordless phone base station and turn off the handset phone by disconnecting the battery. With the phone disconnected in this way, use your wireless network. If the signal is greatly improved, the phone was contributing to the interference.

- **Interference from building structures**—Concrete walls, brick walls, large metal objects, TVs, and other metal structures also can create interference with the signal. Although you can't change those structures (and you probably don't want to because the goal of adding a home entertainment network is not to reconfigure your house!), you can try some simple actions that might help your signals bypass some of those structures. The best thing to try is locating your router to a different position in the room. Put it up as high as possible and nearest to the center of the house as you can. This move might help, and consider that if the router is on the ground next to a floor-standing PC, or with the PC between the wireless router and the other devices in your home, the PC might be the "big metal box" that reduces quality of reception.

If the preceding actions do not help (and they might not), you can generally improve signal reception in your home by adding a "signal booster" device.

Almost all wireless routers sell devices called access points or signal boosters that you can locate between your wireless router and other wireless devices to boost the signal. They are literally signal amplifiers that take the signal from the wireless router and resend it from where they are located (at midpoints in your home) to help the receiving device get a full-strength signal. The location of the signal booster is totally dependent upon the layout of your home and the structures and devices in it. If you use such a device, experiment with different locations for it to find the best placement and improve reception for the greatest number of devices.

If a signal booster works for some locations and not all locations, you might be faced with adding more than one signal booster in your home.

One problem with such devices is that some only work with the same brand of wireless router you are using. Be sure to check your owner's manual to see whether that is the case, and buy the same brand if so.

Access points and signal boosters help you with signal strength and reception better than any other actions, but they do add about $100 to the cost of your home entertainment network.

Using the Wireless Network Utilities

The wireless configuration and management utility that comes with your wireless adapter helps you understand and control your wireless connection. Figure 8.15 shows a wireless configuration utility menu along with the status of a wireless connection for a laptop using a wireless notebook adapter card. It allows you to make changes to the settings of your wireless adapter.

FIGURE 8.15

Wireless connection menu showing full information about the network adapter.

The wireless configuration utility provided for almost any wireless adapter allows you to monitor your wireless connection and also to change important settings, such as which networks are available to you. (You might find that a network from the house next store shows up!) It also shows statistics and general networking settings.

The site monitoring menu is especially helpful in understanding the type of network you are on, such as support for 802.11b and 802.11g, supported rates, signal strength, and the channel the computer is using.

If your performance is still poor after you've tried relocating your PC or antenna, be sure to check the statistics using the utility program to track whether the location changes improved network performance.

Another utility that might come with your wireless network adapter is shown in Figure 8.16. The wireless network connection menu appears as an icon in the lower-right corner of the Windows taskbar. When you click on it, you see a number of important statistics about the wireless connection your computer has made, including the following:

- **Status**—Whether you are connected or disconnected.

- **Network**—The name of the network you are connected to.

- **Duration**—How long you have been connected.

- **Speed**—The Mbps for your connection.

- **Signal strength**—How strong your network signal is.

- **Packets**—How many packets of data were sent and received during the session.

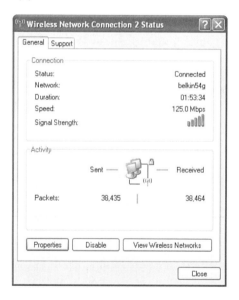

FIGURE 8.16

The wireless network connection status menu showing vital statistics about your network connection.

After you get familiar with these two wireless network utilities for your wireless network adapter, you can monitor performance and change settings to increase performance and security.

Using Wired and Wireless Connections

With your PCs connected to your broadband router using either a wired or wireless connection, all your PCs are protected by the firewall from your broadband router, and they all have access to the Web through the Internet connection provided by the broadband router.

If you are using a mix of wired and wireless devices and a non-Windows XP firewall, you might run into situations where your wirelessly networked PC or device cannot connect with your network. Be sure to check your PC-based firewall software and make sure it is not blocking access. You can add the IP address of the device to your list of allowed devices to remedy the problem.

If you find that the PCs using wireless network adapters perform poorly due to signal strength, you can add a signal booster to increase the signal, or you might also choose to make a wired connection if possible.

As attractive as a wireless connection is, a wired connection still offers the best overall performance, lowest cost, and the most secure form of networking between devices. When possible, use a wired connection.

When using a wireless connection, be sure to enable WEP or Wi-Fi Protected Access (WPA) security. They encrypt data between the devices on your wireless network, making it hard for devices from outside your network to tap in to your data. You should also change the name of your network (the Service Set Identifier [SSID]) from your web-based router controls so that your network has a unique name—which also helps keep devices that do not have that name from using your network.

Summary

You can easily add PCs to a home entertainment network that uses a broadband router. For a wired connection, the process is as simple as connecting an Ethernet CAT-5E cable between the router and the PC. For wireless network connections, you must have a wireless broadband router and an appropriate wireless network adapter card for each PC that you want to connect to the network wirelessly.

To install a wireless adapter, you must first install the wireless network drivers and utilities and then shut down your PC and add the wireless network adapter. After restarting your PC, Windows recognizes the new hardware and completes the installation using the drivers that were installed. At that point, your PC can access your wireless network.

Adding TV and Media Extenders to the Network

Now that you've learned how to create a secure home entertainment network using firewalls and antivirus and spyware software for your PCs, the next step is to learn how to add non-PC devices such as TVs, stereos, and media extenders.

Until now, the home entertainment network you have been putting together has been a fairly conventional home network consisting of PCs, a high-speed Internet connection, and a broadband router. Each of those is required before you can effectively build a home entertainment network that brings the media on your PCs and the Internet to the TVs and stereos in your home.

To begin, let's take a look at the home network you've built so far. Figure 9.1 shows a connection to the Internet using either DSL or a cable modem, a main "hub" PC, and a wireless router.

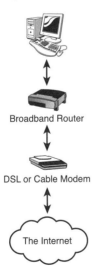

Broadband Router

DSL or Cable Modem

The Internet

FIGURE 9.1

A home entertainment network starts with at least a main PC, a router, and a high-speed connection to the Internet using a DSL or cable modem.

With this basic configuration, you could easily expand the system to include TV view-ing, digital video recording of TV shows, and purchasing and playing music from the Internet or your own audio files on your PC. Figure 9.2 shows how adding a TV tuner card, a TV, and a home stereo or powered speakers would convert your basic home PC into a home entertainment center.

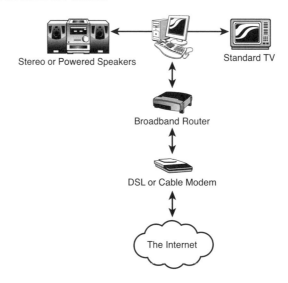

Stereo or Powered Speakers

Standard TV

Broadband Router

DSL or Cable Modem

The Internet

FIGURE 9.2

By adding a TV tuner card and connecting a TV and home stereo or powered speakers to your PC, your system becomes a digital home entertainment center.

For many homes, the configuration is the start of a home entertainment network, and you can use the broadband router to add PCs and TVs or stereos to the network at any point in the future. One of the best ways to start is to expand your main PC to be capa-ble of playing video files on a standard TV, recording TV programs, and playing them back.

Adding a TV Tuner Card to Your PC

Many computers being sold today, such as Media Center Edition PCs, come equipped with a TV tuner card. If you have a PC that does not have one installed, this section looks at adding one to your desktop, tower, or laptop PC.

A TV tuner card is essentially the same device as a TV tuner inside a TV. It "tunes" TV signals from a TV source such as an antenna, cable, or satellite set top box, or even a VCR or analog port of a camcorder. It tunes the signals by standard channels and con-verts those signals into a digital form that your computer can play or even record.

Once you install a TV tuner card, you can watch and record regular TV on your PC.

Desktop or tower PCs can use an internal PCI TV tuner card. If no PCI slots are available, they can use an external USB TV tuner card, and those are the type that you would use for a laptop computer.

Installation on a Desktop or Tower PC

Before you attempt to install an internal TV tuner card on a desktop or tower PC, be sure to open your PC (following the instructions in the manual that came with your PC regarding expanding it or adding cards) and check to see if you have an open PCI slot.

Figure 9.3 shows a series of open PCI slots on a tower PC, with the metal panels covering the slots from outside of the PC removed. Your PCI will have other cards in the slots, and you will want to check if a slot is open. Figure 9.3 shows how they look when empty.

FIGURE 9.3

Open PCI connectors inside a tower PC.

If you have an open PCI slot, the next step is to purchase a TV tuner card. There are a number of different configurations of TV tuner cards, and depending on what equipment your PC currently has, you might want to purchase a simple TV tuner card or a video card that has a TV tuner built-in. There are also TV tuner cards that offer an FM tuner in addition to the TV tuner connection. This is highly recommended for a home entertainment network because you will be able to listen to FM broadcasts with the TV/FM tuner.

You might also want to consider the purchase of a combination card such as an ATI All-in-Wonder card that combines a video card with a TV and FM tuner card. Such combination cards will use the AGP slot of your PC—that keeps your PCI slots open for other uses.

FIGURE 9.4

TV tuner PCI card with connectors for accepting a TV signal.

Figure 9.4 shows a typical TV tuner PCI card. It has connectors for

- **Antenna In:** For connecting a standard coaxial antenna cable
- **S-Video In:** For connecting an S-Video connector such as those used by set top boxes (such as a digital cable or satellite receiver) and VCRs
- **Composite Video In:** For connecting a RCA-type composite video connector such as those used by set top boxes and VCRs
- **RCA-type Audio In:** Stereo connectors for the audio-out connections from a camcorder, set top box, or VCR

Figure 9.5 shows a PCI TV tuner card that has the same basic TV-in connectors as the card shown in Figure 9.4, but adds an additional coaxial connector for an FM radio broadcast antenna. You will need an FM antenna to receive signals, and they are easily found in electronics stores such as Best Buy or Radio Shack.

FIGURE 9.5

TV tuner card with an FM tuner for receiving FM radio broadcasts.

Once you have decided on the best TV tuner card (and one with an FM radio tuner is highly recommended), the next step is to install the card in your PC.

Just as when installing a network adapter card, the setup process usually will involve using the supplied CD-ROM setup utility to install the TV tuner drivers and TV (and FM radio if so equipped) applications on your PC.

> **TIP**
> If your desktop or tower PC does not have any available PCI slots for an internal TV tuner card, use a USB TV tuner. You might also be able to replace the video card on your PC with a new one that has both video card and TV tuner features.

After the installation of the drivers and applications, you will shut off and disconnect the power cable of your PC and install the card in an open PCI slot. Open the PC, remove the metal plate covering the slot on the back of the PC, position the card over the connector, and gently press the card into the slot until it fits snugly in the connector and has a proper fit on the back panel of the PC.

After replacing the cover on the PC, you can connect a video source such as a coaxial antenna cable, or S-Video and audio cables to the card. If you use a coaxial antenna connector, you do not need to connect audio cables—it carries both the video and the audio signals.

After turning your PC back on, you can launch the TV player application and following the users manual, learn how to tune channels, create channel presets, and even use an onscreen program guide that most TV tuner cards supply. If you have an FM tuner, you will also be able to listen to FM broadcasts and set FM presets of your favorite stations.

Installation on a Laptop

With the limited expansion ports on a laptop, if your laptop does not already have a TV tuner, you can add a USB TV tuner. This would also apply to a desktop or tower PC without any available PCI slots.

Figure 9.6 shows a USB TV tuner card connected to a laptop. Unlike the number of options found on an internal PCI TV tuner card, the USB tuner usually is limited to a coaxial TV antenna connector and a single S-Video connector and mini-stereo audio connector. These are adequate for most any situation, but make sure that your TV source can work with the connectors on the USB TV tuner that you purchase.

FIGURE 9.6

USB TV tuner card connected to the USB port of a laptop.

As you can see in Figure 9.6, like any device you add to a laptop, the TV tuner is large and clumsy and, although it does the job, is not as elegant as a built-in TV tuner. If you are purchasing a new laptop, look for one with a built-in TV tuner.

Installation is simple using the provided CD-ROM for installing drivers and the TV tuner application and possibly an onscreen program guide. After installing the software, you simply plug the TV tuner in to the USB port and then connect a TV source. Using the TV viewing application, you can watch or record programs, use the onscreen guide to schedule recordings, and make presets of your favorite stations.

Viewing Video on a TV from Your PC

With the addition of a TV tuner card to your PC, you will be able to watch TV, record TV, and make TV a part of your PC experience.

As great as adding TV viewing is, watching TV on a computer monitor or laptop screen is not the best experience. TV should be viewed on a TV, so the next task is to be able to connect your PC to a TV to watch TV programs, videos, and video content from the Internet, such as rented movies or music videos.

Many new PCs and laptops have begun to include a TV-out port. Media-centric PCs and laptops—including great media PCs such as Media Center PCs—have TV connectors that allow you to view videos and DVDs on a TV connected to your PC. If you have one of those newer PCs, you are all set. If not, you will want to add a video card with TV-out to your existing PC.

Your current video card will support standard *VGA* (*video graphics adapter*) and will connect to any computer monitor using a 15-pin VGA connector.

You will want to replace that video card with a video card that continues to have a VGA connector plus a TV connector. Figure 9.7 shows a video card containing both connectors.

FIGURE 9.7

Video card with both VGA and TV connections.

Unlike a TV tuner card that has ports for both audio and video signals, the video card only has a video port for the TV signal. The audio signal will come from your audio card—not the video card.

Most video cards that have TV-out use an S-Video connector, but some do offer composite RCA-type connectors. The latest models also offer a *DVI* (*digital video interface*) connector. Newer flat-panel plasma or LCD TVs are now using DVI ports, and some also include standard VCA ports. If your TV (or computer monitor) uses a DVI port, be sure that you get a video card that has a DVI port for TV signals.

Depending on the video card, you might need to install drivers or utilities prior to installing the card. Your card will most likely come with a CD-ROM containing the required drivers and utilities, as well as instructions for installation. Most cards will take you through a process as follows:

- Run the installation or setup software that came with the video card prior to installing the card in your PC. It will install any drivers required by Windows and add any utilities that will help you make adjustments to the video or display device.

- The setup routine will instruct you to install the new card in your PC.

- When you restart your PC, Windows will detect the new hardware and launch the Found New Hardware Wizard. Allow the wizard to automatically find the appropriate drivers. The setup routine you ran prior to installing the card has placed the drivers in the correct file locations for Windows to use.

- Once the wizard finds and installs the required drivers, it will notify you that your new hardware has been installed and is ready for use.

Once installed, connect your TV to the video card using an S-Video or DVI cable (depending on your card and TV), and connect the audio-in of your TV to the audio-out/speaker connection on your audio card.

Using the provided instructions, you will need to set the display properties on your PC to view your PC on the TV, your computer monitor, or both if you desire.

Making Audio Connections

After getting TV signals in and out of your PC, the next thing to consider is audio. Most all PCs have audio ports or audio cards so you might be all set, but it's good to examine just what type of audio ports are available on your PC.

Figure 9.8 shows a good audio card choice for PCs. It includes

- **Line–in:** This port allows you to bring line-level signals such as those from a set top box into your PC.

- **Line-out:** This connection allows you to send a line-level stereo signal to a set of powered speakers or headphones.

- **Mic-in:** This allows you to add a microphone for recording your own voice or music.

FIGURE 9.8

Audio card provides audio connections to powered speakers, TVs, and home stereos.

- **Digital Out:** This sends a pure digital signal to a surround sound amplifier or digital amplifier. This port can be labeled "S/PDIF" (Sony/Philips Digital Interface) or can also take the form of an optical TOSLINK connector.

- **Surround Sound:** This adds the surround sound signals to powered surround sound speaker systems.

Each PC on your home entertainment network should ideally have a sound card that supports both stereo and surround sound audio. It is also good to find one that has a digital out signal since newer TVs and powered speaker systems support digital signals.

Connecting your TV, powered speakers, or home stereo to your sound card is simply a matter of using the line-out and/or surround sound ports to the TV, speakers, or stereo. As with all audio from a PC, use the utilities provided and Windows Volume control panel to make sure that the audio levels are properly set.

Figure 9.9 shows a typical audio connection from a PC with an audio and video card connected to a TV. Audio cards on PCs will most often use stereo 1/8'' mini-plug connectors, whereas TVs and set top boxes will use RCA-type audio connectors. You will need an audio cable that has a stereo 1/8'' mini plug on one end and RCA stereo connectors at the other end to make the connection.

With a good audio card, you can connect your PC to a variety of devices that match your media habits. For the most part, a good idea, regardless of whether you will be listening primarily to TV or to music, is to connect your PC to a good set of powered speakers.

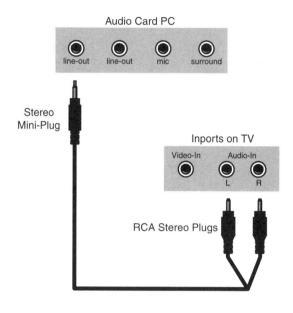

FIGURE 9.9

Making an audio connection between a PC audio card and the audio input connectors on a TV.

> **TIP**
>
> You can find terrific powered speaker sets for your home entertainment network for well under $100. At such a low price, you can add powered speakers in most any location where you have a PC or media extender in your home.

Powered speakers have come a long way, and you should be able to find a great set (stereo or surround with five speakers and a sub-woofer) that will serve as your sound system for music and TV viewing.

When you use your PC as a primary TV, the powered speakers will play TV audio. When you listen to music files, the powered speakers will play music. This is the start of how a properly configured PC becomes your home entertainment center. It plays music, DVD audio, TV audio, and with a good set of speakers, makes games rumble and roar.

Where you once had a home stereo, a TV playing its own audio with its inadequate speakers, and games playing through the small speakers on a TV or the PC, a great set of powered speakers, complete with surround sound and subwoofer, will become your primary sound system.

When you are purchasing a new PC, you should look for one that will give you the best audio experience possible. New PCs and motherboards incorporating Intel High-Definition Audio are now entering the market and will give you the latest audio technology without needing to upgrade or add audio cards in the future.

Using Media Extenders

With the basic understanding of how you can connect a TV to your PC and use your PC for viewing live TV—and TV that you have recorded—you are at the starting point of what makes a home entertainment network different from a PC home network. The ability to play and record music and TV turns a PC from a workplace device into a home entertainment center.

Now, since it works great with your one primary computer, you can use the home network you have created to share your TV, video, audio, and picture files with other TVs and stereos in your home.

Notice that there is no mention of PCs?

Although you can add other PCs in your home and use them in essentially the same way as your primary PC with a TV tuner, video card and audio card, and share media files, that's really not necessary. It might be better to simply connect other TVs and powered speakers in the house and use the network to play media files from your primary PC.

Not only is that the best possible method, but it's also the one that costs the least. Adding additional PCs in most rooms in your home could be pretty expensive. And you might not need "computing" power in all the other locations in your house.

What is needed is a way to "extend" the media files from your PC to other rooms in your home to play on TVs and audio devices.

The answer is called a "media extender." Answering the preceding need to play media throughout the house without additional PCs, media extenders are network devices that are essentially mini PCs with wired or wireless connectors, having the capability to connect to a TV and display menus of your media content on the home entertainment network and allowing you to play those files on a TV or stereo connected to it.

Media extender devices generally cost about $200 for video and audio playing and as low as $100 for playing audio only.

Figure 9.10 shows a media extender from D-Link. It works wirelessly or wired, plays video files, music files, picture files, and even media from the Internet. It connects easily to the network, your TV, and to any audio system including the one on the TV, a home stereo, or a set of powered speakers.

The Media Lounge is attractive and looks like any piece of home entertainment equipment such as a DVD player—in fact it's the same width as DVD players and stereos. It blends right into a home entertainment rack. It comes with its own remote control, and you operate it using the remote control for all functions.

FIGURE 9.10

Front view of the Media Lounge media extender from D-Link.

Figure 9.11 shows the back panel of Media Lounge. It has connections for S-Video, composite video, component video, as well as stereo audio and coaxial and optical digital connectors for surround sound systems. It also has an Ethernet port for wired network connections and an antenna for its built-in 802.11g wireless adapter.

FIGURE 9.11

The back panel of Media Lounge features most all connections possible for connecting it to a TV or audio system.

Installing a Media Extender

Once you purchase a media extender, you should identify where you want it to be located and place it there—but don't turn it on yet. You can make the connections to the TV and the audio system you will be using, but don't connect it to the network or power it on at this time.

Using the setup CD-ROM that comes with the media extender, run the setup routine. It will install a media player that the device will use to play media from your PC/server, and it will also take you through the process of adding your media extender device to your home network.

The media player is a unique application, and each media extender has its own media player, but they all use the TV as a menu into the media files on your server PC. Without installing and running the media player that comes with the media extender, it won't be able to find and play media files on the network.

Once you have installed the Media Player software for a media extender such as Media Lounge, you will select which files you will allow it to view. Figure 9.12 shows the PC-side menu of Media Lounge and how you select what media files you want to be able to play on the Media Lounges you have on your home entertainment network. (You may use more than one.)

FIGURE 9.12

Using the media extender's application to identify which media files you want to make available to the media extender.

Figure 9.13 shows the menu from which you can choose exactly what file types you want to make available. A folder or drive that you have chosen might contain a number of file formats that are not desirable for viewing, such as GIF files from Internet graphics. By clicking the ones that you want to view and deselecting the ones that you do not want to be included, you will create a menu list on the device that is easier to navigate and doesn't contain unwanted files.

FIGURE 9.13

You can limit the file types that can be viewed on the media extender, making menus and media files easier to find.

After identifying the file locations and file types, your media server is ready to provide media files to the media extenders on the home entertainment network. The next step is to connect your media extender to a TV and a speakers, and then connect it to your wired or wireless network.

The process is simply one in which you go through a setup wizard that identifies if you will be using a wired or wireless connection, and then searches for the network. Once the network is found, it then searches for available media servers (because there might be more than one from several different computers in your home entertainment network).

Figure 9.14 shows the initial setup wizard for the Media Lounge media extender. You can use a setup wizard, or go into the menu and make adjustments for the network manually.

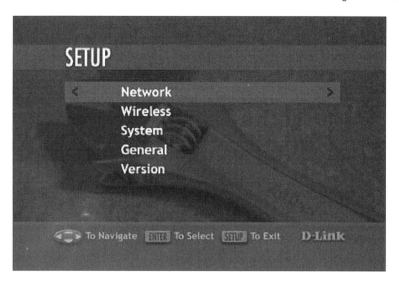

FIGURE 9.14

Main setup menu for the D-Link Media Lounge.

After the settings have been made (and adjustments generally only need to be made if there are firewall restrictions on your broadband router), the media extender will restart, make a connection to the network, and then connect with your media server software on your PC.

Once connected, you will see the main menu as illustrated in Figure 9.15 showing the choice of viewing video, music, photo, or radio menus.

Playing Files on a Media Extender

After you have reached the main menu, each menu button will bring you to a list of the files you have selected in your Media Server software on your PC. The files are displayed in a typical PC folder metaphor of files in folders, and you will find the user interface very TV like, but also similar to using a PC.

Music plays in sequence or randomly, picture files play as a slideshow, video files play one by one, and radio allows you to tune to stations.

When you make changes or add files to the folders you have selected in your Media Server application, the changes will instantly be made available from the media extender menus. All the files you are viewing or playing are from the main PC or whatever file server you have chosen on your home entertainment network.

FIGURE 9.15

Main menu for the D-Link Media Lounge allows you to play video, music, Internet radio, or view photos.

Figure 9.16 shows a music menu displayed in a Media Lounge screen. The advantage of playing music with a TV interface is that you can see the playlist and visually navigate your music files.

FIGURE 9.16

Music menu from the D-Link Media Lounge media extender.

Using a Media Center Edition Extender

The D-Link Media Lounge is an example of a media extender that works with any Windows XP PC. It has a nice TV-centric feel and installs easily on a home network.

If you have a Windows Media Center PC, running the Windows XP Media Center Edition operating system, you might prefer to use a Windows Media Center Edition Extender.

Windows Media Center Edition is a totally TV-centric version of the Windows XP operating system and is one of the best media PCs you can find. They have been designed to play and record TV, play DVDs, video files, music libraries, Internet radio, FM radio broadcasts, media content from the Internet, and have one of the best slideshow players for digital photos to be found on any computer.

Windows Media Center is an easy-to-use, TV-like version of Windows, and when in Media Center, your PC is all about media playing. When you want to use your PC for traditional computing, you simply return to Windows XP, and it's computing as usual.

Figure 9.17 shows the TV-centric environment found in Media Center. It's a fluid, moving, easy-to-navigate interface.

FIGURE 9.17

Microsoft's Media Center is found only on PCs sold as Windows XP Media Center Edition PCs.

After you become accustomed to using Media Center for media playing, it would be hard to imagine using any other user interface, even on a media extender. The good news is that Microsoft has created a media extender operating system that looks, feels, and acts just like Media Center. Once a Media Center Extender is connected to your home network and attached to a TV, you would swear that you were looking at a full PC version of Media Center. It even uses the exact same remote control.

Figure 9.18 shows a menu from a Media Center Extender. As you can see, it is hard to tell the difference between the PC version and the media extender version of the user interface.

FIGURE 9.18

Menu from a Media Center Extender as displayed on a TV.

Installing a Media Center Extender is extremely simple. You connect the box to the network (they work with a built-in wireless connector, or you can use a wired connection), and Media Center will recognize the extender and begin sharing all files with it from your PC.

Figure 9.19 shows a Media Center Extender from the front. It's a simple, small box that you connect to your TV and audio system the same way that you would any other media extender. Figure 9.20 shows the connectors on the back panel of a Media Center Extender, and its connections enable it to connect to virtually any TV.

About the only thing that Media Center Extenders don't do (and the PC version of Media Center does) is play DVDs over the home network. Copy protection issues restrict DVD playing across the home network, and it is basically the only feature missing from the main PC-based Media Center version.

FIGURE 9.19

Front panel of a Media Center Extender.

FIGURE 9.20

Back panel connections on a Media Center Extender.

If you have a Windows XP Media Center Edition PC, be sure to use a Media Center Extender. It is the perfect way to add TVs and music to your home entertainment network.

Using Audio Extenders

The final category of media extender focuses only on music files. Network music players connect to your home entertainment network, search your PCs for music files, and use a very simple LCD panel to navigate your music files. You attach the network music player to your network and to a set of speakers or stereo, and you can play your music from anywhere in your home.

These devices cost less than a media extender that connects to a TV and also allows playing video, recorded TV, and, most importantly, offers a highly visual user interface to navigate your music files. Because you might not have a TV in all locations where you want to play music, a network music player might be the best solution.

The advantage of network music players is that they are simple, small, and cost between $100 and $150 (about half of video-based media extenders). There are even models that have their own set of speakers.

Network music players might be a good solution for you if all you are looking for is a way to play music from your PC in various locations in your home—and in locations where a TV might not be practical or available.

Start with a full media extender, and if you are limited by a lack of a TV in the location, choose a network music player.

Summary

The primary PC, or any other PC on the home entertainment network, should be capable of tuning in TV signals and recording them, as well as playing video or recorded TV to a TV set connected to the PC. This is done by installing a TV tuner card and a video card that supports TV-out. If possible, get a TV tuner card that includes an FM radio tuner.

A good audio card will allow you to have stereo or surround sound by simply attaching a high-quality set of powered speakers.

Once you have a home network in place, you can add media extenders to turn your TVs and stereo equipment into remote devices that play media from any PC on your home entertainment network.

Limitations of Media Extenders on Wired and Wireless Networks

Media extenders are essential devices for building a dynamic—and inexpensive—home entertainment network. Because a media extender is one of the primary devices you will be using in your home, it is important to understand that they have their limitations. They are inexpensive compared with computers, for example, and they can't do all the things a computer can do.

Because media extenders use a wired or wireless network to play video, music, Internet radio, or streaming media and also display picture files, some of their limitations are a result of the speed at which a home network can send media files. Video files, for example, are large and can play perfectly with a wired connection, but in a wireless network, they might pause or stop if the wireless signal slows for any reason.

When you understand the mechanics of moving media files over a home network, you can optimize those files to work best with media extenders. This chapter will look at the high-bandwidth demands that video files place on media extenders and will help you create video files in a way that allow media extenders to play them flawlessly.

Because media extenders are some of the newest networking devices around, they each operate in a different way, offer different features, and often require its own media player application to use. This chapter will also look at what media extenders are best at, what type of files they can handle (and which they can't), and what type of media is best played on them.

Understanding the Different Types of Media Extenders

Right now, media extenders all share the same method of connecting to a home network, using a "media player" application to play files from PCs on the network and play them on TVs and stereos.

There are four basic types of media extenders:

- **Wireless audio and video player**—This media extender connects to either a wired or wireless network using its own wireless adapter (most often using the 802.11g standard) and connects to a TV and uses the TV's speakers, a stereo, or powered speakers for audio. It has a TV-based user interface of its own design and visually displays menus for videos, music, and picture files stored on the PCs in your home network.

- **Wired audio and video player**—This version is essentially the same as the previous one, but it only works in a wired network and requires a wired Ethernet connection to the PC or router.

- **Wireless audio player with TV menu**—This media extender only plays music files. Many wireless audio players operate on the slower 802.11b standard, although newer models are now using the 802.11g standard. Even though it is only intended for music playing, it connects to a TV for a visual interface to music file menus and uses a remote control for music selection.

- **Wireless audio player with LCD menu**—This wireless audio player uses files from PCs located in the home network but is standalone and does not use a TV for the menus. It has an LCD screen that you use to navigate music menus, and some models have their own speakers much as a radio does. Current models are available in both the 802.11b and 802.11g standards.

Most all of these media extenders come with remote controls and are easily added to a home network. Audio-only media extenders can work with a set of powered speakers or a home stereo, and some models have their own speakers and operate as a radio does. The devices range in cost from $99 to about $300, depending on whether it is wireless and whether it interfaces with a TV to display menus and play pictures and video.

As exciting as these devices are, you should understand some issues about how well they handle media files, which will be important when you plan your home entertainment network.

Bandwidth Issues with Video and Music Files

It's safe to say that most of the devices I've discussed, whether operating wired or wirelessly, do a great job on most music files and photo files. The relatively small file sizes of photo and music files allow the media extenders to "keep up" with the stream of data coming through the home network.

Wireless networks are totally reliant on excellent reception. When the reception degrades, media files become choppy or stop playing for moments at a time.

If you have made every possible improvement for getting good reception in your wireless network (positioning the router, adding signal boosters, and adding access points), you can take two additional steps when reception continues to fail:

1. Use a wired connection. You will just about eliminate any skips or stops in music files this way.

2. Create media files at a low sampling rate. Music files saved at a lower sampling rate use less bandwidth and are less likely to skip when transmission speeds slow down.

Most media files you create using MP3, WMA, or MPEG file formats use varying amounts of compression. The rule is that the more you compress a file, the more quality you lose. If your file compression is minimal, or you have none at all, the bandwidth required to play it on a media extender might exceed the speed of the wireless network. Figure 10.1 shows this problem.

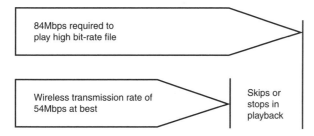

FIGURE 10.1

The best transmission rates of a wireless network might not be adequate for high bit-rate files.

A wired connection is generally fast enough for most files, not just because the bandwidth is higher, but also because it is not subject to interference and slowdowns due to radio signal interference in your home. Figure 10.2 shows how a wired network "keeps ahead" of most files being sent over the network.

A wired network is reliable and it is the best option, but as shown earlier in this book, it is not always practical to have wired connections in many homes. If you are using a wireless connection with a media extender, you will learn that you should create versions of your media files that have a low enough bit rate to play well on a wireless network.

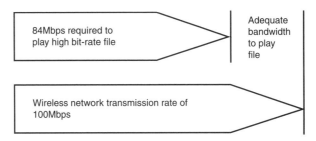

FIGURE 10.2

The reliability and high speed of a wired network keep it ahead of most of the media being transmitted through it.

Here are some examples of video sampling rates; you will see how the bit rate at which a video file is created affects not only how large the file is, but also how capable it is of working on a wireless network. Even when using a 802.11g wireless network, which should be capable of sending most media files reliably, it can slow down at times so that it cannot handle video files.

- Uncompressed video(AVI)—30Mbps

- Compressed video (MPEG-2)—4.5Mbps

These numbers reflect the minimum rate at which the data must move over the wireless network to simply play the video. There is a lot more going on in sending data across the network than the file data itself. There is system management information, competition from other devices on the network, error-checking, and packet management. When they all figure together, it's really hard to play an uncompressed, full AVI video on a wireless network at all. The much smaller MPEG-2 file will play, but only under ideal conditions.

To address this very real situation, media extenders "support" different file formats and don't play formats that are saved at too high of a bit rate for wireless networks. For example, a media extender plays an MPEG video, but not an AVI video. It plays MP3s that are encoded at a low bit rate but not those encoded at highest bit rates. The result is that not every media file plays on a media extender. You need to check the packaging of any media extender you are interested in purchasing to see what file formats, and compression rates, are supported.

A wired media extender supports most file formats, especially when it comes to video. Music files have the best overall support from both wired and wireless media extenders. Picture files work well on virtually all media extenders that can play pictures.

If you find that you have files that do not work with your media extender because of the file format, or the compression rate is not supported by the media extender, consider converting your files. Using Windows Media Player, Windows Movie Maker or Apple's QuickTime (for Apple's ACC file formats for music), open a file and then select Save As and choose a file format that is supported by your media extender. Be sure to read the manual or help files for your media extender to see the list of supported file formats.

Using Photos Files with Media Extenders

Unlike music and video, where bandwidth is an issue of presenting a continual stream of music or video that can't be interrupted, photo files are a different story.

Because the actual photo file does not appear until all the data is received by the media extender, and it can "buffer" the data from the next picture while it is displaying the current picture, media extenders handle photo files quite well.

Occasionally, there might be a slight delay while loading a file, but it doesn't result in the interruption of the experience the way a network slowdown would for video or audio files. When the wireless network slows down for viewing picture files, you simply continue to see the picture you are currently viewing while the next picture is being received. The consequence of a network slowdown for picture viewing shows in the time between pictures in a slideshow.

Some file formats still might not be supported by media extenders. You will be okay if you use JPEGs, but larger file formats such as BMPs and TIFFs (which are uncompressed files designed for maximum quality images) might not be supported, and some extremely large files might not load even if they are in a supported file format such as JPEG. Even JPEG files created by newer digital cameras can be in the 4–5 megabyte range and are too large for a media extender to open.

Comparing a Wired and Wireless Media Extender

To understand how using a wired connection to a media extender is really a plus in general, especially if you are playing videos, let's take a look at two popular models: the D-Link Media Lounge, which was featured in Chapter 9, "Adding TV and Media Extenders to the Network," and Hauppauge's Media MVP. (The MVP stands for music, videos, and pictures.)

Shown later in Figure 10.11, the Media Lounge sells for about $200 and offers both wired and wireless connectivity. The Media MVP, shown in Figure 10.3, sells for about $100 and only works with a wired connection. Each is a capable media extender—easy to set up, attractive in a home entertainment center, and easy to use with good performance. Each comes with a remote control and makes using media files from your PC as easy as surfing regular channels on any TV.

These are great examples of how, and why, home entertainment networks are possible because they eliminate the need for PCs all over your house and greatly reduce the cost of your overall home entertainment network while adding features never available before in home entertainment centers.

Each device hooks up to a TV for the user interface, and each requires a small "media player" application to be running on a PC. If your main server PC is not on, they cannot connect to their media server applications.

Media MVP Wired Media Extender

First, let's take a look at the Media MVP.

FIGURE 10.3

The Media MVP here is sitting on top of a standard-size VCR.

As you can see in Figures 10.3 and 10.4, the Media MVP is a small unit, about the size of a portable CD player, making it possible to tuck it away on a shelf or place it on top of a TV. Because it does have an infrared port on the front of the unit to communicate with its remote control, you need to keep it in the "line of sight" so that the remote control can send signals to it.

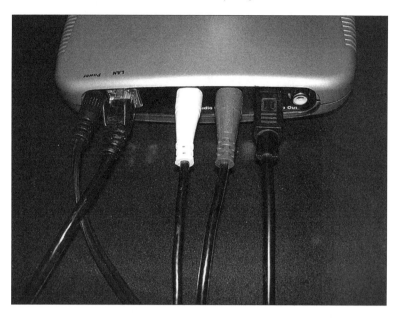

FIGURE 10.4

*The back panel of the Media MVP has connections for power, Ethernet port, S-Video, compos-
ite video, and RCA-style stereos.*

The back panel has the basic connectors needed to connect to a TV and sound system
(TV, stereo, or powered speakers) but lacks component video or digital-out connections
for surround sound. Considering its price and overall perform-
ance, it's fine for connecting to most TVs that do not have those
connections. Because most audio and video files are not surround sound, it should suffice for almost all the media you play.

Figure 10.5 shows the main menu that appears when you turn on
Media MVP. Just like the device itself, the user interface is
extremely simple, visual, and easy to navigate. The choices are
to go to music, video, pictures, or the setup screen.

> **TIP**
>
> You should attach any media
> extender to a TV that supports
> more than one video connection.
> Some TVs have several video con-
> nections. You do not want to have
> to reach back and change cables
> each time you want to use the
> media extender!

One of the first things you notice when using Media MVP is that
it is fast. With a wired connection running at up to 100Mbps, it
does not experience clipping or drop-outs when playing music or videos. And because
it uses a wired network connection, it plays MP3s without hesitation, regardless of
their sample rate.

FIGURE 10.5

The main menu of Media MVP is simple and easy to read on any TV.

Figure 10.6 shows the music menu of Media MVP, which like all the menus and the user interface is simple and highly readable, even on small TVs. This menu design is a real plus when you use a media extender on older or small sets: A good user interface for any media extender keeps things simple and readable.

FIGURE 10.6

After you choose which music folders you want in the media server, you navigate to them by album name and then by song name.

One nice feature is that after you get your music playing, you can switch to the pictures menu and start a slide show while the music continues to play. Playing music and pictures simultaneously is a great feature, although you can't synchronize the pictures to any music play list.

Pictures are also easy to use, and after you choose your folders from the media server application, you choose them by folders and then by the individual photos. The photos are previewed as thumbnails, and then you view them one-by-one or in a slide show. Figure 10.7 shows the pictures menu.

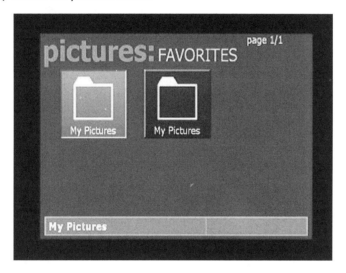

FIGURE 10.7

You navigate to pictures using the same folder and files system used in Windows XP.

Videos are as easy to reach as music and pictures after you set the desired folders on your server PC from the media player application.

Media MVP plays MPEG-1 and MPEG-2 videos without a hitch. But, it does not handle full uncompressed AVI files, which are too large even for a wired network, in most cases. Figure 10.8 shows the menu for navigating to video files.

If a file folder you select contains only video files that are not supported such as full-size AVIs, you see the message in Figure 10.9, indicating that no files are available for viewing. If the folder contains both supported and unsupported files, you will be able to open the folder and when you attempt to play an unsupported file, you will see a "file not supported" message.

FIGURE 10.8

Navigating to video files uses the same technique as music or pictures—files and folders.

FIGURE 10.9

If your folder contains video files that are not supported, the screen indicates that there are no video files—even though you know there are video files in the folder.

This message brings up one of the key issues of media extenders, even when using a wired connection: If you plan to play video files throughout your home on media extenders, be sure that your media files are in a format that is supported by the media extenders. Each media extender comes with a full list of supported file formats, and you might want to keep this list in your thoughts when creating video files. If you are using a mix of wired and wireless media extenders, store your media files (or at least copies of them) at the lowest common denominator that works on each media extender.

> **TIP**
>
> If you want to be able to play all your video files on your media extenders, but you don't want to lose the high-quality video files that you started with, save your original video as an AVI for the highest possible quality and then also save a second file as an MPEG-1 or MPEG-2 file. That way, you'll have versions that your media extenders can handle.

Adding files to the list of media that the media extender can use is as simple as selecting from a list of file folders and adding them to a favorites list from the media player application on your PC, as shown in Figure 10.10. This process is important because you might have a large number of files on your server PC: Navigating to them on a TV using a remote control is better with a favorites list.

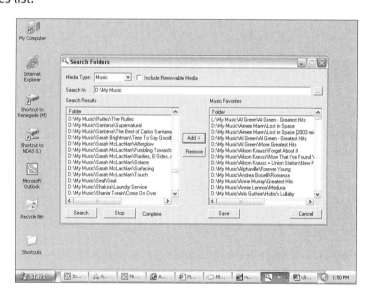

FIGURE 10.10

You add media files for playing and viewing from your main server PC by selecting files and folders of media.

You perform all the operations described here by simply attaching a Media MVP to a TV and turning on the device. There is no lag time, and files load quickly and play seamlessly because of the wired connection. Except for limiting your media playing to

167

supported file formats, you should have an excellent experience with a wired media extender such as the Media MVP.

Media Lounge Wireless or Wired Media Extender

Already introduced in Chapter 9, the Media Lounge from D-Link is an exciting media extender because it operates wired to a network or with its own internal 802.11g wireless adapter. Looking like any slick consumer electronic device, it plays music, videos, and pictures and also includes the ability to play Internet radio.

Figure 10.11 shows the Media Lounge from the front: It has a slim case that is the same size as most DVD players and home stereo units, so it fits right into a home entertainment center. About the only thing that gives it away as a network device is that it has a small antenna for its wireless adapter.

FIGURE 10.11

A small wireless network antenna is about the only thing that distinguishes Media Lounge from any other consumer electronic device.

The back panel has connectors for audio out, digital audio out for surround sound equipment, and video out for composite, S-Video, and component video. It's a full-featured device when it comes to connectors. It also has a connector for the wireless antenna and an Ethernet port.

When you power on the device for the first time, it takes you through a setup routine where you decide whether you are using a wired or wireless connection. Unless you have a special home network configuration, the device looks to your router for a Dynamic Host Configuration Protocol (DHCP) assignment and then connects to the wired or wireless network.

At this point, and this point applies to both devices covered in this chapter, you run into a problem with the Windows XP Firewall. The firewall initially blocks these devices, and you have one of two choices: Turn off the firewall (which is not recommended) or allow the installation routine for the media extender to add the device to the list of allowed devices from the Windows XP Firewall menu. The setup and installation programs for media extenders give you the option of modifying firewall settings, and because it is a trusted device, choose Yes for this option.

Figure 10.12 shows one of the important screens from the installation procedure: connecting to a media server.

Media Lounge requires that you install and run its Media Server application on your PC for Media Lounge to access media files. You launch Media Server on your PC. In addition to allowing you to list which files you want to share with Media Lounge, it is the active application that serves the media files to it. You can have more than one PC serving media files, so this screen is where you decide which media server you want to use.

FIGURE 10.12

You need to select a media server when using Media Lounge.

One frustration with using Media Lounge is that because it is designed to operate as a wireless media extender, it does have limits on the files it supports. For example, MP3 and WMA files that are created at too high a bit rate do not play, although if it were a completely wired media extender, they would. The same is true for video files that are saved at too high of a bit rate: You are limited to file formats that work both in a wireless and a wired connection.

When you attempt to play music files, Media Lounge lists the filenames, as shown in Figure 10.13. As shown in Figure 10.14, if the files are not supported because they do not have the correct MP3 format, you get an error message. This part can be frustrating at times, and the limitations of wireless file access apply to the device even when in a wired mode.

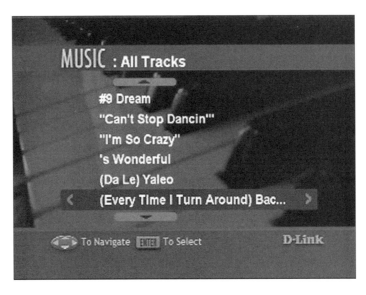

FIGURE 10.13

MP3 files appear as a list when you enter the music menu.

FIGURE 10.14

If the file format is not supported, you get an error message asking you to refer to the user manual for a list of supported file types.

The same error message appears when you attempt to play video files that are not supported. As with all media extenders, it does have a limit on how large a media file it can play through a network—especially a wireless network. A good solution is to create media libraries (even if they are simple low-bandwidth copies of full-band media) for playing on these devices.

Picture files play well wirelessly on Media Lounge, even when they are large JPEGs. Figure 10.15 shows a JPEG loading, and rather than indicating the file is too large or will not display, a circular clock in the middle of the screen shows the progress of the image loading.

FIGURE 10.15

Even larger JPEG files play, but if the wireless network is slow, you get a time bar to show that it is indeed loading.

In general, when used wirelessly or wired, Media Lounge is a sophisticated media extender with a classy user interface, and it is easy to use after you get past the wireless or wired setup screens. One feature it includes is the ability to play Internet radio, as shown in Figure 10.16. For its $199 price, it's not much more expensive than dedicated Internet radio extenders for PCs!

The device ships with a choice of several Internet radio portals (such as AOL Radio and Napster), and if you are a current subscriber to any of the services, the radio service is free. If you are not a subscriber, you get a free 6-month period to use the radio service.

FIGURE 10.16

Internet radio from AOL and other portals is included with Media Lounge.

The wireless and wired networking features, the ability to play music files and Internet radio, and the ability to play videos and view pictures make a great example of an excellent media extender. It brings together all the media that you use PCs for—without a PC. It puts all that media where it belongs: on TVs and home stereos or powered speakers.

Using Media Extenders Makes Sense

Using the two devices as examples of media extenders you can use right now in your home entertainment network, you start to realize that media extenders make perfect sense.

Yes, network bandwidth limits the size and types of files that you can play, but in reality, the quality of TVs and the quality of music files it can play are more than you need for almost any home entertainment experience.

Media extenders are truly what changes a PC-based network, where you need to connect clumsy and expensive PCs together to share media, into an elegant and inexpensive home entertainment network. Their ability to use TVs and existing stereos and audio devices make the media files on your PC useable just about anywhere in your home where you have a TV.

Although you can purchase a media extender that plays only music, those are best for locations where you do not have a TV. Because the prices are so close for a media extender that plays video and audio and for an audio-only device, if you have a TV where you want to play music, go for the full media extender because it will serve music and video too. The user interface is better on a TV.

Overcoming the Limitations of Media Extenders

With all the benefits that the current generation of media extenders offer, they are a essential component of your home entertainment network. By understanding what limitations they have (which are largely issues of network performance and bandwidth), you can easily overcome those limitations.

The following are some suggestions that will help you get the right media extender and manage your media files to work correctly with it:

- **Use a wired connection for video**—If you want to use a media extender primarily to play video files, consider using a wired connection. The high bandwidth required to display just about any video file with good quality on a TV is best distributed using a wired connection that can maintain up to 100Mbps. If you use a wireless connection, you need to save your video files at such a high level of compression to play without pauses or full stops.

- **Save files in the right format**—Be sure that the files you want to play on your media extenders are in the supported file formats for the media extender. Each media extender provides a list of supported file formats, and you should check before purchasing one whether you can play your files. If you have an existing library of files that are not supported, you can convert them to the correct file format, although that process can be long and tedious if you have a lot of files. When creating any new files, be sure to save them in a supported file format. If quality is an issue, you can save a copy of the file in a compressed format that you can play on your media extenders (such as a JPEG copy of a TIFF picture file for media extender play).

- **Get the right media extender**—If you want to play music at only one location and videos in another location, get the right media extender for the job. Media extenders come in versions just for music and versions that can play music, video, and pictures. When shopping, remember that a media extender that can play video can also play music. If the prices are close and you have a TV that you can use to display the user interface, go for the media extender that can play the greatest number of file formats. Also be sure that any wireless media extender, even if only for music playing, also has a wired connection to give you that option if you need it at some point.

- **Mix and match**—You can have different types of media extenders in a home entertainment network. They do not all have to be the same brand. You can have a music-only media extender in one room and a video, music, picture, and Internet radio media extender in another room.

Successful media playing with media extenders is largely about a reliable network connection and files that are in the correct file format and that are compressed enough to play on the media extender.

If you match your network connection (wired or wireless) to the media type (music and pictures versus video), you can overcome the limitations of media extenders in a home entertainment network.

Summary

Media extenders are essential devices in any home entertainment network. They allow you to access media content from PCs and the Internet without the need or expense of additional PCs.

Although they are great media players, they do have a limit on what types of files they can play, especially in a wireless network. Knowing the file types that you can play and building libraries of playable media files provide a practical answer.

Media extenders come in wired and wireless versions; a wired media extender provides the most reliable media playing at the lowest cost.

MANAGING A HOME ENTERTAINMENT NETWORK

PART III

Sharing Files and Adding Users

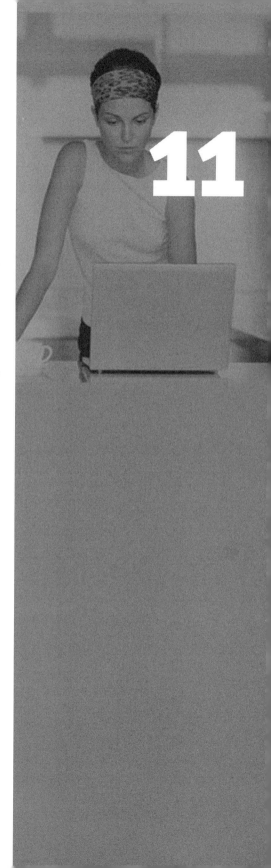

11

By bringing all of your PCs, TVs, and stereos together using home networking equipment to create a true home entertainment network, you can begin sharing media files between the devices. This allows you to distribute all the video, music, and pictures that had been stuck on your PCs and put them where they belong: on TVs and audio devices.

Once you have brought your equipment together in a home entertainment network, the next task is to begin to manage the sharing of files between devices and to begin to control how each user on the network can access those files. You can, for example, turn off certain content such as music files at a certain time of the day so that kids focus on homework rather than listening to tunes.

This chapter shows how to share files between computers, create users on the network, and helps you begin to manage access to your media content in your home.

Adding Your Computers to the Network

Except for media extenders (which have their own media servers for getting media files from PCs; sharing files between computers is a separate activity), you can have a home network in which you can share files between computers, or even in which no files are shared—the router could just be sharing an Internet connection between PCs.

With the release of Windows XP, and even more so with Windows XP Service Pack 2, file sharing is extremely easy to turn on and manage.

In a totally secure home environment where anyone in the home can use any computer and you are not worried about file access, you can set things up where any user can reach any file on any computer. Because that might not always be the case, you can also set things up, for example, where users can either access files but not change them, or not access them at all.

Here are the steps that will work best for your home entertainment network, and each will be detailed in the sections that follow:

1. Set up a workgroup for your home entertainment network and add your computers to the network workgroup.

2. Turn on file sharing and device sharing.

Although you don't have to create a workgroup, you will find that if you want to create different levels of access in your home (business group, family group, or all users), this is the best way to do that.

File sharing lets you decide which drives, folders, or individual files can be shared.

Once you do this, your home entertainment network can take advantage of all your file storage on all devices and allow you to get at files from anywhere in your home—provided that you have established the correct security settings to access those files from other devices.

Let's take a look at creating the workgroup first.

Creating a Workgroup

First, you will want to learn whether you have an existing workgroup on your computer that was installed when you added your router or wireless network. If a workgroup is in place, you will want to make sure that each computer on your network uses the same workgroup name and becomes a part of the workgroup. Each computer in the workgroup will have a name, and you can decide on the name for the workgroup and for each computer on the network.

Figure 11.1 shows a control panel using the Windows XP Classic View that is reached by

1. Clicking Start from the bottom left corner of your Windows desktop and then choosing Control Panel.

2. Clicking the System control panel from the menu or set of icons.

3. From the System control panel, clicking on the Computer Name Tab.

Any of the preceding actions must be done by the system administrator, who, unless you have created different user accounts on your computer, will be the default user. If you only have one user account on your PC, and you have not changed any user or network settings up to this point, you are the default system administrator.

If you prefer, you can change the name of your computer on the workgroup to make it easy to identify to other users on the network. From the Control Panel, choose Change to change the computer name, and then from the menu that pops up, enter a descriptive name that contains no spaces, and click Finish. You can also add a description of your PC such as "PC in the bedroom." This is shown in Figure 11.2.

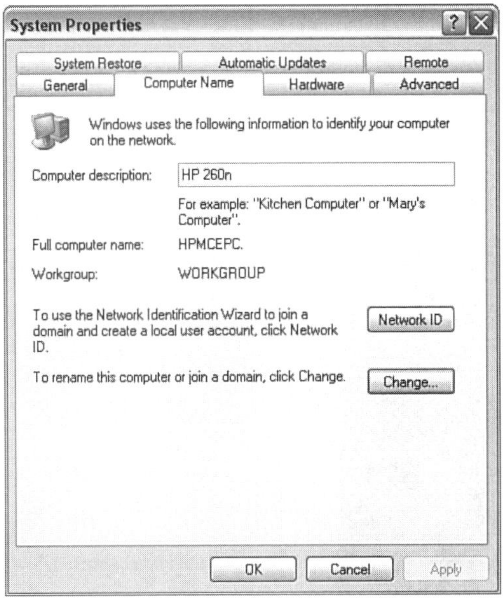

FIGURE 11.1

The computer name and workgroup control panel are where you join a workgroup and name your PC.

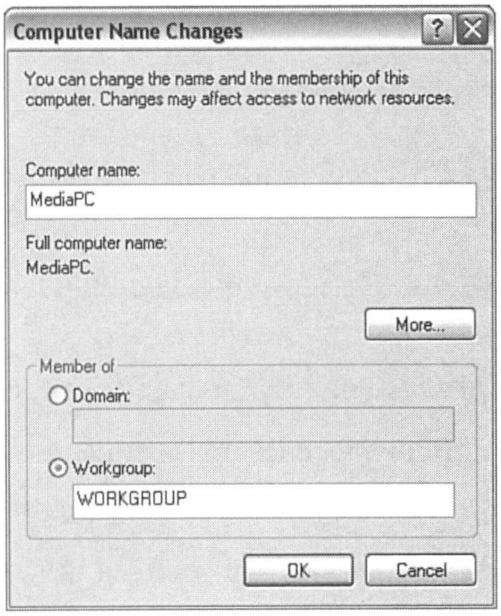

FIGURE 11.2

You can change the name of the computer or the workgroup. Here the computer name is being changed.

Adding Your Computer to the Network

Finally, as shown in Figure 11.3, you should choose to identify your computer as a part of a network. This will make it easier for your computer to become part of the home entertainment network, and it's a simple process of starting the Network Identification Wizard by choosing to obtain a Network ID from the control panel, and then telling the Wizard that your computer is part of a home network.

FIGURE 11.3

The Network Identification Wizard will add your computer to the network.

To add your computer to a network, follow the steps in the following order when using the Windows Classic view:

1. Click Start from the bottom left corner of your Windows desktop, and then choose Control Panel.

2. Click the System control panel from the menu or set of icons.

3. From the System control panel, click on the Computer Name Tab.

4. From the Computer Name Tab, click on the Network ID button.

5. The Network Identification Wizard will appear. Click Next from the menu shown in Figure 11.3.

6. Because you are building a home network, choose This Computer Is for Home Use and not Part of a Business Network from the next menu in the wizard.

7. From the next menu that appears, click Finish. Your computer has been added to a network using the workgroup name and computer name you have established. You will need to restart your computer for the changes to take effect.

Once you have made these settings, you will know the name of your workgroup, and will have named your computer and obtained a Network ID. After all these steps are completed, you must restart your PC for the changes to take effect.

When you added a network router, it connected your computer to the Internet through a network connection. The creation of your home entertainment network, where computers share files with each other, requires the preceding steps.

Setting Up Wireless Networks

When you use a wireless network, there is a quick and easy way to create the home network using a new wizard found in Windows XP Service Pack 2. It not only adds your computers to the network, but it also helps make all required settings and security settings for the firewall to mix wired and wireless computers on the network. To use this wizard, go to the Control Panel from the Start menu. You will see two important wizards listed in the Control Panel: Network Setup Wizard and Wireless Setup Wizard. This Windows Classic View screen is shown in Figure 11.4.

If you are not using Windows XP Service Pack 2, it is strongly recommended that you update your version of Windows XP to Service Pack 2. If you are not using Windows XP Service Pack 2 or a previous version of Windows, you will need to use the Network Setup Wizard for both wired and wireless network configurations.

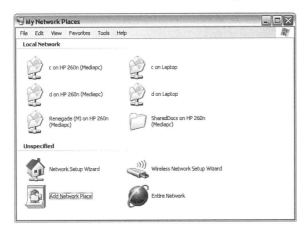

FIGURE 11.4

Network Setup Wizard and Wireless Setup Wizard are reached from the Control Panel, which is reached from the Start menu.

If you are using an all-wired network, you can choose to use the Network Setup Wizard, and it will take you through the process of adding your computer to the network. Then you can use a storage device, such as a floppy disk or a USB storage device, to transfer the network settings to every other computer on the network using the same settings and identifying each computer correctly.

Because your home entertainment network will most likely be mixing wired and wireless connections, let's look at using the Wireless Setup Wizard.

Begin by clicking on the Wireless Network Setup wizard icon. You will arrive at the menu shown in Figure 11.5. The first menu will tell you that you are setting up a wireless network that will add security features called a Wireless Infrastructure Network.

FIGURE 11.5

The first menu in the Wireless Network Setup Wizard will tell you that you are creating a wireless security-enabled network.

After clicking to continue, you will then see the screen shown in Figure 11.6 asking you if you want to add your computer to an existing wireless network. If this is the first time using the Wireless Network Setup wizard and the first computer you are setting up, choose to create a new wireless network.

If you choose to add a computer to a wireless network, as shown in Figure 11.6, you will be asked for a network name (*SSID*—which stands for *Service Set Identifier*, which is a name for your network). All the computers on your network will use this network name to work with each other. Choose any name you like up to 32 characters long without spaces.

You can also have the wizard automatically assign a "network key." The network key is either *WEP* (*Wired Equivalent Privacy*) or *WPA* (*Wi-Fi Protected Access*), and because not all routers and wireless devices support WPA, you have both options. Network keys encrypt the data that is transmitted between devices on your wireless network to help secure the data from being used by anyone outside your network.

FIGURE 11.6

If this is the first computer you are adding to the wireless network, choose to create a new wireless network. If you have an existing network, choose to add your computer to the existing network as shown here.

For the initial setup, have the wizard automatically assign a network key. You can change the settings at a later date if you need to. WPA is the preferred method of network key (it provides a higher level of network security), and if you know that all of your devices can support WPA, check the "Use WPA" box at the bottom of the screen. If you are unsure, check the packaging and manuals for your devices, or leave this box unchecked for now.

The next screen will ask you whether you want to create your network by saving all the network settings on a USB flash card, or to set up each computer on the network manually. It's best to use the USB flash card method because all the network settings and information about each computer will be stored on the flash card and you will not have to type it in on the other computers you will be adding. This screen is shown in Figure 11.7.

> **TIP**
> If you don't have a USB flash card, you can use another storage card such as a SD or Compact memory card or even a floppy disk. What is important is that you have a common storage card or disk that can be read by each computer you will be working with.

If you chose to use a Flash drive, you will then see the screen shown in Figure 11.8 instructing you to insert the flash drive along with an illustration of how to insert the device. You will also see a menu to choose the drive letter for the portable storage device you will be using. It is good practice to know the drive letter your USB flash drive or other portable storage card uses before getting to this screen.

183

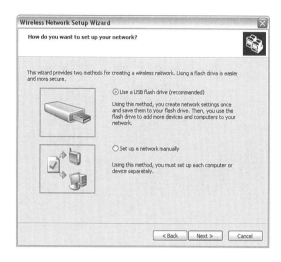

FIGURE 11.7

If you have a USB flash drive or other storage device that can be used on each computer, select to use a flash drive. If not, select the manual option.

FIGURE 11.8

If you chose to use a USB flash card, this menu will allow you to choose the drive letter and complete the process.

After you have inserted the flash or memory card and identified the drive letter, click Next, and the network settings will be made to your computer and a complete copy of the network settings will be stored on the card.

These settings will include the network name and security identification for your wireless network, and the Wireless Network Wizard makes the settings to your computer and each new computer you add to the network. The Wireless Network Wizard is new to Windows XP Service Pack 2, and it makes a very complex process very simple.

If you do not have a portable storage device that will work on each computer, such as a USB flash drive, you can choose the manual process of setting up the wireless network, where you will print out the information each computer and device will require—including your broadband router—and then make the settings manually on each device.

Figure 11.9 shows the screen you see when you choose the manual option, and there is a button for printing the network setting information and instructions to copy the information to every other device on the network.

FIGURE 11.9

When you choose Manual settings, you must print out a page with all the required network settings to copy to each device on your network.

After you have been through the preceding process on the first computer, you will need to go to each additional computer on your home entertainment network and repeat the process of naming it, making sure that it is on the same workgroup, identifying it to the network, and finally running the Wireless Network Setup Wizard.

If you are not using a wireless network, you can choose to use the Network Setup Wizard. This Wizard will name your workgroup and computers in the same manner as the Wireless Networked Setup wizard, but it will not add the network security features for a wireless network.

If you use a wireless router, be sure to use the Wireless Network Setup Wizard for all computers, even if they are connected via a wired connection. If you are using a wireless router, but all your devices are connected to it via an Ethernet cable, the router is still capable of sending data and you will want to use the security features enabled by the Wireless Network Setup Wizard.

After you have completed this process, all the computers in your home will be on the same network, in the same workgroup, and each will have a name and description to help you identify it. At this time, you may start to turn on file sharing between the computers on the network.

Setting Up File Sharing on Each Computer

In order to share media files between computers and other devices such as media extenders, you must first turn on file sharing from each computer on the network that you want to share files from. You can set up file sharing to share entire drives, or just particular files or folders from any drive on your PCs.

If you use a PC for both regular computing and also store a lot of media files on it such as music and video, you can choose to simply share the media files, but not share the business or other files. Assuming that you will want to make all files available to any user or device on the home entertainment network, the process of setting up file sharing on each PC is as follows.

The decision to share a whole drive and all the files on it, or just particular files or folders on a drive is up to you, but the process is essentially the same for either.

Sharing Drives on the Network

To share a hard drive and all the folders and files on it with other device on the network, you must turn on file sharing for the drive.

First, from the Start menu, go to My Computer as shown in Figure 11.10. You will see a list of the drives on your PC, such as the C drive, D drive, and any other drives that you might have attached such as portable drives or CD-ROM or DVD drives.

Next, choose a drive that you want to share on the network by selecting it, and from the File menu in the top menu bar, select Sharing and Security. This will present you with the Properties control panel for that drive, as shown in Figure 11.11. From the drive Properties menu, you will be able to set sharing levels for the drive.

To share the hard drive, follow these steps:

1. Click on the Sharing tab from the drive Properties control panel.

2. Go to the Network Sharing and Security area of the menu, and click the boxes to Share the drive on the network, and if you prefer, allow other users to change the files on the drive.

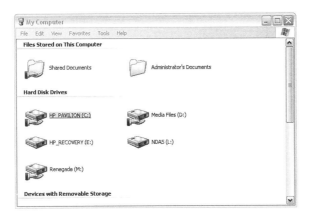

FIGURE 11.10

My Computer lists all the drives that are attached to your computer.

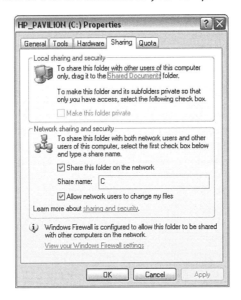

FIGURE 11.11

Properties control panel for a hard drive where you can set its sharing and security.

3. If you prefer, you can also give the drive a name that is descriptive rather than the simple drive letter. You name the drive by entering a name in the Share Name box on the menu.

4. Click OK to finish the sharing settings for the drive.

Note that at the bottom of the Control Panel, there is a message that Windows has enabled the firewall to share the drive. This is because you have followed the steps listed earlier of letting the Microsoft network wizards add your computer safely to your network with security features enabled. This also protects your drives on the network with the Windows Firewall.

After you have made the settings and clicked OK to finish, your drive will be in a shared mode. If you look back to Figure 11.10, you will see that some of the drive icons in the My Computer folder have "hands" under them. This is the icon for a shared drive. This lets you easily see which drives are being shared on your network.

Sharing Files or Folders on the Network

If you do not want to make a full drive available to other users on the network, you can select to only share folders, or even files on a drive. The process is essentially the same as sharing a hard drive. Set file or folder sharing using these steps:

1. From My Computer, select the drive by clicking on it to open the contents of the drive.

2. Select the folder or file you want to share, and from the File Menu, select Sharing and Security.

3. From the File or Folder Properties menu that appears, select the Sharing tab.

4. From the Sharing menu, choose to share the file or folder from the Network Sharing and Security menu area. You can choose to not allow others to change the file. This is useful if you do not want the files modified in any way, or accidentally erased. This option will only allow other users or devices to open and view the file.

5. Click on "OK" to complete the sharing process.

6. If you choose to make individual files or folders available to the network rather than the entire contents of a drive, you must go to each folder or file that you want to share and repeat this process.

TIP

Files, folders, and drives that are shared on the home entertainment network are only available when the computer they are on is powered on. Be sure that any computers you want to share files with are on and available to the network to share their files.

After you have completed setting either drive or file/folder sharing for each computer on the home entertainment network, you should go to the My Network Places folder from the Start menu and you will see all the drives that are available to any computer on the network, as shown in Figure 11.12.

The networked drives will have a folder icon, and the folder icon has the folder connected to a network pipe. You can click any of these folders to look at the contents inside.

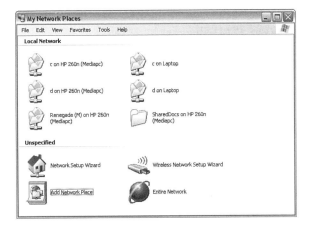

FIGURE 11.12

All shared drives and resources on the network can be viewed from the My Network Places folder.

When you are accessing data from a shared drive on the network, you can open the folders from the My Network Places, or from any file menu, choose Open, and then select My Network Places the exact same way that you would choose My Documents. Figure 11.13 shows a File Open menu with My Network Places selected. You can open files by navigating into the drives and finding the files you want.

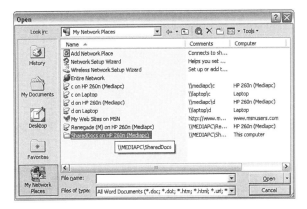

FIGURE 11.13

You can open files from the shared drives on the network by choosing My Network Places from any File Open menu.

At this point, you have added your computers to the home entertainment network and have made drives, folders, or even just files available to other devices on the network.

Repeat this process for each computer, and you will have all of your media content available for all access points and devices in your home.

Saving Power with a Network Drive

As mentioned previously, to share media files across your network, you need to have the computers on which those drives, files, or folders are located turned on and running. This can use a lot of electricity when those files are shared among many PCs. In addition to using electricity, in places such as a bedroom, the slight noise of a fan running from a computer in the room can be a nuisance.

One option for sharing files across a network is to use a network drive. A network drive is a standalone hard drive that has its own Ethernet port or wireless adapter and connects directly to the network router without being directly attached to a PC. You store files on the network drive, and it will serve files to the network on its own, and it is not a part of any PC on the network.

Figure 11.14 shows the NetDisk network hard drive from Ximeta, Inc., which attaches directly to an Ethernet port on a wired or wireless router. Once connected, you install a small driver application on each PC on your home entertainment network. Once the application is installed to the PC, the NetDisk looks and acts as any local hard drive to the PC running the application.

The benefit of a network hard drive is that you can store files on it that can be shared by a number of PCs, and you can access the files from any PC on the network—even when the PC that originally stored the file on the network drive is turned off. It is a true shared network device.

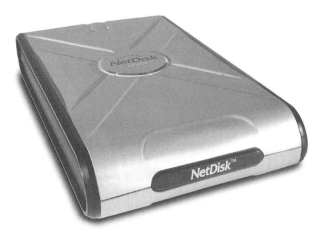

FIGURE 11.14

A network hard drive from Ximeta, Inc. enables storing files on a standalone hard drive connected to the network and shared by any number of PCs.

The drive can only be accessed by PCs running the network drive application. Because most media extenders require a Media Server application running on a PC, they cannot directly access files from such a network hard drive.

If you use one main PC (such as the PC connected to the router) and it runs the application for the network drive and the media servers for media extenders, you can use the network drive to serve files to media extenders as long as the main PC remains on.

Installing and using a network hard drive requires the following steps:

1. Connect the network hard drive directly to an Ethernet port on the router using an Ethernet cable.

2. Turn on the power to the network drive, and be sure to always leave it turned on.

3. Install the driver application by running the network drive setup program on each PC on the network.

4. After the driver application for the network drive is installed and running (it will launch automatically each time you start your PCs), go to the My Computer menu to view the drive and its contents.

5. Store files on the network drive from any computer on the network.

Most network drives are plug-and-play devices and do not require any special network IDs or modifications to your security settings. In addition, they are installed as shared drives. Once installed as part of your network, you can treat the drive as you would any local drive that is located on your PC.

Assigning Users to Your PCs

With all of your drives and files open to the home entertainment network, there might be situations in which you don't want access from certain locations or by certain users.

Although this is more often associated with accessing files (or to limit the changes that can be made to a computer regarding adding programs, deleting files, and changing system settings), it is also good for managing access to media content in a home entertainment network.

You can limit the ability to change files or access to files by setting up "users" on your PCs.

When you set up your Windows XP computer for the first time, it defines two basic users: a system administrator, and a guest. As the person setting up the computer the first time, you are the system administrator, and you can assign new users and define what level of control and access you want to assign to them.

You can certainly choose to not add users. When your computer is turned on, you—or whoever is using the computer—logs in as the administrator with full access to all features and can make any changes possible to the machine.

If you want to be the only person who can configure or modify the computer, you can assign yourself a password so that only you can log on to the computer as the system administrator. All other users can log on as guests, and you can establish how much access guests have to your computer. However, guests will not be able to make any changes to the system files, add or delete programs, or make any major changes to the system without your permission.

To password protect your administrator account, use the following steps:

1. From the Windows Start menu, go to the Control Panel menu and select User Accounts.

2. From the User Accounts menu, choose Change an Account, or you can use the icons of the existing accounts on the bottom of the menu. To add a password for the administrator, choose to add it from the Change an Account menu or double-click on the Administrator icon.

3. Choose to Create a Password from the menu.

4. Enter, and then reenter your password in the fields provided on the menu, and then fill in a password "hint" that will allow you to easily remember your password. Because this is the password for the Administrator account, it is very important that you remember this password.

5. Click on Create Password to complete the procedure.

The next time you use your PC and log in as the administrator, you will be prompted for your user password.

You can also create user accounts, as shown in Figure 11.15, where users can log on to the computer and have greater access to features and settings. When you turn on the PC, you will see a list of user accounts, and each one can be password protected so that only that user can use that account.

To create additional users, perform the following steps:

1. From the Windows Start menu, go to the Control Panel menu and select User Accounts.

2. From the User Accounts menu, choose Create a New Account.

3. Enter the name for the new account and click on Next.

4. If this is the first new user account, you must first create your own Computer Administrator account with full access and system privileges.

5. Once you have created the Administrator account, repeat steps 1 through 3, enter the name for the new user account, and click Next.

6. Using the onscreen choices, choose the level of modifications the user account can make to the computer.

After creating your user account, you can also repeat the steps for adding a password to the user account as described previously. As the system administrator, you can also turn off the user account, modify the access levels, or delete the user.

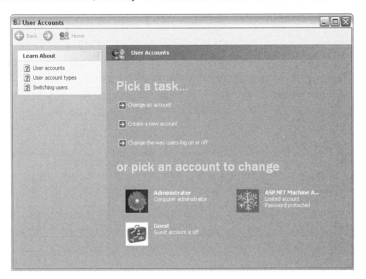

FIGURE 11.15

User Accounts menu is reached from the Start menu, and then the Control Panel.

After you create user accounts, you can then control the very large network of files and drives that you have made available to your home entertainment network. This will allow you to restrict access to certain drives or files by children or guests in your home, and also to be sure that files aren't easily moved or erased.

With a "Limited" status for a user or account, the user can add or change his own password, as well as create, add, delete, and view files he created in his own My Documents folder and view files from a Shared Documents folder.

With a good strategy for storing files (such as in file folders for Music, Pictures, Video, and Recorded TV), you can make controlling access to media files easy to manage. For example, if you don't want users to delete media files, place shortcuts to the media folders and media files in the Shared Documents folder. This folder only allows the files to be opened, but not deleted.

The centralized location of files that are for viewing on the home entertainment network makes it possible to allow users to not only view shared files, but also to create their own files and save them in their own My Documents folder.

Combining good file storage management with user accounts allows you to control who can view files, who can add or modify them, and who can delete them.

You can have a home entertainment network without assigning any users, but having user accounts is good practice if there are many different users. You can revert back to administrator access by any user at any point in the future by returning to the User Accounts control panel and changing user access status levels.

Summary

Once you have connected all of your PCs and media extenders to your home entertainment network, you will want to activate your computers on the network and turn on file sharing so that your files can be reached throughout your home.

This is done by running the Network Setup or Wireless Network Setup Wizards from the My Network Places folder for each computer on the home entertainment network.

When your PCs are part of the network, you can turn on file sharing for the files, folders, or entire drives on each PC.

For a further level of control over all the files across the PCs on the network, you can assign users who have limited access to files or deny them the ability to modify or change the files.

Creating a Media Server Strategy

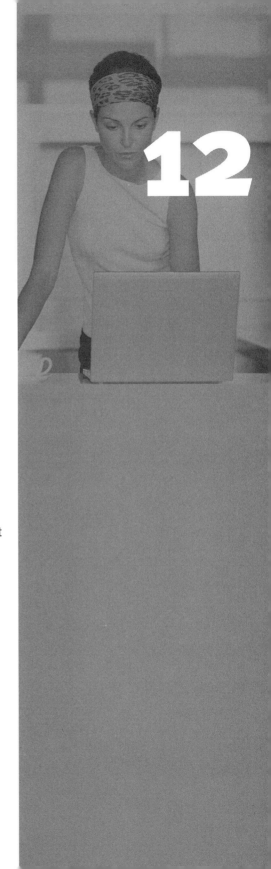

Your home entertainment network not only brings all your computers together to share content and media files, but also adds new types of networked devices such as network hard drives and media extenders. It's an exciting new way to use computers, and it turns your home into one giant, networked entertainment center.

In a conventional home, PCs are capable of storing large amounts of media files including music, photos, recorded TV programs and video files from your camcorders. All of those files are essentially bound to viewing or playing from PCs. A digital home entertainment network allows those files to be accessed from PCs, but also from any TV or audio device when it is connected to a media extender.

The use of a PC to be a media server greatly increases your ability to access the media files you have created virtually anywhere in your home. The key action is to simply think of media stored on your PCs as content for viewing when, and where, you wish.

Because you will view most of the media content you access on TVs rather than computer monitors, you will use a different type of computer interface: TVs.

TVs are getting to the point where they are essentially the same as computer monitors. Newer TVs come in the form of High Definition TVs (HDTV), Liquid Crystal Display TVs (LCD), and plasma display TVs. Chances are that you will still be using a lot of standard tube-style TVs—the types you've been using for years.

The difference between a TV and a computer monitor is interesting. Each is really good at something the other isn't. Here are the main differences:

- **TVs**—Standard TVs are good at playing TV but terrible at displaying even a 640×480 resolution computer screen. TVs are low-resolution devices but have been engineered to display moving video. We are also accustomed to viewing video on TVs, and that's "the way TV looks."

- **Computer monitors**—Whether they are LCD flat panels or cathode ray tube (CRT) computer monitors, monitors are great at displaying detailed, high-resolution graphics such as text and graphics. Because they display a lot more information each second at a high resolution, they are capable of being used both as a computer monitor and also for TV viewing.

The questions concern how to bring the "look and feel" of TV to computing devices and how to navigate into video and music using computer interfaces on a standard TV. These issues have presented challenges, challenges that are addressed correctly in a home entertainment network using media extenders and TV-centric PCs such as Windows XP Media Center Edition PCs.

One of the reasons the use of media extenders is such an important development for home entertainment networks is that they take the complex navigation of files and directories from the computers on the network, find only the media files, and display them in a simple, TV-centric user interface that works perfectly on any TV.

Figure 12.1 shows how simple and elegant a media extender interface can be. Note that everything you want to pull off your PCs in the way of entertainment content is on a TV screen that gets you right to where you want to go.

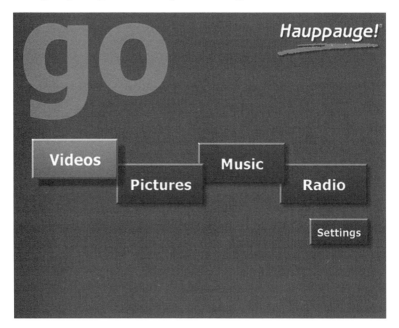

FIGURE 12.1

The Media MVP user interface brings to a TV screen a simple user interface for accessing content from a PC.

Although you can simply connect a TV to a PC, using the standard Windows XP user interface on a TV isn't the best experience. There is one answer for connecting your TV directly to a PC for viewing media content, and that is a Media Center PC with Windows XP Media Center Edition.

Figure 12.2 shows a typical Media Center screen. This screen works exactly the same— and looks fantastic—on either a computer monitor or a TV screen. The entire user interface was designed to be both device- and resolution-independent so that it looks and feels the same on any display. Just like media extender interfaces and experiences, it is limited to accessing media content, not offering traditional computer applications.

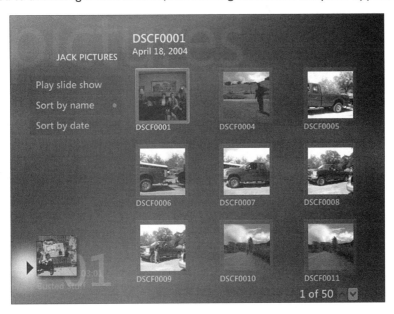

FIGURE 12.2

Windows XP Media Center Edition PCs have the perfect user interface for viewing and navigating media content on a TV or a PC monitor.

As you start to think about what your home entertainment network is really about— playing media from your PCs on your TVs and stereos—you should start to think about the user interfaces used by media extenders and Media Center Edition PCs. They all have the following qualities:

- **Simple**—They have large type with little information onscreen at any one time.

- **Easy to navigate**—Designed to be used with a remote control, the simplicity of the user interface does not require anything more than the cursor keys and "select" key from the remote control to get to the content you want.

- **Well organized**—Media Center Edition PCs and media extenders organize all media content by video, music, and pictures (and radio if available).

Now comes the whole point of this chapter: If you are using a world of PCs and media extenders that have a simple, easy-to-navigate user interface organized by type of media, the organization of your media files should follow that same strategy.

Organizing files and file sharing privileges is the most important tasks you face after putting your computers and media extenders into a home entertainment network.

Creating a Media Server

The preceding section explains why it makes sense to organize your media in a simple, intuitive, and easy-to-navigate file structure. Media extenders and TV interfaces all work better when your files are organized in that way. The PCs that store the media files your media extenders will access must be turned on and be running media server applications. Media server applications are programs on the server PC that send media files to the media extenders you have added to your home entertainment network.

This means that if you have spread your media content across more than one PC, all those PCs need to be on and running most of the time for the media extenders to play the media stored on them.

The main PC that is connected to your broadband router is the best machine to do the following:

> **STRATEGY**
>
> Because media extenders get their content from the hard drives connected to PCs, the PCs have to be on for the media extender to access the data. A good strategy is to have one main PC act as a "media server" to all media extenders. This setup makes file organization simple, and only one PC has to be on for all devices to access media files. Using a network hard drive attached to the router as the central storage space is also a good strategy for allowing all other PCs to add content to the media library.

- **Run media server applications**—Media extenders require media server applications to be running. Have your main PC run those applications and leave it on all the time, or your media extenders will not be able to access content.

- **Manage access**—Assigning users or access levels is best done from the main PC, and you can manage and even log file access on your home entertainment network.

- **Store media files**—Because the main PC is on all the time and is acting as the media server for the home entertainment network, it is the best place to store almost all your media content.

- **Record and store TV shows**—Your main PC is also the best place to record and store TV shows and serve them to all the media extenders and other PCs.

When you consider all these list items, you should start thinking about making your main PC a "media server." Figure 12.3 shows the home entertainment network from a media server perspective and the role the media player serves in your home entertainment network.

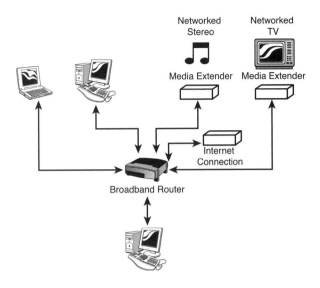

FIGURE 12.3

By configuring your main PC—the one connected to your broadband router using a wired connection—you have one main access point for media files.

In addition to being a server, the main PC is directly connected to your router with a wired connection. It uses that wired connection to serve media to both wired and wireless devices.

There are other ways to serve media. It's okay to spread your media files across PCs or to use a network hard drive connected to the router for all PCs to share and add content to. In fact, it might be a good use of disk space. At least for now, if you are going to use media extenders, which generally can call content from only one media server application at a time, it remains the best practice to put all your media files in one simple place—your media server.

Whether you configure your home entertainment network in the manner described here or you prefer to distribute your media files across devices, the following section will be helpful in making it easy to find, play, and manage your media files.

Managing Your Media Files and Libraries

Because media extenders and even full-blown media PCs such as Windows XP Media Center Edition PCs use a common media-based metaphor for navigating media files, you should think about organizing your files the same way. Think of grouping your media into directories that conform to the following structure:

- **Video**—Organize all your recorded TV and video files such as home videos from your camcorder or videos that you have downloaded from the Internet into one directory or folder labeled Video.

- **Music**—If you are currently using the My Music folder on your C drive in the My Documents folder, you can continue to do so, but consider that a large music library is best stored off the C drive, which is for program and system files. (You might want to restrict access to it for safety reasons.) It is also good to put music files on a separate drive, such as a D drive or an external hard drive, so that they do not compete with the operating system functions of the C drive. Place all your music in a shared directory or folder labeled Music.

- **Pictures**—The same rules that apply to music files are good to apply to picture files. Most pictures tend to end up in the My Pictures folder in the My Documents folder. It is good to move those to a directory called Pictures on another drive.

Now, think of the simple user interface of a media extender. It looks for videos, music, and pictures. If you put all your files together in the same way that a media extender organizes them, it will be easy to tell the media extender and its media server application where to look for media files.

Is it a good practice to put all those files in one folder or in one place? Yes. As long as you have good backup practices or keep another drive where you can copy all those files on a regular basis, it is a good practice.

> **TIP**
> It's okay to put shortcuts from various file locations into three main folders (video, music, and pictures), but be sure that all those files are from your main server PC. If the files are from other PCs on your network, those computers need to be on and running to access those files.

Because you are using Windows XP, you can also use some of the great techniques it offers, such as creating a folder and then placing shortcuts in that folder to other file locations and placing as many subfolders within it as you wish. You can let your video, music, and picture folders simply contain shortcuts to wherever your media files are located on the network. The goal is to have one main folder where all media files can be accessed by a media extender.

Figure 12.4 shows a classic method of putting all your media files, including shortcuts, into a main folder called Media Files and then three folders for video, music, and picture files. With this method, you can also turn sharing and access privileges on or off to just three main folders rather than dozens of separate folders.

Using shortcuts, you can also create different folders within any of the primary media folders. One folder can have sharing privileges set to allow modifying and deleting, and another folder can be set to allow only viewing. As the system administrator, you have a great deal of control over the management of files by users on a network when you put the power of file sharing and users together in managing the media folders.

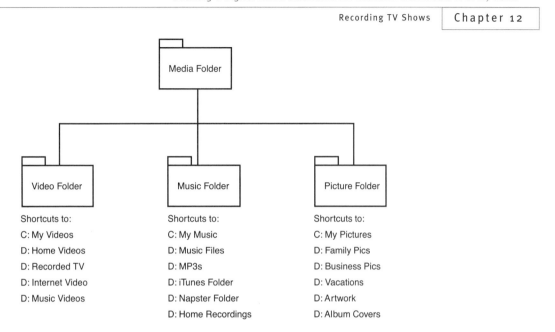

FIGURE 12.4

Organize your media files in one main media file folder and then three subfolders for video, music, and pictures.

You will develop your own file and serving preferences as you begin to work with your home entertainment network, but the file structure in Figure 12.4 is a good way to start. It can be as simple as creating the folders and placing shortcuts in them. Try it first, and see whether that works well for your way of managing media files.

Recording TV Shows

If you installed a TV tuner card in your main server PC, you can record TV shows. The ability to record TV shows and then serve them to other media extenders and PCs in your home is an exciting part of a home entertainment network.

Depending on the TV tuner card your computer has, you can choose where your TV recordings are stored. If at all possible, save your recorded TV programs as MPEG-1 or MPEG-2 files. MPEG video files are compressed video files that work best with media extenders and are supported by almost all media playing software, such as Windows Media Player, and also by the media players used by media extender devices.

Recording your TV shows as MPEG files makes it possible to view them anywhere on your home entertainment network. Since TV shows are actually quote low in their resolution, storing them as MPEG-1 files offers a good blend of capturing the original TV display quality while keeping the file size small. This allows you to save lots of MPEG-1 files on your hard drive. MPEG-2 files allow you to save TV shows at the same quality as a DVD but the increase in quality also means the file size is larger. Since most TV broadcasts are not equal to the quality of a DVD, it makes good sense to use MPEG-1 for TV recordings.

Now it's time for a great question: If you use a media extender connected to a TV anywhere in your home, why watch a TV program from the PC server? Here are some great answers:

- **Time shifting**—Time shifting is the ability to watch a TV show when you choose, not just when it is playing. The benefit of watching a recording of a TV show is that you can watch it anytime you want.

- **Stop, pause, or replay**—With a recording, you can pause the show, stop it, and come back later or replay favorite scenes.

- **Skip commercials**—Okay, you're not supposed to do this, but it is really easy using the fast-forward button on the remote control to skip past commercials. If you see a commercial with an 800 number or product information that you want to jot down, stop and get that information.

- **Use one main receiver**—If one TV uses a digital cable box or satellite cable box but other TVs in your home don't, you can record the program and watch it on a TV set that doesn't have a set top box attached. Because there is usually an extra monthly charge to use additional set top boxes, this tip makes good sense.

- **Control who watches what**—If you want to control what programs your kids watch, you can record shows for them and only allow viewing of programs from your PC server. You don't even need to connect cable or satellite to their TV sets. Think about the control that offers!

All of these list items are great reasons to record TV shows and serve them to media extenders and other PCs in your home entertainment network.

Scheduling TV Recordings

Each TV tuner has its own unique TV recording software, and most come with an electronic program guide (EPG) for scheduling recordings. Figure 12.5 shows the excellent EPG that comes with Windows XP Media Center Edition PCs. You can set up recordings once, weekly, or everyday or use a number of different ways based on the show name, type of show, actor, or character.

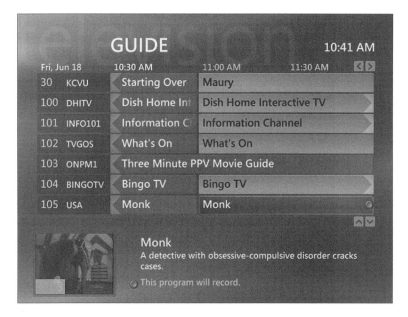

FIGURE 12.5

Using the EPG that comes with your TV tuner software, you can schedule recordings of TV shows.

Although the software for scheduling and recording TV shows varies depending on the manufacturer of your TV tuner card, the process of recording and saving a TV show is pretty consistent between them. It follows this process:

1. Before recording any TV shows, use the file settings or preferences menu of the TV viewer and recording software (often called PVR or personal video recording software) to set the file format that you want to save the recording as. You should choose a common file format that is supported by your media extenders (such as MPEG-2). You should also test that the selected file format plays well on your media extender before recording too many shows.

2. Also before recording any TV shows, from the same file settings or preferences menu, choose the location where you want to save your files. If you created a media folder, select to store recorded TV shows in a TV Shows folder inside the Video folder. If you have options for file naming conventions (such as using the name of the show from the EPG), select the preferences that allow you to best identify the recorded TV show.

3. Schedule recordings of TV shows using an EPG if one is provided with your TV recording software. To schedule a recording, you generally just click on the show

and select to record one time or record the series. Good EPG recording programs allow you to create a series recording of only new shows, all shows, any occurrence, or a one-time recording. It might also offer the option of automatically deleting older episodes after a specified number of episodes are recorded. This setup allows a daily show to start "recording over" itself after 5 episodes, for example.

4. Confirm your scheduled recordings by looking at the menu that lists the shows you selected to be recorded. This step helps you confirm that the shows you want to record are on the list and even remove some if hard disk space is getting tight.

5. You can schedule shows by time, date, and channel if your TV recording does not come with its own EPG. Using any popular web-based TV listings, you can find the dates, times, and channel numbers for shows you want to record.

6. Check the reception of TV channels on your TV tuner card to make sure that all connections were properly made. If you are using remote devices to change channels on a set-top box, change channels manually to be sure that the device is attached and working properly.

The most important action you can take regarding TV show recording concerns its file format. If your shows won't play on media extenders or other PCs, then they will be little use in your home entertainment network.

Recording More Than One Show at One Time

> **TIP**
>
> Do you need to record two different TV shows at one time? Use the TV tuner cards in two separate PCs to record the shows, or find out whether your brand of TV tuner card recording software supports the use of two TV tuner cards at one time, which allows you to record two shows at once on the same PC.

There is one limitation on most PCs that use a single TV tuner card. TV tuner cards can tune to only one TV show at a time. That means you can't record two different shows that are on at the same time. This situation is where having more than one PC with a TV tuner card helps. Each can be recording a different show at the same time, and you can then save the recording to your main video file location.

The latest version of Windows XP Media Center Edition (2005) allows for the use of two TV tuner cards, so it is possible to record two different shows at the same time—as long as you have two separate TV tuner cards in your PC and each is attached to a separate TV source, such as a cable box and a satellite box.

Watching and Recording Shows at the Same Time

One of the things that you can do is record one show while you are watching a show that was recorded at an earlier time. You can even start watching the show that is currently recording using a bit of time-shifting, where you wait about 15 minutes to begin watching the show that is being recorded so that you can skip past commercials.

In a home entertainment network, you might face a situation where you are recording a show and two or three media extenders are watching recorded TV show files. If you have a fast hard drive (7200 rpm or faster), this should not be a problem. Hard drives use buffers and manage data requests to allow viewing multiple videos at one time— but every system has its limits.

If you have a home entertainment network with two or more media extenders, the best thing to do is put it to the test. Record a few TV shows, and then while one show is recording, play recorded shows on the media extenders in other rooms to see whether they all keep up and play without pauses or glitches. If you are using a wired network, it should work well. If you are using a wireless network, that might not always be the case.

At a minimum, you can watch a show while one is recording and watch at least two shows if no show is recording.

Making the Move to Nonlinear TV

Using your TV tuner card and watching shows after they are recorded allows you to make the move to nonlinear TV viewing. As detailed earlier, you watch TV when you want, not just when it's on, so you don't have to run home to watch a show. You can also pause your viewing to take a phone call or get a snack.

Nonlinear viewing is also a great way to think of TV in the same way you think of music or digital pictures. They are files that you can watch, share, and erase when you choose. You can even offload your favorite TV shows to DVDs if you have a DVD burner, so you can build DVD libraries of TV shows.

When you really embrace nonlinear TV and use recordings, it also helps you preview shows that you might or might not want your family to watch. If you have children, it's a great way to screen TV programming and keep tabs on what they watch.

Children also love to watch shows over and over. If you have a child, you probably have seen VHS tapes of Barney or Disney movies wear out because they get a lot of repeat play. Digital TV files are there when they want to watch them, and they don't wear out!

TV in a home entertainment network is most often viewed as recordings, not live broad-casts. You can always watch the news, weather, or sporting events in real time. You still have live TV, but you have the luxury of time-shifting, recording your favorite TV shows, and watching them any time and anywhere in your home that you have a media extender.

Deciding Who Can View Files

With good file management and the strategies listed in this chapter, you can easily manage who views media files in your home.

As mentioned earlier, it is possible to hook up a TV just to a media extender, but not an antenna or satellite or cable box. When it comes to managing what kids watch, this setup provides a whole new level of control.

Most homes have open access, where anyone can get to all media on the PC server. If you have children, you can control access in a number of ways, and this section will examine them.

Limiting File Access on Media Extenders

One of the simplest ways to restrict file access comes from using a media extender. Because a media extender relies on a media server application running on the server PC for the file list it can view, you can simply limit the files or folders a particular media extender can play.

This strategy applies to pictures, music, and videos. For example, suppose you want to restrict what content you want a child's room to play. By not connecting a live TV source to the TV in that room and by relying only on the media extender for content from the server PC, you can create a media list of the music and TV shows that you allow.

Figure 12.6 shows a typical media server file list. Simply create a list of permitted music, recorded TV shows, pictures, or video and your TV in the kids' room will have only the content that you want them to access.

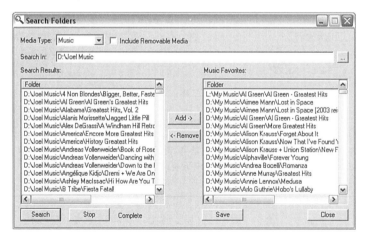

FIGURE 12.6

By choosing the media you want kids to access, you can use media extenders to limit what music, video, and pictures they access.

Depending on your brand of media extender, you might be able to create multiple "media servers" that allow custom viewing lists. If you have a media extender that requires multiple media extenders of the same brand to use a common media server, you can still establish parental controls.

Working with User Settings from Windows XP

If you are only using PCs in a home entertainment network to access files, you can use different settings for each user. That allows you to select certain folders each user can access, which can be a great way to set user access to media content if you only use PCs to view media in your home.

Restricting access to media files when using media extenders connected to a home entertainment network requires a different strategy if you wish to restrict file access. Most media extenders are not connected to the user settings, and when the media server application is running, it is available to the media extenders on the home network.

One of the ways you can use user settings to control access is to make sure that only the system administrator has access to the media server applications for the media extenders. This setup prevents children, for example, from going to the main PC and adding media content to their media extender.

Because most newer media extenders also allow some form of connection to Internet sites such as radio stations, you can choose which Internet sites the media server application can reach. It is important that only the system administrator make changes to the media server application.

Many TV tuner cards come with player software that does have parental controls to limit viewing based on the rating system for TV shows. This software works great when you are viewing the shows from the PC running that particular playback program but does not work when the file is saved and viewed as an MPEG file on other computers or media extenders.

You can manage access to users in a limited way, but because the whole area of home entertainment networks is relatively new in practice, some of the controls you might want are yet to come. Be sure to upgrade your software and the firmware on your media center devices as new controls become available.

Summary

With the goal of a home entertainment network being to view videos and pictures and to listen to music, start organizing your media files into folders for video, music, and pictures.

Media extenders use a simple, TV-centric user interface that most often uses the same categories of video, music, and pictures. The better you organize the files, the better the TV experience of navigating to media files will be.

You should also begin the practice of recording TV rather than viewing it live. You then can take advantage of viewing recorded programs anywhere in the home entertainment network time-shifting programs, and moving to nonlinear TV viewing.

Finally, you can effect some forms of viewer restrictions by making access to TV or music available only through the home entertainment network, rather than through cable or satellite TV sources or traditional stereos.

Adding Media Content from the Internet

Your home entertainment network has been built to distribute video, recorded TV shows, music, and picture files to PCs and TV and stereos connected to media extenders throughout your home. Because your network also has full-time access to the Internet, you can add an amazing quantity of media content from there including movie rentals and music you can purchase.

It's really easy to access the Internet from a PC, but media extenders are a different story. They do allow access to Internet content, but not in the traditional way of accessing it from a web browser.

This chapter looks at how to find, download, buy, and share content from the Internet using your home entertainment network. It even shows you how to put as much of it as you can on your media extender devices connected to TVs.

Including Internet Access in Your Entertainment Mix

As good as the Internet is for data and finding information, it very quickly has become the best place for getting media. At the time of writing this book, Apple's online iTune's music store has become the largest single seller of music in the world—bigger than any retail chain. The way we get media—all media including TV shows—is starting to change entirely because of high-speed access to the Internet.

The Internet is exceptionally well-suited for

- Listening to and purchasing music
- Listening to radio shows from all over the world
- Viewing movie trailers
- Finding, buying, and sharing pictures
- Sharing your own photos with friends and family

- Renting full-length movies to view on your home entertainment network

- Viewing news segments from leading newscasts

- Watching broadcasts of sporting events you can't see from your home location, including game highlights

Much of the previous might be "old news" to you as someone who actively uses their PC for media. It's a new situation to get Internet content that works with TVs. The goal is to get all of the preceding off a web browser and onto TVs around your home connected to media extenders.

PC Content Displayed on TVs

One thing you learn very quickly when you connect a TV to a Windows XP PC and use it to view the standard Windows XP desktop (or any programs running on it) is that it is almost not viewable. PC monitors are designed to display data with a non-interlaced mode at a minimum of 640×480 pixels. The non-interlaced part means that each second you are seeing all the lines of resolution, making the image very clear and sharp.

TVs are nowhere near the minimum level of resolution of a computer monitor. They display video at 320×240 pixels of resolution, and in an interlaced mode. This means that it takes two separate passes of display (at a 30th of a second each) to create a full image on the TV screen. The two sets of lines from each pass (odd and even scan line fields) allows you to perceive them as one image because they appear so quickly. It's a low resolution display system designed over a half a century ago and does not display the detailed, text-heavy screens used in computing.

As a result, if you attempted to display a web browser on a TV connected to the TV-out port of a PC or a media extender, you would have a very hard time seeing any of the text. Also, there would be scrollbars since most websites are now designed for viewing on displays showing at least 800×600 pixels.

The video files, such as recorded TV programs that you have saved, are recorded at 320×240 pixel resolution and play back exactly the way they should—on a TV.

Media extenders—as shown in Chapters 11, "Sharing Files and Adding Users," and 12, "Creating a Media Server Strategy"—have their own unique TV-specific user interfaces and use the right colors, fonts, and graphics for a TV display. When they play videos or display photos, because the videos are usually at TV-specific resolution and photos can be sized to fit the screen, they look great. Menus for music are created for the TV environment, and the overall experience is excellent on TVs.

When using a PC connected to a TV, or a media extender connected to a TV, rather than going to websites, you really will want to play media content from the websites, not the website itself.

Media extenders and TV-centric PCs such as Media Center Edition PCs use custom links to websites that are designed specifically to be viewed on a TV. Since the arrival of

WebTV (now known as MSN TV Service), a number of websites have created TV-specific versions for Internet-on-TV devices. The problem is that such sites are not generally available directly from a web browser—you need the specific device such as an MSN TV box for accessing the TV-centric websites.

This tradition continues with media extenders (some of which offer access to Internet content that is formatted specifically for TV display) and Windows XP Media Center Edition PCs. One of the benefits of using a Windows XP Media Center Edition PC is the nice mix of web content available from its Online Spotlight feature. All the content from the Internet featured in Online Spotlight is perfect for viewing on TVs—but only if you have a Windows XP Media Center Edition PC or a Media Center extender connected to one in the home entertainment network.

For your home entertainment network, it is best to continue to use a standard PC and PC monitor to visit websites and pull content from them for viewing on your media extenders and PC-driven TVs.

Using MSN TV to Access Internet Sites

Media extenders deal with using content from the Internet in a creative way. They pull media off the Internet (such as Internet Radio) and use their own interfaces to display the information.

This works very well, and as time goes on, you will see the arrival of media extenders that do the same for videos from the Internet.

Right now, if you really want to use your TV to access Internet content, you can purchase an MSN TV box. It is the next generation of the old WebTV box that connects to the Internet and uses only websites that have been formatted for WebTV or MSN TV. Because your home has at least one PC, and perhaps more, this seems like an unnecessary device, but it is available if pure Internet-on-TV is what you need in a certain location.

TIP

You can get a "viewable" screen with a TV connected to your PC displaying the standard Windows XP desktop. After connecting your TV to the TV-out connector of your video card, right-click anywhere on the desktop, and from the pop-up menu, click on Properties. From the Display Properties menu, change the screen resolution to its lowest setting— which most likely will be 640×480. If your video card installed TV settings, you might also have a setting for 320×240. Use the lowest resolution setting that is available to you. Next, click on the Appearance tab, and from the bottom of the menu, choose Large Fonts. The combination of a low screen resolution and using larger fonts will make it possible to display and read type on the TV. If your video card comes with custom settings for TVs, be sure to use any adjustments those settings might offer. Finally, be sure to adjust the brightness and contrast of your TV—it helps. If you really want to use your TV as your computer display, you will need to purchase a dedicated PC-to-TV device such as a video scaler that will produce a standard TV signal of the Windows desktop and Windows applications on most any TV.

Content from the Internet Using Media Extenders

Because you will most likely have high-speed Internet access in your home and you will have your PCs networked, you will be able to access the Internet wherever you want. As previously described, it might not be good to attempt to display websites on TV screens connected to PCs, but if you have computer monitors in place (such as using only a computer monitor to watch media, or both a computer monitor and a TV are connected to a single PC), you will be able to use the Internet whenever you want.

One of the things that many media extenders offer (which is actually a live connection to the Internet) is Internet radio. This allows you to play steaming audio from Internet radio stations from virtually any place in your home where you use a media extender.

INTERNET RADIO

One of the best sources of media content for your home entertainment network is Internet radio. Not to be confused with standard broadcast radio, Internet radio is distributed over the Internet using streaming audio that can be played using standard media players such as Windows Media Player 10. Some Internet radio services require a special player, but most work with Windows Media Player.

Although there are often subscription fees for commercial-free Internet radio services, many are free of charge. The free stations might have commercials, but not as many as off-the-air radio broadcasts.

The biggest benefit of Internet radio is selection. There are hundreds of stations and just about as many music, talk, news, and sports radio formats. Some broadcast radio stations have even begun offering their shows on Internet radio too. Imagine listening to a college football game broadcast—even if you live hundreds of miles from the station broadcasting the game. With Internet radio, you can listen to a wider range of radio than your local market could ever broadcast.

If you are using a media extender that includes Internet radio, it will usually offer you a free trial subscription to an Internet radio service. If you are using a PC and a Web browser, a good way to find Internet radio stations is to visit an Internet radio portal such as www.live365.com or www.shoutcast.com. Portals bring together a large selection of stations, genres, and formats—most commercial free and at no charge.

If you are a subscriber to AOL, be sure to use AOL Radio. The same is true if you are a subscriber to Napster, MSN, or a user of iTunes or Launch.com. They all have a large selection of Internet radio content you can tap in to.

Figure 13.1 shows an Internet radio station being played on a Windows XP Media Center Edition PC media extender. What is nice about this is that the user interface of this media extender is very friendly and displays all critical information about the station and the music or talk show playing. This example shows how media extenders do a great job of bringing media content from the Internet to your TV set.

FIGURE 13.1

Internet radio is a full TV-like experience when using a Media Center Extender, which only works with Media Center Edition PCs.

If you don't have a Windows XP Media Center Edition PC and are using Windows XP and another brand of media extender, you can still get great access to Internet radio. Figure 13.2 shows the radio menu from the Media MVP media extender, and although the user interface is a bit bare bones, it quickly tunes to Internet radio stations and allows you to easily add any Internet radio station to a list of favorites using a web browser on your PC, and then add them to a My Radio folder in your My Documents folder.

For now, most media extenders have limited access to Internet content except for Internet radio. Media Center Edition PCs using Media Center extenders do have the capability to play Internet content from the Media Center Online Spotlight area as shown in Figure 13.3. It brings news, sports, weather, movie rentals, and music sites to the Media Center extender—all formatted to work perfectly on a TV.

Although Media Center Edition PCs and the extenders for them offer the best media-extender and TV-centric online experience, other media extenders are making strides—even if it is limited to radio at this time. As you will learn in the rest of this chapter, much of the content you will be able to view on a media extender is content that is downloaded from the Internet and stored as files that can be viewed or played on a media extender or TV connected to a TV.

STRATEGY

If you are using media extenders, they will allow you to tune in to Internet radio stations, which is a real-time experience because you can't record radio the same as you would TV shows. Use your PC to access the Internet to download video, pictures, and music and use your media extender to access that content once it has been stored on the server PC.

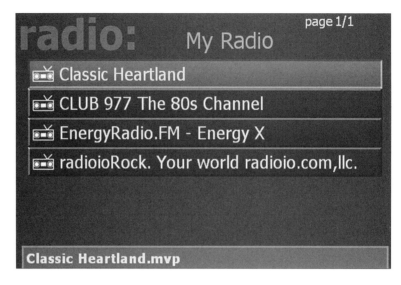

FIGURE 13.2

Internet radio station playing through a Media MVP media extender displayed on a TV screen.

FIGURE 13.3

Media Center PCs using Media Center extenders have a great assortment of TV-formatted media that can be played on TVs through the extender.

Finding Great Internet Media Content

Beyond the Internet radio stations that can be reached using most media extenders, the Internet is a great source of media content that is perfect for playing on a home entertainment network.

Because most media content from the Internet is actually pretty low-bandwidth, it is extremely well suited for access by the 100Mbps speed of a wired network connection and the 54Mbps speed of a wireless connection using a 54g (802.11g) wireless router.

Since media extenders seem to be limited to accessing Internet radio for the near future, most of your use of media from the Internet will be limited to

- **Playing Internet media** on PCs that are connected to your networked PCs that can use a regular web browser.

- **Storing media** that is downloaded from the Internet on a regular PC and then playing it as files on media extenders.

That's not too bad of a compromise. You will have at least one PC in your home entertainment network, and you can use it as your search engine for Internet media.

In some instances, you will be able to use a network PC for viewing and playing steaming media. When you can purchase or download a file, you can make those files available to all of your devices—PCs and media extenders.

So, with a full understanding that there is a whole world of wonderful videos, music, and pictures just waiting for you to access them, and understanding that not all of them can be saved to play at a future time on your home entertainment network, and some can be saved or purchased so that they can be played at a future time, let's look at some of the best places to find media.

> **WARNING**
> One of the caveats is that much of the music and video that you can view or play on the Internet is "Streaming Media" and cannot be saved as a file. Much of that content may be purchased, and then you can view it on your other devices, but be aware that not all Internet media can be saved as files on your server PC.

The following sites show Media Extender/TV-centric versions when available, or web versions when they are great places for downloads and purchasing media.

Finding Music

Music comes in three main categories:

1. Music you can **listen** to as radio stations.

2. Music you can **download** for free or preview.

3. Music you can **purchase**.

Depending on your musical interests, and budget, the preceding three categories actually are an incredible combination. One of the problems with buying music, especially

CDs, is that you couldn't really be sure if you liked all the songs on the CD, or even that the one you might have heard on the radio was the song on the CD.

Listen to Radio First

With the three preceding methods, you can listen to Internet radio, which, unlike most broadcast radio stations nowadays, actually displays the name of the track and the artist plus the name of the album it's from. Most radio stations even contain a link to go and buy the CD. (Hey, who needs to buy CDs anymore?)

That helps identify music, and also because Internet radio offers an almost unlimited selection of genres and music formats, you will be able to hear music you wouldn't normally hear on broadcast radio.

Figure 13.4 shows a small example of the many radio stations and formats found on an Internet radio portal called SHOUTcast. All the stations are easily added to your My Radio folder for use on media extenders, and the selection is well suited to most all musical tastes.

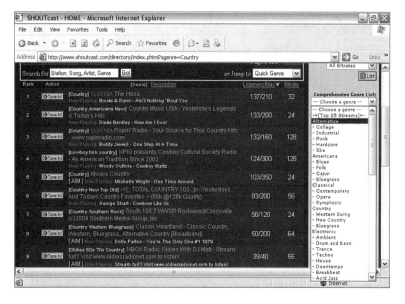

FIGURE 13.4

SHOUTcast.com is just one of many Internet radio portals that connects you to an amazing number of Internet radio stations.

You can use Google or Yahoo! to search on Internet Radio Portals. The portals are best because they list a lot of radio stations. You can also use Microsoft Windows Media Player, which allows you to access Napster Radio or MSN Radio but beware: They are staring to charge for commercial free access! One of the best radio sources is iTunes from Apple, which is a media player, online store, and a great Internet radio source. Be sure to check it out since it's becoming the standard for all other online music sites.

With some time on the radio, or even from your own knowledge of music and artists you like, the next step is to go to online music stores to preview music and to music sites where you can download music free.

Preview Music Next

Online music stores are there to sell you music, but they are also great places to preview music. Most every album featured in an online music store such as Napster or iTunes offers a 30-second preview of the songs you are interested in. Many even offer free downloads of promotional music. Before you purchase any music, preview it to make sure that it's what you are looking for.

In addition to online music stores where you can purchase and preview music, a number of websites still offer free music downloads. The days of illegal "sharing" of music files, such as the early days of Napster, are quickly fading for legal reasons, but a number of sites still feature artists who want you to download their music, legally, so that you grow to like them and eventually purchase their music.

Figure 13.5 shows a surprise spot for some really good free and legal MP3 downloads: Amazon.com. It has an area (not well promoted) that has a good selection of MP3s from known, as well as not so well-known, artists. It's actually easy to find. Go to Amazon, choose the music tab, and on the top bar of the music screen will be a button for free downloads.

FIGURE 13.5

Free, legal MP3 downloads are still available, even from Amazon.com.

As with all Internet content, use search engines to find free Music or free MP3s. But, beware: Most of the search results will bring you to sites that are music stores—not really free MP3 sites. Using a bit of caution and persistence, you will be rewarded with some great music that you can download free as MP3 files that you can play across your home entertainment network.

Buy Music Last

After you have listened to Internet radio, found free music downloads, previewed tracks at online music stores, and you know what you want and are ready to purchase it, pull out your credit card and discover the new age of music buying.

More than any other online music store, Apple's iTunes Music Store (www.itunes.com) has changed music buying. By offering most of the popular music on the market today for online purchase, and allowing you to buy any track for a very reasonable 99¢ or the whole CD for $9.99, it's THE way to purchase music.

With a great selection, a great media player, long music previews, and a great price, it's hard to imagine going out and paying between $11 and $19 for a CD any longer.

Figure 13.6 shows a menu of music that can be purchased song by song or by the entire album on iTunes. You can go there, buy songs, and you can play them on up to 10 computers in your home. The lack of harsh restrictions on playing them in a home entertainment network (and also moving them to portable devices such as iPods and burning CDs for your car or portable CD player) have changed the industry in a way greater than even the original Napster.

So, why is an Apple product being featured in an all-Windows PC book? Simple. Apple has versions of iTunes (which is an application that resides as a program on your PC) for Windows. It's totally compatible with Windows. As the largest online store (at least right now), it also features the largest number of artists to choose from.

Other equally good deals are now available from online stores such as Napster, Launch, MSN Music, RealRhapsody, and MusicNow, so be sure to find a service that you like best—and, most importantly, has the artists you like. Each online music store has a limit on how many artists work with their service. That's why it's good to shop the music stores before you begin using them.

Finally, you can always trudge out to Wal-Mart and buy a CD for $13.99 and bring it home and rip it to your PC server for all your devices to access. (But hey, even Wal-Mart has an online music store selling tracks for only 88¢ per song!) Maybe give the online stores a try before your next CD purchase!

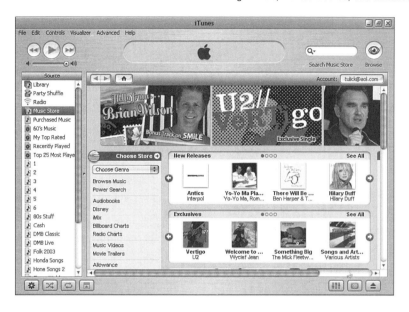

Figure 13.6

Apple's iTunes Store has changed the way the world buys music, and is very "home entertainment friendly" regarding how many different devices can play a purchased track.

Finding Videos, Rental Movies, and Enhanced TV

The success of music online, and the arrival of high-speed Internet access, has made it possible for you to watch all kinds of video content from the Internet and even rent movies to watch just as if you went to a video store and rented a DVD.

There is a lot of video content on the Internet, and most of it is in the form of streaming video that cannot be saved as a file on your PC.

How do you know if a video file can be saved as a file on a PC? It's an easy process: Start playing a video from virtually any website that has videos that you can watch and begin playing the video. Whenever possible, choose the Windows Media Player format for playing the video. As shown in Figure 13.7, go to the File menu while the video is playing and look to see if the Save As menu item is highlighted. If it is dimmed out, it simply means that it's a streaming video that you cannot save as a file on your PC for sharing with your home entertainment network.

In addition to being able to possibly save a file you are viewing, a large number of websites offer the ability to download video files. Sometimes they are free, and others charge for downloads.

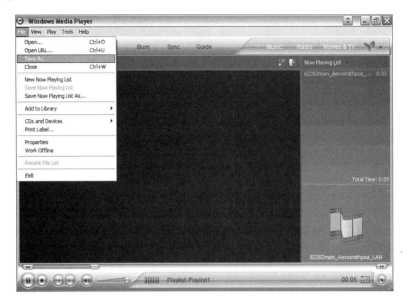

FIGURE 13.7

While watching a video from the Internet, you might be able to save it as a file on your PC. Go to the File menu in Windows Media Player and if the Save As menu item is highlighted, you can save the file.

Because video clips and movies are generally copy-protected content, more sites are using streaming video formats so that their clips can be viewed—but not saved.

A growing number of movie rental websites have begun to offer full-length download-able versions for first run and recent movies (and also libraries of old movies) as rentals.

For a fee (generally around $4.00), you can rent a movie online, download it your server PC, and watch it in your home for a limited period of time, usually 24 hours. This works well if you have broadband access, and even with high-speed Internet, it does take quite a while to download—often as long as the movie is in length.

The movie rental site downloads a small application to your PC that manages the ability for you to view the movie, and for how long. When the rental period is up, the movie is no longer playable. These services get better and better, and they are from companies backed by major movie studios. You can download a rental movie, watch it as often as you want in your home, and never have to leave the house to go to a video store.

Figure 13.8 shows the Movielink website, where you can rent movies online. You set up an account, download the application, and start the download. Even though the download does take a while, you can start watching the movie a few minutes into the download.

Some good online movie sites to visit include Movielink, CinemaNow, and AtomFilms. This is a new category of online service, and it is growing, so also do a regular search for "online movie rentals."

FIGURE 13.8

Online movie rental sites, such as Movielink.com, allow you to download movies to view on your home entertainment network for a standard rental fee.

With movie rental sites, a large number of websites that include video clips that can be saved, and the growth of broadband Internet service, the future for downloading videos for your home entertainment network makes the Internet a great source for video content.

INTERACTIVE TV IS AVAILABLE

Another growing area of interest for TV fans is the development of TV shows that allow you to interact with the shows using your PC and watch them on a TV connected to your PC. Called interactive TV, it's one of the things you can really have fun with using your home entertainment network.

For example, you can watch a live TV show and view it on your TV, and if you have the computer in the same room, play along or find additional details from the companion website for the show.

Finally, most all TV shows have their own websites that allow you to find show schedules, view clips and trailers, and bring the TV and PC experience together like never before.

Adding News, Sports, and Weather to the Mix

Some of the most mature areas of content on the Internet are news, sports, and weather. A quick visit to CNN.com, MSN.com, or ABC.com will reveal a wide mix of text, graphics, radio, and video versions of these important topic areas.

If you have a Media Center Edition PC running Windows XP Media Center, it's online spotlight area will allow you to access TV-centric versions of some of the best news, sports, and weather sites available. Unfortunately, these sites are only available in their "TV" form to users of MSN TV Internet devices and Media Center PC users.

For the most part, you should think of adding news, sports, and weather in two very effective ways:

- **Tune to Internet Radio:** Make presets for Internet radio stations that feature news, weather, or sporting events. A really popular feature of Internet radio is the broadcast of college games that are usually only available in the location of the games. They are often available on Internet radio. Save good news and sports radio stations as favorites, and use the Radio feature of your media extenders to access those stations.

- **Record Shows:** An easy method for having information programming is to schedule regular, daily recordings of your favorite news shows so that you can watch them when you choose. You might be off to work too early to catch all of the *Today* show, so record it and watch it later when you get home. Recording TV is one of the best ways to capture news, sporting events, or even weather forecasts for playing throughout the home entertainment network.

Sharing Pictures from the Internet

One of the easiest things you can share on every device (except audio-only media extenders) is pictures.

If you store your pictures using any of the popular online photo services with friends and family, it's a great place to store and share pictures. Once you use a popular online photo service such as "You've Got Pictures!" from AOL or even online photo processing services from retailers, such as grocery or drug stores, you have access to a huge collection of photos.

To view all of those photos on your home entertainment network, be sure to go to the online photo albums, select the ones you want to have on your home entertainment network, and download them into the Pictures directory that you created.

For now, access to pictures from the Internet to media extenders is just starting to happen. Kodak has developed a picture service designed for use on Media Center PCs using Media Center through the Online Spotlight area, and it's a good preview of what's to come with online picture sharing—putting pictures on TVs for all the family to see.

Downloading pictures from Internet-based photo albums might be an extra step, but it does allow you to turn any room in your home with a PC or TV attached to a media extender into a multimedia photo album.

Using Email on Your Home Entertainment Network

Email is one of the original "hot ideas" for Web TV and other TV-based services that have come and gone over the years. It really boiled down to the fact that the TV is not the best place to view text documents, it's hard to type in a living room setting, and it's a very public display of your emails.

Although most media extenders do not offer any sort of email function, some instant messaging (IM) applications are starting to appear. As with so many new features in a home entertainment network, Microsoft is offering the use of MS Messenger on Media Center Edition PCs. You can literally IM people in your home, or over the Internet, with this feature. Instant messaging allows quick and easy conversations between users of PCs through the Internet, and although a TV is a great place for IM sessions, this feature might not be as easy to use on a remote control number keypad (such as with cell phones) in which letters are entered using repeated pressing of a number key.

Although you might not have a computer in every room in your home, your home entertainment network has at least one PC, probably more, and you can continue to use all the Web browsing and email clients that you normally would with any PC.

Email and even Web browsing removes a bit of the "entertainment" aspect from your home entertainment network, but it's highly likely it will be incorporated in the not-too-distant future.

Thinking About Web Access

As discussed throughout this chapter, websites have developed so strongly to be PC-centric in their design and function that they are not really suited for the TV-centric world you are creating with your home entertainment network.

Take a look at Figure 13.9. It's Launch.com, a fantastic music site that has music videos for just about every popular artist on the market. It's one of the best examples of Internet video ever. It's video-on-demand. You select an artist, listen to his music, see a full-length music video, and even buy his music from the site. But, you can't save the videos to your PC—they are streaming videos that can't be saved, and right now the site is pure Web—not a site that can work on a media extender.

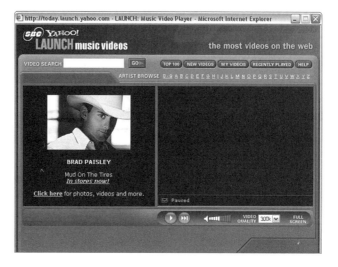

FIGURE 13.9

Watching a full-length music video on Launch.com, you see that the video is great quality that can fill any screen with a high-speed Internet connection.

Launch is a site you can use for PCs connected on your home entertainment network. The full-screen video it's capable of can be viewed on a TV connected directly to that PC. Try it: It's a great experience, and you'll probably never watch the standard TV network versions of MTV or CMT again!

Right now, some amazing media content from the Internet is just that—Internet content that requires a PC and a web browser to view it properly. Although you might have media extenders, don't forget that the PC is also a great entertainment device. You just might have to sit a bit closer or use it to control the TV connected to it.

Summary

There is a great deal of entertainment content on the Internet. Music, movies, videos, Internet radio, and picture sharing are all media files that you should put to use in your home entertainment network.

Content from the Internet comes in two main forms: content you play on your PCs or media extenders and cannot be stored on your server PCs, or content that you can save as files on your server PCs and play when desired.

Not all entertainment content from the Internet is formatted for viewing on TVs, and some is best viewed from PCs on the home entertainment network. By searching for Internet radio stations or movie rental sites that allow you to rent downloaded movies and finding videos, you will be able to add new types of content that have never been available for TV viewing before to TVs in your home connected to media extenders.

Working with Portable Entertainment Devices

Your home entertainment network doesn't need to be limited to the "home" any longer. Portable entertainment devices are extremely popular and allow you to take the entertainment content that you've put together for your home entertainment network with you wherever you go.

Examples of portable entertainment devices include

- MP3 players that use non-moving memory chips to store music files

- iPods, Zen, Rio, and other hard-drive equipped portable music devices

- Portable media players that allow you to play music, video, TV shows, and picture files

- Pocket PCs, PDAs, and Palm Pilots

- Camcorders and digital cameras that record movies

All of the preceding devices can, at a minimum, obtain their media content from your server PC, but they can also provide content for it. A digital camera that can record a 30-second MPEG movie is a source of entertainment content.

This chapter takes a look at how to connect these devices to your home entertainment network and when possible, make it an active part of the network to access content in your home or even provide content to it.

Working with Portable Audio Devices on the Network

Most current audio devices are not networked devices. They are designed to simply connect (usually through a USB port) to a single PC for the purpose of transferring audio files. That's okay. Portable audio devices allow you to take the music files you have assembled on your server PC on the road.

Working with MP3 Players and Hard Drive–Based Players

If you have an MP3 player (with internal memory, a memory card, or an internal hard drive), you know that it will have come with some form of media player program that will allow you to move MP3 files to the device and often "check in or check out" the files if you are following the legal procedures of licensing music for use on portable devices.

The problem with many portable devices such as MP3 players is that each comes with its own media player software, and each time you install a media player, it wants to become your "default" media player for all media played on your PC. This is not what you want to have happen.

Think of it this way: You create a perfect home entertainment network, and you're using Windows Media Player 10 or iTunes as your primary media player; then you purchase a little MP3 player and install the required software. The next time you click on a music file, up pops some arcane media player designed for that device, and not the media player you normally use.

So, there are some simple steps you can take to avoid this:

1. When you are purchasing an MP3 player, make sure that it can work directly with Windows Media Player. If you are not sure, visit the Windows Media Player website (www.microsoft.com/windows/windowsmedia) and click on the list of supported portable media players to see if the MP3 player you are interested in is supported and can work directly with Windows Media Player.

2. Next, avoid installing the media player software that comes with the MP3 player entirely. If you purchased an MP3 player that works directly with Windows Media Player 10, you will be able to attach your MP3 player to your PC with a USB cable and use Windows Media Player 10 for moving files in and out of the device.

Figure 14.1 shows the portable device screen from Windows Media Player 10. You reach this screen by launching Windows Media Player 10, going to the Tools menu, and choosing Options. You will see a control panel with several Tabs, one of them being Devices. Click on the Devices tab, and you will see the menu shown in Figure 14.1.

From the Devices menu, click on the Add button, and you will be sent to a Microsoft web page that has a large listing of most of the portable music and portable media players on the market, and will allow you to add devices that can be used to transfer music files to and from your MP3 player using Windows Media Player.

The Microsoft website showing devices that can work this way is shown in Figure 14.2.

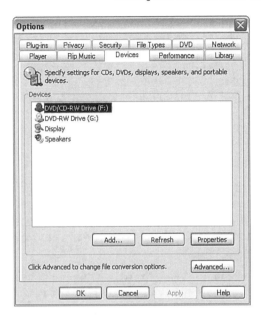

FIGURE 14.1

The portable Devices tab from the Options menu in Windows Media Player 10.

FIGURE 14.2

If your portable music player is listed, select it, and it will be added to Windows Media Player as a supported device allowing you to use Windows Media Player rather than the player that came with your device.

Your device might not be supported, and you might still need to install the media player software that came with your device to manage the transfer of music to it.

If your portable audio player is supported by Windows Media Player 10, one nice feature is that you can connect it to a PC anywhere in your home and access music files from anywhere on the home entertainment network from the MP3 player.

Working with iPods

iPods have become the most successful and popular portable audio players on the market, and the good news is that they work perfectly with Windows XP. In fact, an iPod is a networked device that can be attached to any PC on your network, and you can access files saved on it from other PCs on the network.

For example, you can connect your iPod to a laptop in the bedroom, and using iTunes (the media player application that comes with iPod and is recommended either as a primary media player or along with Windows Media Player on every PC), you can access music and files from the iPod using Apple's Air Tunes media extender.

The Air Tunes media extender is a device that simply plugs in to any electrical outlet and makes an audio connection from the Air Tunes media extender to a home stereo or powered speakers. It is a wireless media extender (54g, 802.11g), and once it is recognized by the network, iTunes will find and display it in a pop-up menu on the bottom of the iTunes screen. You can select any playlist or music you want to play at that location from iTunes.

Air Tunes also allows you to connect a USB device such as a printer to the network. For $129, it's a great media extender if you like iTunes and just want to network music.

A little known fact about iPod is that it can be used as a portable hard drive. In that mode, you can store almost any type of media file on it (although it won't be capable of directly playing files stored in this manner—including music files).

When used as a hard drive with media files, it is a network-ready device. Figure 14.3 shows how an iPod, once connected to a PC using its USB or FireWire connection, becomes a "drive" on the My Computer folder in Windows XP.

To make sure that your iPod can share its files, you need to right-click on the iPod drive icon from My Computer and choose file sharing just as you would any other drive or directory. Once you do so, the iPod will be shown on the My Network Places directory of other devices on your network.

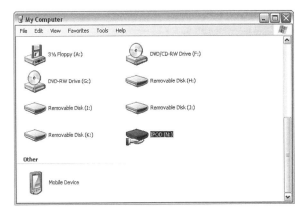

Figure 14.3

iPods are network devices and are recognized as a device/drive by Windows XP, as shown here on the My Computer screen.

In the current release of iTunes, an iPod is a local device as far as music management to the computer the iPod is connected to, but future releases are expected to turn the iPod into a fully network-capable music device.

For the most part, portable music devices are about taking music from your home entertainment network and playing them on the road as mentioned previously. The next generation of portable media players represent a much more exciting future—one in which they become an active component in the home entertainment network and allow you to take TV shows, videos, music, and pictures from your network with you wherever you go.

Better Than MP3s: Portable Media Players

The newest portable media devices on the market are termed *Portable Media Players* (*PMPs*). If you are planning on purchasing any type of portable media player (even if you're thinking about an iPod), consider what these devices offer:

- **Music:** Portable Media Players feature music playing, but unlike MP3 players, they have a full video interface and can even play music videos.

- **Video:** Portable Media Players have a high-resolution video screen that can play full videos that you move from your server PC or download from the Internet, as well as your home videos from your camcorder.

- **TV Shows:** You can bring your TV shows with you. These players allow you to record TV shows on your PC and play them on the device.

- **Pictures:** With a great color display, portable media players make a perfect picture album, and you can create slideshows that play along with music.

- **Pocket Size:** Although about as large as a Palm Pilot or Pocket PC, they are still very portable and smaller than a portable CD player.

Even more impressive, these small devices—with full-color screens that use a large internal hard drive for storing about 80 hours of video and music—retail for well under $500, which puts them in the same price range as an iPod.

Figure 14.4 shows a few of the newest portable media players that work with Windows Media Player 10 and Windows Media Edition PCs. Called Windows Portable Media Players, they attach as part of your network and integrate with Windows XP to transfer media to the devices with little effort.

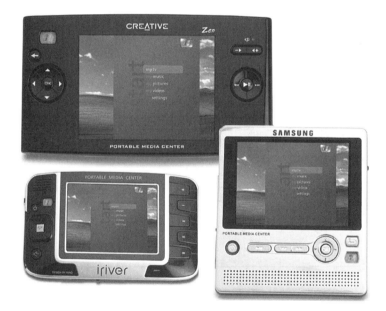

FIGURE 14.4

These Windows Portable Media Players are networked devices that play music, video, TV shows, and pictures. This is the future of portable media playing, and these devices are available now.

The portable media players shown in Figure 14.4 are designed entirely to integrate with Windows Media Player 10 and with Windows Media Center Edition PCs. TV shows recorded in Media Center and all media that plays in Media Center can be transferred and downsized to play on the portable media players that contain a user interface that is virtually the same as Media Center.

If you are not using a Window Media Center PC, don't fret. A number of other portable media players offer similar features—the ability to allow you to carry your TV shows, videos, and music with you in a device with a quality color display and costing under $500.

Figure 14.5 shows an RCA Lyra Audio/Video Jukebox. Containing a 40GB hard drive, it is designed to use media from your home entertainment network. Similar to the preceding Windows Portable Media Players, it uses a video screen as a user interface to music and all media stored on it.

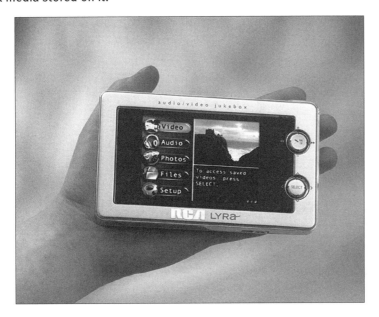

FIGURE 14.5

RCA Lyra Audio/Video Jukebox uses your media files combined with its own unique user interface to create a portable media player.

All the preceding portable media players attach to your PC via a cradle or USB connector and have a sync program that not only moves files to the devices, but also puts the media in the correct formats for file size considerations and to play properly on the device. For example, a full-size video file is transferred and converted automatically to the proper screen size for the device.

Portable media devices really are a new development in your home entertainment network. By putting your favorite TV shows and music on them, you can view them out in the yard, anywhere in your home, and, of course, you can take them with you wherever you go.

Pocket PCs Are Media Players Too

If you have ever used a Pocket PC using Windows Mobile operating system, you will know that these small, handheld devices have a lot of power, storage, and a really good color screen. Unlike Palm Pilot devices, they have color screens and integrate seamlessly with Windows XP. Even better, when you add a wireless networking card to a Pocket PC, it becomes an instant part of your home network if you are using a wireless router.

Pocket PCs contain their own version of Windows Media Player, so they can play music and videos. If you have a large enough storage card installed in the pocket PC, you can move TV shows, videos, picture files, and music to it. If you use Windows Media Player, it will help you move any media file to a Pocket PC, even downsizing files as it transfers them to the device.

Figure 14.6 shows a 20-minute movie playing full screen on a Pocket PC, and the results are excellent. To create the file, it was a 6GB AVI file opened in Windows Movie Maker 2.0 and saved as a movie for Windows Pocket PC full screen. The new file, which was 48MB, was moved to a compact flash card in the Pocket PC, and the movie was viewed in Windows Media Player for Pocket PC.

FIGURE 14.6

A 20-minute full-screen movie playing on a Pocket PC.

To move a movie, a TV program recorded on your PC, or any other media file to your Pocket PC, simply drag the document to a Pocket PC Documents folder in your My Documents folder. When you put the Pocket PC in the Sync cradle or use a Sync cable, the files are moved automatically to the Pocket PC.

If you are in your home and would prefer to simply access your entertainment content from a Pocket PC, you can use an 802.11a, 802.11b, or 802.11g wireless network adapter card. (They come in Compact Flash and SB card varieties, depending on what type of expansion port your Pocket PC has.) Using Internet Explorer, Windows Media Player, or Picture Viewer on the Pocket PC, you can access content wirelessly from your Pocket PC to get at all of your PC-based content.

If you simply want to move content onto a Pocket PC, it's as simple as setting the Pocket PC in its Sync cradle. The ActiveSync application that comes with the device manages the transfer of files based on your specifications of what type of files should be shared between the Pocket PC and content on your home entertainment network.

Figure 14.7 shows the file synchronization menu that allows you to establish which file types, including data and media, should be synced whenever you connect your Pocket PC to the network.

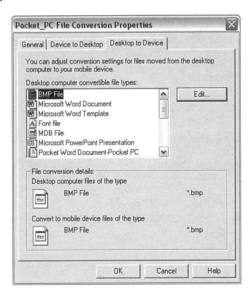

FIGURE 14.7

ActiveSync for Pocket PCs converts and moves files between your home network content and your Pocket PC.

If you are Palm Pilot user, there is some progress on that platform. In much the same way as with a Pocket PC, you can move media files such as pictures and MP3 files, but it's not nearly as good as using a Pocket PC for a number of reasons.

Pocket PCs are Windows CE based and share file formats with Windows XP and feature programs that are the same as you would find on Windows XP, such as Windows Media Player and Internet Explorer. Palm Pilot devices use programs that can read Word, Excel, and most media formats, but they are not as integrated as the applications on a Pocket PC are.

Recent Palm devices are capable of playing media files, but they require special applications on both the PDA and your PC. As part of a home entertainment network, they lack the media integration that Pocket PCs offer.

Getting Files from Digital Cameras and Camcorders

One of the great sources of content for your home entertainment network is that which you produce: your digital pictures and videos.

If you have a digital camera or digital camcorder, you will want to make all of those pictures and videos a part of your media files. Moving pictures from the device to the PC server is actually pretty easy, and there are a few tricks that can make it even simpler than your current method.

First, let's look at getting pictures from a digital camera.

Moving Pictures from Your Digital Camera to Your PC

Most digital cameras come with the following:

- A memory card slot for a compact flash card, SD memory car, memory stick, or other memory card slot
- A USB connector port for connecting your digital camera to your PC and using a supplied picture management program that moves the files to your PC and helps you view them on your PC

Okay, think this one through. If you use the supplied USB cable and connect your digital camera to your PC, you will need to install a special program that will attempt to totally control your picture management experience, will only work on that PC, and in reality is not needed at all to get your pictures from your digital camera to your PC.

If your camera is relatively new, you might be able to simply avoid installing any of the software that comes with the camera (unless you want the image editing software most cameras come with) and connect your camera to your PC using the provided USB cable. Once connected, Windows XP should be capable of recognizing your camera as a "device with removable storage" from the My Computer folder.

To see whether you can move picture files from your camera to your PC in this way, follow these steps:

1. Using the USB cable that comes with your digital camera, connect the camera to your PC.

2. From the Start menu, select My Computer.

3. If your camera is recognized by Windows XP, you will see your camera (and its name) listed as a Device with Removable Storage.

4. Double-click on your camera's icon, and you will see a folder for the files in the camera.

5. Move, copy, or delete the files.

Although directly connecting a digital camera to your PC and being able to access its memory card is the best way to manage copying, moving, or deleting files on the digital camera, not all cameras are recognized by Windows XP.

If your camera is not recognized in the manner described previously, a good solution is to simply take the memory card out of your camera (regardless of the format of the card), and put it in the card slot of a media reader that your computer might already have, or you can add to your computer's USB port.

Figure 14.8 shows a feature most new computers come with—a memory card reader. This one features a card slot for virtually every card format on the market.

FIGURE 14.8

A built-in memory card reader drive on a newer PC that can read most any memory card on the market.

If your computer does not have a built-in memory card reader, you can purchase a memory card–specific reader that attaches to a USB port or a multi-card reader that attaches to a USB port. A number of different memory card formats are on the market including Compact Flash I and Compact Flash II, SmartCard, Secure Digital, and MemoryStick. You will need to be sure that you get a single-card or multi-card reader that works with the memory card format for your digital camera.

Figure 14.9 shows a compact flash card (type I and II) reader. It inserts in the USB port, and the card goes in the slot on the front. If you can't place it easily in a USB port because of the location of the port, it comes with a USB extender cable.

FIGURE 14.9

A compact flash card reader that attaches to a USB port.

Using a USB cable and a special program is way too complicated, and it requires you to have the program installed on any computer you want to transfer pictures to. A simple memory card reader is a much better way. A portable reader can go from computer to computer, and because it is viewed by your PC as a drive, you can share that drive with all other devices on your home entertainment network in a shared drive mode.

To transfer pictures using a memory card reader, you take the memory card out of your camera, insert it in the card reader, and at that point, treat it as any other drive on your PC. You can open the drive folder, use any program you like, such as Adobe Slideshow or Microsoft Picture and Fax viewer to view the pictures, or simply copy or move the pictures to your Pictures folder that you use for all of your pictures on the network.

By moving your pictures, it also takes them off the memory card and retrieves space so that the card is empty when you return it to your camera.

The goal is to get the pictures from your camera to your network Pictures folder. The preceding process is the simplest way, and you can use the photo editing and sorting programs you like—not the one that came with your camera.

Getting Video from Camcorders

If you have a digital camcorder (MiniDV or Digital8), moving your movies to your PC's network drives is a slightly different process than with digital cameras, but it's actually very easy.

You will need to connect your digital camcorder to your PC using a FireWire (IEEE 1394) cable. Your camcorder does come with a connector for this digital cable, and it will be labeled by one of three names:

- iLink
- FireWire
- IEEE 1394

The terms all represent the same standard of cable and connector, so your camera might have an iLink port, and you might end up using a FireWire cable. As long as they have those names, you are using the right connectors or cables.

FIGURE 14.10

An iLink port on a Sony digital camcorder with a 4-pin cable about to be attached.

The port on your digital camcorder will be very small, often referred to as a 4-pin cable. Figure 14.10 shows a 4-pin port on a Sony digital camcorder with a 4-pin cable about to be attached. Depending on your computer, you might have a 4-pin connector, or a larger 6-pin connector cable. You will need to make sure of the following to be able to transfer video between your digital camcorder and your PC:

- That your PC has a iLink/FireWire/IEEE 1394 port and that you know what size connector it has—4- or 6-pin.

- That the cable you use to connect the two devices has the right match of pin-sized cables—4-4, 6-6, or 4-6. Most likely you will need a 4-6 cable.

If your PC or laptop does not have a iLink/FireWire/IEEE 1394 port, you will need to add one. They can be purchased as a PCI expansion card for PCs, or a PC card for laptops. Figure 14.11 shows a PC Card FireWire adapter for a laptop.

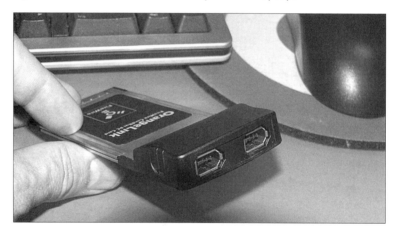

FIGURE 14.11

FireWire/IEEE 1394 PC Card adapter for a laptop.

Once you have the right cables, and you have the correct port on your PC, you will need to use a video editing program that supports digital video capture. You computer might come with such a program, and it is most likely that your digital camcorder came with a special program for both video editing and video capture.

If you want to take the simpler route, you can use Windows Movie Maker 2 that comes with Windows XP. It allows video capture, does a great job, and is very easy to use. Chapter 17, "Programming Your Own Media Network," looks at capturing videos using Windows Movie Maker 2.

Whether using Windows Movie Maker 2 or the video editing and capture program that came with your digital camcorder, you will be able to import your video, and then edit it and save it as a file. The type of file you save it as has a number of important considerations.

For the highest quality, save it first as an AVI file, uncompressed. This will allow you to edit and create "master" video files that are the highest quality. From them, you can create lower-bandwidth copies that are also lower in quality.

For media extender devices, and especially wireless networking of video, make a copy of your movie as an MPEG file. You might have to try a number of MPEG settings before you reach a setting that plays perfectly on your network.

Using Older Analog Camcorders

If you don't have a digital camcorder and are using an older analog camcorder or have your home videos on VHS tapes, don't fret. Since you have added a TV tuner card to your PC, simply connect your camcorder or VCR to the video-in port on your TV tuner card, tune the TV player to S-Video or line-in, and use the same TV recorder software that came with your TV tuner card to record your analog tapes. Store them as MPEG files, and they are ready for play on your home entertainment network.

Attaching Network Printers

Now that you've attached portable audio players—such as MP3 players and iPods, Windows Portable Media Players, Pocket PCs, digital cameras, and digital and analog camcorders to provide content to your home entertainment network—the last thing you will want to do is make sure that you attach your photo-quality printer (or any printer, actually) as a network printer.

You will want to be able to make photo prints or print just about anything from any PC or device in your home. Your printer can be changed from a "local" printer, which only works with the PC it is attached to, to a network printer that can be used by the devices on the network.

This has many advantages. First, it means that you can save money by not having a printer attached to every PC, and it also allows you to print from anywhere, even from a wirelessly networked Pocket PC.

To change your printer(s) to networked devices, be sure that it is attached to a PC (preferably your main server PC or where you do most of your PC work), and do the following:

1. From the Start menu, go to the Control Panel, and then to Printers and Faxes.

2. Once you are at the Printer and Faxes control menu, select the printer you want to change to a networked printer.

3. From the File menu, or by right-clicking on the printer icon, you will see a Sharing menu item. Click on it.

4. Select Share this Printer, as shown in Figure 14.12.

FIGURE 14.12

Choose Share this Printer from a selected printer from the Printer control panel to turn your printer into a network resource.

After you have done this, click OK; then go to any program from any other networked PC and choose Print. The printer will be listed as a printer on the network and will be available.

You might need to have your printer installation disk the first time you use the printer on other PCs. The printer drivers will be needed to use the networked printer, so have it handy the first time it is used.

Summary

With a home entertainment network, you will be able to use portable devices to take content from your media library on the road with you. MP3 players, iPods, Windows Portable Media Players, and Pocket PCs are all great additions to your entertainment mix.

The connection of the devices is largely done with USB connectors, but some connections can be wireless too.

Digital cameras use memory cards that make it easy to transfer photos from the cards to your Picture folder to make all of your pictures available to the network. It is best to use a card reader rather than the picture transfer application and USB cable that came with your camera.

Digital camcorders require a FireWire connection and cable to move video from the camcorder to your PC, and you can use the applications that came with the camcorder or simply use Windows MovieMaker to transfer the video.

Finally, you will want to change your printers to network printers so that they can be used by any PC or device on your home entertainment network.

GOING BEYOND THE PC NETWORK

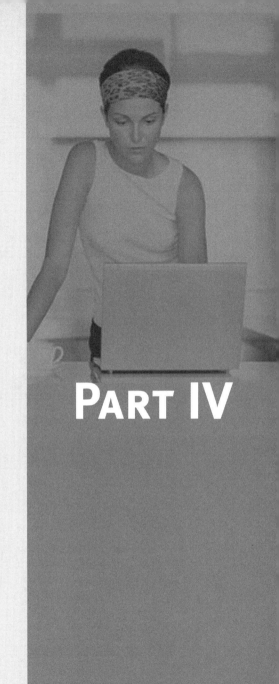

PART IV

TV Sources: Cable, Satellite, Antennas, and DVDs

A home entertainment network is really about bringing two worlds together: the home entertainment devices you have always used (TVs, DVD players, and stereos) and a PC-based home network.

When you combine them, you have a classic scenario in which the sum is far greater than the total of its parts. The integration of traditional TV sources, music, and pictures stored as a digital file structure on PCs allows you to share them on a network to truly create a new type of home entertainment center—one that is better since it unlocks content that was once only on one TV or on one PC and opens it to any device in your home entertainment network.

This chapter looks at how to get the content from TV sources (cable, satellite, and broadcast, as well as DVDs) into digital files that can be used on the home entertainment network.

Deciding on a TV Source

The number of choices for where you get your TV programs seems to be growing daily. Right now, the main sources of TV programming comes from broadcast, satellite, and cable TV. As you build a library of TV content or share TV programs on your home entertainment network, you will need to connect your TV sources to your PCs. The following sections look at how you work with each of the different TV sources available to your home.

Antenna Reception

For many people, a rooftop or well positioned antenna in the home is a great source of free TV. The quality of the signal depends on where you live, so don't count it out. It's free, and it's changing. Recent changes by the FCC have mandated that all TV broadcasters begin broadcasting both analog and HDTV (high definition TV) signals to their markets.

I live in a remote part of Northern California—an old mountain cowboy town where they trade horses and there's just a few gas stations, a few feed and tackle stores, and lots of pickup trucks. But the one thing it does have is great broadcast signals for both traditional analog TV and HDTV. I don't need cable or satellite service in my little town to get good TV, but it is limited to broadcast networks.

Maybe one of the reasons it's good here is that there are no high-rise buildings, and it's big sky country where the signals can roam free and say "hi" to the horses and cattle along the way. When I first moved here, I decided to buy an antenna at Radio Shack and see if I could get a station or two. It worked so well that for a year I just used my antenna.

Perhaps your location may get perfectly good broadcast reception, and it's strongly recommended that if you can, be sure to have an antenna for your home entertainment network.

Here are the reasons why:

- **It's good to have more than one TV source:** As you learned earlier in the book, you can record one show while watching another or even record two shows at once if your PC has dual TV tuner cards. It's smart to have two TV sources. Broadcast represents local stations, and when cable or satellite is down (or they turn you off because your check arrived 4.8 seconds late), you can switch to your antenna.

- **The price is right:** Because it's free, you can't beat the price. If you have lots of TVs and PCs with TV tuner cards, an antenna is the lowest price option for people who primarily watch broadcast network TV and live in an area where there is good reception.

There are some strong drawbacks. Reception is top on the list. If you can't receive most stations without static or ghosting, then even free, it's no bargain. The other reason is the number of choices for programming. Broadcast TV is limited to the major broadcast TV networks, a local PBS station, and maybe a Fox or UPN station too.

If you do choose to use an internal or rooftop antenna, connecting it to a TV or to the TV tuner card of your PC is extremely easy. The connection uses a single cable, called an antenna cable or a coaxial cable. Figure 15.1 shows a coaxial cable connector about to be inserted into a TV tuner card.

The coaxial connector has a single wire pin in the center and a threaded connector collar for securing the connection and acting as the ground wire. Some antenna cables are "quick connect" types that snap on and do not require threading. They work, but you would be best to use a threaded connection.

FIGURE 15.1

A coaxial antenna cable about to be connected to the TV tuner card of a PC.

One of the other really nice advantages of antenna connections in practical use is that if you have dual TV tuner cards, or have a PC with a tuner card that is recording a show and you would like to continue to use a TV sitting next to it to just watch a show without going through the PC, you can take one lead from an antenna and use a splitter to make two connections from your one antenna to send the TV signals to two devices such as the TV tuner card on the PC and the TV itself.

Figure 15.2 shows a simple coaxial splitter. You attach your antenna cable on the single side, and then additional coaxial cables (splitters come in versions for as many as four connections) to the other side. There is a limit to how many splitters you can use without losing signal strength. For those instances, there are amplified splitters you can use, but chances are a simple splitter will do the trick for sending the signal to a TV and a PC.

One final thought on antenna TV sources: Always have an antenna around that you can connect to a TV if needed. A simple set of "rabbit ears" costs about $5 and is a good investment. If your cable or satellite goes out and you need to hear the news or weather, you'll be glad you have a pair around to use.

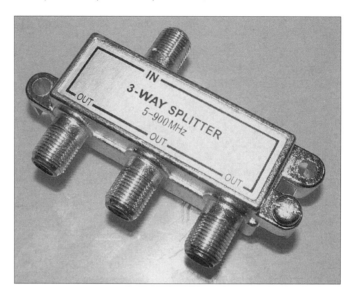

FIGURE 15.2

A coaxial splitter allows you to make two or three antenna connections from one antenna lead.

Using Cable Service

Cable is undergoing a major change in America. It started as a reliable way to bring broadcast TV to homes with a quality signal by obtaining the best reception possible at the broadcast antenna source, and then sending that signal to homes through a cable. Great idea! And for millions of homes with poor antenna reception, it was a hit.

The cable that they used to go into a home had a lot more bandwidth than the three or four local stations would ever use, so cable began to really get big when it started carrying cable networks. Cable networks were only available through cable, rode on the bandwidth the cable could carry, and offered cable an advantage because it could offer at least 40 channels, and in some cable systems up to 120 cable channels—most all of which could only be seen if you subscribed to cable.

Now, cable has competition from satellite services (covered next), and the cable companies have begun to respond to the digital signal of satellite (and the larger number of channels satellite services can offer) by making the switch from analog to digital cable.

Digital cable can fit more channels into the same bandwidth; it delivers digital signals (although signals do get converted back to analog to play on your TV); and it will offer interactive TV, VOD (video-on-demand), and other related services such as high-speed Internet service using the digital "pipe" cable providers run into your home. But it all comes with a price.

Cable rates are going up, and there are some simpler considerations to think about beyond price in a home entertainment network, including

- **You need a set top box:** Digital cable requires a set top box to convert the digital signal into an analog signal that can be used by your TV. Set top boxes are a pain, and no matter how it's marketed to you, you end up paying for them. If you have several rooms where you want TV sources, you will need several set top boxes. That adds expense, and you will need to set up your PC's TV tuner card to somehow control the set top box to change channels.

- **Use analog cable if it's available:** If your cable operator still offers analog service, which doesn't require a set top box, that's the best option for some of the locations in your home. The picture is about the same quality, and you won't pay the premium for digital service, which is largely you paying the price for cable companies' build out to all digital. With analog cable, you can make a direct connection and control channels directly from a TV or TV tuner card.

The advantages of cable are a reliable TV selection, a large channel offering, and a mix and match of digital and analog cable in a home. A good practice is to get digital cable in one room, and then "TV Ready" cable in all the other rooms.

> **TIP**
> Even though they will never recommend it, most every cable service allows you to "mix and match" digital cable and analog cable in your home. You can put digital service in one room with a set top box and use TV ready analog cable in all other locations, and you'll save a lot each month on your cable bill.

If you have digital cable, you can set your PC's TV tuner card to control the set top box and then be able to record the premium and VOD programs a digital set top box service offers. You can use a direct connection to other PC tuner cards and TVs in your home with standard analog cable. Making such connections is detailed later in this chapter.

If your cable system has moved to all digital, you'll be stuck using set top boxes, so be sure that's the actual case and not a marketing practice cable operators are using to get the most money from you.

Finally, if you are in a larger city or have just moved into an area, you might have a choice of a number of cable service providers. Check the Yellow Pages, or better yet, call your local utilities board. Cable service is regulated by cities or counties, and the local government or utility board will tell you every cable service that can connect to your home or apartment. In a competitive market, shop for the best value.

The Sky's the Limit with Satellite

The fastest growing and most exciting development in TV sources is satellite TV service. Even up here in the wilds of Northern California, I've succumbed to the large channel lineups and great deals satellite TV services offer.

If you live in a location where you can mount a small satellite dish to your home or apartment with a clear view to the sky (at least the Southern part of it), you can get satellite. About the only times it doesn't work is if some building is obstructing the view from the satellite dish and the sky, or if there are trees; and in cold climates, a lot of snow on the dish can interrupt service sometimes.

For most homes, satellite is easy to install. Figure 15.3 shows my little dish attached to a fence around my patio. It was just the easiest place to install it, and because it doesn't snow here much, my reception has been perfect. A satellite dish can mount to a wall, a window, or a roof and has a small transponder that picks up the signal captured by the dish and sends that signal to set top box receivers inside your home.

FIGURE 15.3

A small dish mounted somewhere on your home or apartment that has a clear view of the sky is about all that you need to get satellite TV service.

One important thing to know about satellite TV services is that they are not "TV ready" like analog cable, where you can simply run a coaxial cable from a jack on the wall to your TV or PC's TV tuner card. Each location where you have satellite TV in your home will require a receiver, which is a set top box. Depending on how many receivers you have in your home, you will need to be sure to get the right type of transponder on your dish antenna.

Figure 15.4 shows a two responder antenna configuration. The two round shapes on the device are each a transponder that picks up the signal bounced off the dish. If you wanted a four receiver setup in your home, you would need an antenna with four transponders. If you want to keep costs down, think through how may locations you will want satellite receivers so that you only have to install your transponders one time.

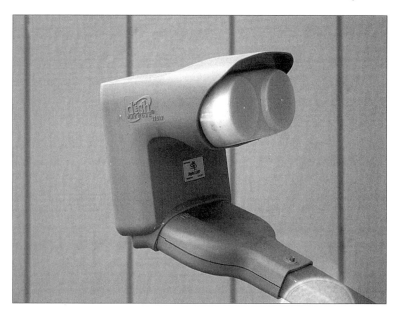

FIGURE 15.4

The number of transponders (the round receivers in this picture) correspond to the number of receivers you can use in your home.

Once you have your antenna installed (and this is best done by getting one of the free installation deals when you sign up for services because it can be tricky to do yourself), you will need to locate receivers in your home. The installer will run a cable from each transponder to a wall jack in your home and connect it to a satellite receiver set top box.

The receivers vary. You can get a simple one that just tunes to channels, or, even better, get one with a digital video recorder to record about 100 hours of service. Even though your PCs will be recording shows, it doesn't hurt to record them on the receiver's digital video recorder first, and then transfer them to your home entertainment network. Think of it as a bonus hard drive!

Figure 15.5 shows a Dish satellite receiver (a digital video recorder version) sitting in a bank of (too many) entertainment devices in my den. It's the device sitting on top of the two VCRs and under a standalone DVD recorder and a D-Link Media Lounge media extender. Not seen in the photo is the fact that all of that equipment is sitting next to a Windows XP Media Center PC. Dish is the primary source for TV signals to the home entertainment network, but I also use it to copy programs directly to the DVD recorder and also to the TV.

FIGURE 15.5

The Dish receiver fits right into both the location of entertainment devices, and the home entertainment strategy of putting TV content wherever it's needed.

After getting a satellite receiver installed, the only really tricky part is getting your TV tuner card to change it's channels.

TIP

If you have a set top box that uses an IR remote control, you are in good shape. (This applies to both cable and satellite service set top box remote controls.) If you have a UHF connector, you may be able to obtain a small converter or device from either your TV tuner card manufacturer—or from Dish, DirecTV, or Voom—that will convert the UHF signals into IR signals for you. You will need to check with the service provider or the TV tuner card manufacturer for an answer on this problem, so do it before you decide on the type of receiver or brand of TV tuner card.

Because it's a set top box, it uses a remote control to change channels. In this instance, some dish receivers use IR remotes, and some use UHF remotes. That can be a problem.

Better TV tuner cards use a small remote device that takes the place of the remote control for turning channels and even turning the receiver on and off. It's a small IR transmitter that you place in front of the set top box. When you schedule a recording on your PC, it's the IR transmitter, not the remote control, that changes the channels on the set top box for you. As you can see, it's an important device and makes it possible to schedule recordings without you being there to manually change channels.

Even with all the installation and changing of channels when using a TV tuner card in your PC that you need to deal with when using a satellite service, the benefits of satellite are worth it. Here are some good reasons why satellite TV services have become so popular:

- **Works most anywhere, and you can take it with you:** Dishes are easily installed in most homes and locations, and if you move you can take the dish with you and stay with the service. That is not always the case with cable, where you may have to change service providers.

- **Channel Selection:** Satellite services offer more than 500 channels of service, and now offer great sports packages, ethnic channels, and a growing selection of music channels, which is great for recording music in your home entertainment network. Depending on the size of the city you live in, local channels might be available too.

- **Reliability:** Any service might have interruptions, but it has been reported that satellite services tend to be highly reliable because they are not affected by breaks in cables from construction or old equipment.

- **Cost:** No TV service is cheap, but satellite service offers a lot of channels, including local channels, generally for less than the same channel lineups from cable services.

Whether you use broadcast TV, satellite, or cable service, you will need to connect those TV sources to your TV tuner card using the following steps.

Connecting a TV Source to a TV Tuner Card

Adding a TV source to your PC's TV tuner card falls into one of the following two categories:

- **Antenna or cable without a set top box:** This is a very simple connection in which you only need to connect the antenna cable or coaxial cable provided in your home by your cable service directly to the antenna coaxial connector of the TV tuner card. The TV tuner card can change channels without the need for any other device.

- **Cable or Satellite service with a set top box:** This is a more complex connection. You can connect a set top box to a TV tuner card with an antenna connection (coaxial cable) or sometimes with an S-video or composite video connection and audio cables. This will depend on the set top box and if it offers S-video connections. That enables your TV tuner card to receive the video and audio, but it cannot tune the channels because the set top box is only sending one channel to your TV tuner card—not all channels as with an antenna or standard cable. You will need to connect a remote device from your TV tuner card to your set top box to enable your TV tuner card to change the channels.

Making Standard Cable and Antenna Connections

To connect an antenna or standard cable (that does not require a set top box), you will use a standard coaxial cable. As shown in Figures 15.1 and 15.2, if you want, you can use a splitter to make a connection from a single antenna or standard cable lead to both a TV and a TV tuner card on your PC.

The length of coaxial cable in your home might be an issue. Generally, cable systems will make sure that the signal to your TV's location is strong enough for a good signal. The cable system uses a series of signal amplifiers to ensure a strong signal. If you are using a splitter, the location of your PC is farther from your antenna than the TV, or when using an antenna the picture is just weak or fuzzy, you might need to use a signal amplifier.

Signal amplifiers for coaxial cable runs can be purchased at most any electronics store such as Radio Shack and will help boost the signal when using long cable runs from a cable or antenna source.

The coaxial cable connects directly to the antenna connection on the TV tuner card, as shown in Figure 15.6. Once you connect the cable, use the TV player software provided with your TV tuner card to make sure that the connection has been made correctly and that you can view TV channels.

FIGURE 15.6

Standard cable and antenna connections are made using coaxial cable connected to the antenna connector on a TV tuner card.

Making Set Top Box Connections

Using a TV tuner card to obtain a TV signal from a set top box and to control the changing of channels is a more complex task. It will require

1. Making a connection from the set top box to receive the video and audio signals

2. Connecting a remote device to change channels on the set top box

3. Connecting a remote sensor to allow you to change the channels on the TV tuner using a remote control

Some TV tuner cards will only accept the video and audio signals, but do not offer the benefit of attaching remote devices for changing channels. You should be sure to use a TV tuner card that offers a remote device for changing channels on the set top box and offers a remote control of its own to allow you to change channels just as you would with a TV or set top box.

The first action is to connect the video and audio from the set top box to the TV tuner card on your PC. Because you are using a set top box, it will only be sending one channel of TV programming to your TV tuner at a time, and this can be done using the standard Antenna Out connection of the set top box to the Antenna connection of your TV tuner card. This connection will carry both the video and audio signal to the TV tuner card and is done with a single coaxial cable.

Some set top boxes enable the same signal to be sent to a TV (or in this case, a TV tuner card) using a higher quality connection such as S-video or composite (RCA-type) connections. In this situation, the video and the audio are two separate signals, and you will need to make a connection for video and a connection for audio.

The best video connection choice for a set top box to a TV tuner card is an S-video connection. If there is only a composite (RCA-type) video connection, you will need to use that connection type. Using an S-video cable (or, if not available, an RCA-type cable) make the connection between the video-out connection of the set top box and the S-video (or composite video if that is the only connection available) of your TV tuner card.

In some cases, your set top box might only have a composite (RCA-type) video out connection, and your TV tuner card might only have an S-video connection. In that case, use a Composite-to-S-video adapter. The adapter might have come with your TV tuner card, but if not, they are available at electronics stores such as Radio Shack.

After making the video connection, you will next need to locate the audio-out connections on your set top box, which will almost always be a set of RCA-type connectors. Your TV tuner card will almost always have a single, stereo mini-plug connection. You will need an RCA-type stereo-to-1/8" mini-plug cable to make the audio connection. If your TV tuner card did not come with this cable, you can purchase them in most any electronics store such as a Radio Shack.

Figure 15.7 shows an S-video cable and an RCA-type stereo-to-1/8" mini-plug cable.

After making the video and audio connections, if your TV tuner card features connections to remote devices for changing the channels on a set top box and for operating a remote control, you will need to connect those devices.

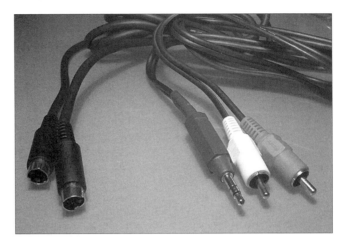

FIGURE 15.7

S-video cable and a cable that enables the connection from RCA-type stereo connector to a 1/8" stereo mini-plug connector for audio connections.

Figure 15.8 shows the remote sensor for a remote control and a remote device that enables the changing of channels on a set top box. The remote sensor for the remote control attaches to the PC using a USB port connector, and the remote device for changing channels connects to the remote sensor.

FIGURE 15.8

A remote device for changing channels on a set top box connected to a remote sensor for using a remote control, which connects to the PC using a USB connection.

The positioning of the two devices is important. The remote sensor for the remote control should be placed on, or near, your TV or computer monitor. It should be in the "line of sight" between the remote control and the display you are using to watch TV.

The remote device for turning channels on your set top box must be able to be located immediately in front of your set top box, next to the IR window that it uses to receive signals from its own remote control. You can usually identify the IR window on a set top box by looking for a small, square, or round glass window on the front of the casing. If it is hard to locate, refer to the user manual for the set top box, and it will have a diagram showing the location of the IR window.

The remote device should either directly attach to the IR window, or be placed immediately in front of it and facing it per the instructions that came with your TV tuner card. Remember, the remote device is turning channels using the same principle and signal as a remote control, so it needs to be placed very near the IR window.

After connecting both devices, start your TV viewing program on your PC, and using the TV tuner remote control, attempt to change channels. If you have made all connections properly, you will now be able to use your PC and TV tuner card to control your set top box.

Mixing TV Sources in Your Home

As you can see from all the preceding descriptions, each TV source has its benefits and perils. One good strategy is to mix and match if possible.

Mixing and matching TV sources, such as digital and analog cable, lowers the overall cost for cable and satellite service and makes it easier to attach cable service to PCs and TVs.

Although you can't mix and match satellite services, you can mix and match the types of receiver boxes in your home. You can have an HDTV receiver in one room, a DVR receiver in another, and a simple channel changer receiver in another. That will also lower your monthly satellite bill.

It is also possible to mix and match cable and satellite services in a home. You might have a great deal on low-cost analog cable, but want the large selection of premium sports and movie channels offered by satellite. Mixing and matching can often give you the best overall solution and the best monthly price.

Finally, be sure to mix and match either cable or satellite service with an antenna connection in your home. When the services go out or are down for a while, you will still be able to get TV off the air. If your reception is good, an antenna is the easiest device to connect to your TV tuner card.

Managing Set Top Boxes from the Network

If you properly connected your set top box to your TV tuner card on your PC, and have a remote transmitter positioned to change the channels and control the set top box, you should be able to schedule recordings and view those recordings from your home entertainment network without a problem.

Once properly connected, a cable or satellite TV service simply becomes a TV source to your PCs and media extenders. Their purpose is to provide a TV signal that can be recorded by your server PC. As long as you can control your set top box from a PC's TV tuner card, you can record and view programs anywhere on your network.

Right now, some media extenders, such as Media Center Extenders that work with Windows XP Media Center Edition PCs, allow you to view a TV source from a server PC on a TV connected to a Media Center Extender. This is a great product because you can have one satellite receiver in one room, and watch a live show from it in another room, where the media extender is located.

Not all TV tuner card TV viewing applications support network viewing. The applications are designed to only view a TV show on the PC that the TV tuner card is attached to.

Think of set top boxes as simple TV sources that are now controlled by your home entertainment network, and you will quickly learn that it is better to let the PC applications control them whenever possible. In the case of TV tuners that do not allow viewing a TV signal on the network through another PC or media extender, think of the TV tuner as a source for TV content that you store as a file on your PC.

The benefit of digital-based TV viewing on a home entertainment network is that you can record the show; then view it anywhere on the network with the full ability to time shift and zip past commercials and view the program when you want. Think of TV shows as files on your network that can be viewed at any time—not just when the show is on TV.

DVDs in a Home Entertainment Network

Throughout this book, DVDs have not been covered to any great extent. DVDs are copy protected and present problems to media extenders. For a number of reasons, mostly legal and very few technical, playing DVDs in a home entertainment network is very much a "wait and see" situation.

Some media extenders allow you to put a DVD in a computer and view it from another room with a media extender connected to a TV, but because it is a digital stream sending copyrighted material to another digital device, the movie and TV industry have expressed concerns that a digital signal is essentially being copied, or at least can be copied by a device at the other end of that signal.

So, for now, DVDs as a network activity are on the back burner. If you want to watch DVDs in your home entertainment network, you might simply want to take the easy solution (and now really inexpensive route since DVD players are so cheap and renting from Netflix and Blockbuster Online is a real value) of connecting DVD players in select locations in your home. If you have a PC connected to a TV in any location, you can use it to view the DVD on the TV using the PC's DVD drive (if it has one).

So, the big question is why can you share and record TV shows, but not movies on DVDs?

TV networks broadcast the signals through the air and over cable or satellite, and the laws still support fair, personal use of that signal. This means that you have the legal right to make a copy or backup for personal use. As long as you are not copying and selling a show, you are within the law as it stands today. But even that might change in this, the day of digital video recorders, DVD burners, and TiVos.

DVDs do not allow duplication in any form, for any reason, and there have been recent court battles trying to define the right to back up a copy of a DVD you purchase for safekeeping, but the entertainment industry has fought hard to restrict any copying of digital media—music or video.

As they say in TV, "stay tuned"—maybe the future of DVDs on home entertainment networks will be brighter. For now, at least, be sure to make DVD backups of the movies and shows you save to your PC if you desire. You still have that right.

Summary

The decision of what TV source to use is less of a technical one in a home entertainment network, and more of a practical one of price, value, reliability, and ease of installation on TV tuner cards and controlling the changing of channels.

A good practice is to find the best TV source for the programs you like and mix that source with broadcast antenna reception as a backup.

DVDs, because of legal issues, are still a gray area in home entertainment networks, and as a TV source, now is not the best time to think of DVDs as TV content you can copy and share on your home entertainment network.

Using Game Consoles, DVD Players, and Digital Video Recorders

16

I f you currently own entertainment devices such as game consoles, digital video recorders, and DVD players, you will want to include them in your home entertainment network. Although most of these devices are not really designed to be a part of a "network," they can connect to the Internet through the network or can provide TV content for the network.

Entertainment devices, such as those listed previously, are designed to be standalone machines that do not need a home entertainment network to operate. TVs, for example, are standalone devices, but when connected to a media extender, they become a network device.

The main categories of these devices are

- **Network Game Consoles:** Network-ready game devices such as PlayStation can connect to the Internet but are not ready to be part of a home entertainment network configuration. The only exception right now is Xbox, which is explained later in this chapter.

- **Digital Video Recorders:** TiVo and ReplayTV DVRs (digital video recorders) can also be connected to the Internet, and they can even be programmed remotely on a PC, but they are still standalone in their design.

- **DVD Players:** Designed to serve one TV, DVD players are standalone devices. As you will learn later in the chapter, there are new DVD players that can connect to a home entertainment network to act as a media extender.

It is important to consider that even with a full home entertainment network in place, you can continue to use your TVs, stereos, digital video recorders, DVD players, and game consoles the same way you always have. They remain useful and fun machines, so the network in no way displaces them.

This chapter takes a look at each of these categories and how well you can incorporate them into the home network you created, as well as how to use them as standalone devices that connect to the Internet through your network.

Connecting Game Boxes

If you are a game fanatic, or at least there are people in your home who are, you know that as an entertainment device, a PlayStation 2 or Xbox keeps a TV occupied for hours on end.

Even more to the point, newer game boxes are designed to connect to the Internet and allow players to battle each other using multiplayer Internet-enabled games. A person can play against another person anywhere else in the world if they are both connected to the Internet.

Game consoles are limited in a home entertainment network because they only

- Connect to a TV
- Connect to the Internet

Game consoles connect to each other through the Internet (even in your home—they do not connect directly to each other) but not to other devices on your home entertainment network, particularly your PCs. The gaming world is divided into two distinct groups: games for game consoles, and games for PCs.

The same game for one device (such as for an Xbox or GameCube) requires the game console or PC it was designed for. Right now, media extenders don't support sharing or using PC games in any way, even from a TV because games require joysticks and paddles or controllers.

So, it is important to think about how to incorporate game consoles in your home entertainment network strategy.

Here are the key things you should consider in locations where you want to locate a game console:

- They need to use the TV, so use a TV that has more than one video source (such as Video 1, Video 2, Video 3). That way, you can put the game console on one video-in port, a media extender, or PC on another video-in port and allow both devices to live in some sort of harmony.

- If the game console can use an Ethernet connector to connect to the Internet and it is in a location that has a media extender or PC that also uses the Ethernet connection at that location, you are faced with having to plug and unplug devices to use that connection or put a small network hub at that location to support two Ethernet connections from one connection. In a home entertainment network, you will most likely have a wireless network, and that might be the best solution if you don't have an open Ethernet port in the room you plan to use the game console in. A number of manufacturers, such as Linksys and D-Link, make wireless adapters for game consoles.

- Your "gamer" will probably want to use the powered speakers that you want to use for your TV experience. Just as with the Ethernet connection, you will need to plug and unplug cables all the time or put a splitter on the powered speakers that can allow two sets of audio connections to be connected to them without having to change cables.

The problem is largely one of sharing resources: the TV, the Internet connection, and the speakers. Although you could break down and buy an extra set of "everything" to avoid the conflict and competition for the resources, the more practical way is to add the following devices at locations where you have a game console and a media extender or PC competing for the TV and audio equipment. They will simply be sharing the TV, which is a network resource, but not in direct connection apart from the home entertainment network.

Sharing the TV

If your TV only has one video-in connector, you can take a very simple approach and put a "Y" adapter on the video-in port. This adapter has two female RCA-type video connectors on one end, and one male RCA-type video connector on the other. Such a connector is shown in Figure 16.1. This eliminates having to plug and unplug the video cables from the game console into the TV. If your game console uses a higher-end connector such as an S-video connector, you can also purchase a Y adapter for S-video connectors.

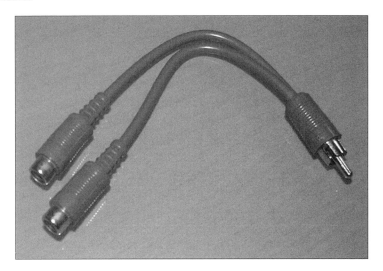

FIGURE 16.1

A simple "Y" adapter will allow two video sources to share one video-in port of a TV.

If you are worried about two connections going into your TV without some protection against overload, you can add a video switcher, as shown in Figure 16.2. Video switchers are available at electronics stores. You connect each device to the back and one cable to the TV. The front panel has buttons for the "A" device, the "B" device, and even more if you have more connections to deal with, and you have a larger switcher.

FIGURE 16.2

If you have the cash and want to play it safe, you can connect multiple video sources to one TV with a video switcher.

Although this is a simple, elegant, and safe way to handle the problem, you might find the $2.99 Y cable a more economical solution.

Sharing the Audio

The same concept described previously for video also works pretty much the same way for audio. Because you will be dealing with stereo, rather than one Y adapter, you get two. That will allow you to create a stereo Y adapter setup.

Y adapters do not degrade or reduce the quality of signal when used properly. If you send the audio signal from one device at one time to the audio equipment, it is the same as a direct connection.

Problems do occur when you have two active devices sending audio signals through each of the two connectors on the Y adapter to the audio equipment. Although it is unlikely you will harm your equipment from two active sources being fed into one device, you will be hearing two audio sources, and there might be a loss in signal strength in each. Here's the rule: When using a Y splitter, only have one active device powered on and playing at a time.

If you decided to purchase a good video switcher as previously described, it might also provide audio connections too, and that will take care of the problem. If not, audio switches are also available and work exactly the same way: You connect the cables to the back, one set to the TV, and press the button of the device you want to hear.

If you are using a good set of powered speakers, they might have their own source set of connectors, which are two sets of inputs. Since so many powered speakers have their origins serving game devices, they are often equipped with their own switchers and that might address your problem perfectly. Just choose which input you need when playing either device.

Sharing an Internet Connection with a Game Console

Sharing an Internet connection located at a networked TV with a network game console presents a different challenge. When you want to connect the game console to the Internet, you can, of course, plug and unplug the Ethernet cable connected to the media extender or PC located at that location and share it between the media extender and the game console, but there are simple solutions:

1. If you can run one Ethernet cable from your router to the location of the TV connected to a media extender where you also want to connect a game console, why not run two Ethernet cables from the router to that location? Running two cables is practical and does not require any additional network hubs or switches.

2. Using the single Ethernet cable running from your router to the location, you can add a network hub or low-cost network switch at the location to allow two or more Ethernet ports to be created from one Ethernet jack.

> **TIP**
>
> If you only have one Ethernet cable running to a location in your home and you need to add another wired device, rather than use a hub that can add complexity and force the creation of a network "bridge," you can use a power line network adapter as featured in Chapter 4, "Getting the Right Networking Gear." You plug one power line adapter in to an electrical outlet by your router and use an Ethernet cable to connect it to the router. By the device you want to add, connect a power line adapter into an electrical outlet and your additional device into the Ethernet port on the power line adapter. Viola! An instant Ethernet port.

3. Most wireless network equipment manufacturers have wireless network adapters that create an Ethernet port for game consoles or other devices that require a wired Ethernet connection. The wireless network Ethernet adapter adds an Ethernet port anywhere in the wireless network to which you can attach the game console. Although this might be the most expensive solution (generally about $80–150 for a wireless network adapter that adds an Ethernet port), it offers the greatest flexibility in connecting the game console or other wired Ethernet device to your Internet connection.

If you have a wireless router, a good solution is to add either the power line adapter, or the wireless Ethernet adapter shown in Figure 16.3.

Using a wireless Ethernet adapter allows you to create a wired Ethernet connection for the game console anywhere in your home. You can connect it to any TV, and you can change its location whenever you want. The following steps are required to add a game console to a wireless network:

FIGURE 16.3

A wireless Ethernet adapter uses the wireless network to add an Ethernet port at any location. This enables a wired connection from a game console or other device that requires a wired connection.

1. Purchase a wireless Ethernet adapter and decide on its location in your home. In most cases, you do not need to run special setup software for this device, but some brands do have a setup disk that sets the router to identify and add the adapter to the network. It will be recognized as a network device by the router.

2. Connect an Ethernet cable from the game console or other device that requires a wired Ethernet location to the wireless Ethernet adapter.

3. Test the connection of the game console or device and make sure that it is recognized on the network and can establish an Internet connection. If it does not, you might need to go into the web-based controls of the wireless router and add the IP address of the device to the list of allowed devices on the network.

Figure 16.4 shows a diagram of how a game console connected to a wireless Ethernet adapter fits into the home entertainment network plan.

The primary purpose of adding an Ethernet adapter to the home entertainment network is to enable the game console to access the Internet. Even if you have more than one game console added to your Internet connection in your home, the two game consoles will use the Internet to play against each other rather than using a direct network connection between each other.

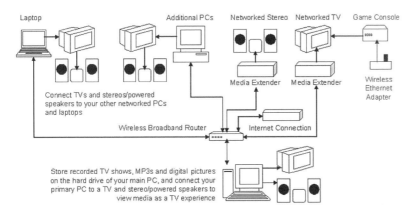

FIGURE 16.4

A game console is added to the home entertainment network by connecting it to a wireless Ethernet adapter.

Game consoles are standalone devices, so although they will need to share resources, they are not truly part of your home entertainment network. However, that might be changing pretty soon. The next generation of game consoles are expected to enable direct connections between each other on a home network. There are even new developments, as shown next, in which using the processing power of the game console has been put to work to turn it into a media extender—a great reason to connect it to your home entertainment network.

Xbox Media Center Extender

Just at the time of writing this book, Microsoft has introduced an add-on device to the Xbox that turns it into a true media extender if you are using the Windows XP Media Center Edition operating system on a Media Center Edition PC. The Xbox, shown in Figure 16.5, is expandable and can connect to the Internet to play games online, play CDs, and with expansion cards, it can play DVDs. Now it is being expanded to be a media extender—but only if you have a Media Center Edition PC running the Windows XP Media Center Edition 2005 operating system.

The Media Center Extender essentially turns the Xbox into a media center that will allow you to use the Xbox to play music, video, recorded TV programs, and access online content from your Media Center Edition PC. When connected to your home entertainment network, the Xbox Media Center extender truly makes the Xbox a part of your home entertainment network, but for entertainment media files—not for games. Games will continued to be played in a standalone mode or online with other players using the Internet connection provided by your home entertainment network.

FIGURE 16.5

Xbox is now offering an option to expand it into a media extender for Media Center Edition PCs.

Expanding the Xbox to become a media center requires that

1. Your Xbox be connected to your home entertainment network through a direct connection via an Ethernet cable to your router. Or, if you have a wireless router and would prefer a wireless connection, you could use a wireless Ethernet adapter to connect the Xbox anywhere in your home. It must also be connected to a TV in the same manner when it is connected for game play.

2. You have a Media Center Edition PC running Windows XP Media Center Edition 2005, and it is connected to your router either as the main PC connected to the router, or another PC connected to the home entertainment network.

3. You install the media extender adapter to the Xbox and run the CD-ROM that provides the Media Center application.

4. Once connected to the adapter and the home network, your Media Center PC will recognize the Xbox Media Extender and enable it to display the Media Center user interface. Then you can play all the media content from your Media Center PC.

Media Center extenders play all the same files as a Media Center PC, except that they do not play DVDs over the network. If you want to play DVDs from your Xbox, you can purchase the DVD expansion kit for Xbox to play them.

Working with DVRs (Digital Video Recorders)

You might already own a DVR (digital video recorder) such as a TiVo or a ReplayTV. If you do, you know that they are not only great video recorders, but they have also been expanded to allow you to play picture and music files pulled from your PC and stored on their own hard drive, making them a distant cousin to a true media extender. They also need to connect to the Internet to get program guide data, and even allow you to program which shows you want to record from work or from any other computer with a web browser.

DVRs, such as current models of TiVo and ReplayTV, use an home network for the following:

1. Using an Ethernet connection and your router to connect to their service's servers to add program guide information, download show information, download advertisements, manage your account information, update the device's software and ROM, and provide remote scheduling of recordings from a web-based interface from any PC.

2. If you subscribe to enhanced service, it uses your home network to pull picture and music files from your PC to move to the DVR and allows you to play pictures and music from the DVR directly—a step backward in a true home entertainment network where you can do that with any PC or media extender.

As exciting as these devices are, they are not yet truly networked devices that can become a part of your home entertainment network in the classic sense. They are standalone devices, and their primary job is to connect to a TV source, such as cable or satellite, and record programs for you on a hard drive.

This doesn't mean that they aren't great to have. Like any other video device that can schedule, record, and store shows, it's a good addition because you can use those recorded shows for viewing on a TV they are connected to when you don't want to fill up hard drive space on your server PC. They are also good all-around video recorders. For some locations in your home, they eliminate the need for a media extender or a PC if all you want to do is to record and playback TV shows at that single location.

The big problem is that if you want to copy a program recorded on a TiVo, for example, to your server PC—you can't—at least not directly as a digital file transfer from the DVR to your PC's hard drive.

You can hook up a video and audio cable set and "play back" the show in real time to the TV tuner card in your PC, but that is so slow and silly that it would have been much better to record the show on the PC in the first place.

But, maybe you love your TiVo or ReplayTV, and if you have one, you will certainly want to use it. The good news is that you can use your home entertainment network to schedule recordings on either device from any web browser on any of your PCs.

Figure 16.6 shows a ReplayTV box. It was upgraded to have 160 hours of recording time, and it's been a workhorse before and during the installation of a home entertainment network.

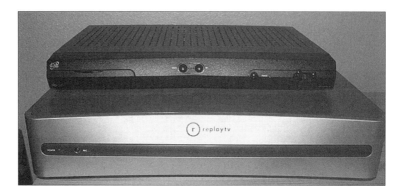

FIGURE 16.6

A ReplayTV DVR connected to a TV and a dish satellite receiver. The device is connected to the Internet with an Ethernet cable connected to the broadband router.

Similar to a PC with a TV tuner card, a DVR is connected to a dish receiver, and uses an infrared (IR) transmitter to turn the dish receiver on and change channels. The problem is that you have to remember to turn it on and schedule recording directly from the TV connected to it.

ReplayTV has a website for users called MyReplayTV, where you can log in to your ReplayTV box (as long as it's connected to the Internet) and view what recordings are there, delete them, and also schedule new recordings.

That scheduling screen is shown in Figure 16.7. What is really handy about using a web browser for controlling recordings on your ReplayTV (or TiVo, which has a similar service for an extra fee) is that when you are at your PC and scheduling shows, if there are any conflicts with how many shows you can record on your PC at the same time, you can jump to your ReplayTV and schedule recordings on that device.

As nice as the remote scheduling features of TiVo or ReplayTV are, it seems that they are attempting to become mini home entertainment networks that include music, pictures, and TV, but they aren't really computers—and there's a monthly subscription fee.

Each of these devices also requires a connection (dial up or Ethernet) to the Internet. The only purpose of this connection is to download program information and, in the case of TiVo, learn a bit about the programs you've chosen to record or watch. And they charge you at least $12.95 each month!

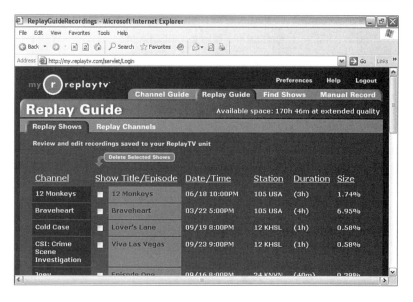

FIGURE 16.7

You can manage your recorded shows and schedule recordings from any web browser at a special website from ReplayTV.

Anything a TiVo or ReplayTV can do, you can do better and with more flexibility on a PC-powered home entertainment network. As DVRs, they are great, but until they can move files between devices and PCs and support media servers, they are dedicated entertainment devices that go against the true future of home entertainment, which is networking with all devices.

Wireless and Networked DVD Players

As mentioned in Chapter 15, "TV Sources: Cable, Satellite, Antennas, and DVDs," DVDs have lots of copy protection and rights issues that have been keeping them out of the home entertainment network mix. There are some advances to report at the time of writing this book.

Several leading DVD manufacturers are introducing what are termed "networked" and "wireless" DVD players.

Be aware that the DVD player is not sending DVD movies to other PCs or media extenders—at least not yet. These DVD players hook to your TV, and using the same principle as a media extender, use a wired or wireless network to pull media content—such as music, home video, or pictures from your server PC—and play it on a TV. They're media extenders!

These are pretty new devices, and at the time of writing, they do look promising as media extenders since they combine the benefit of a media extender with a DVD player. Not bad!

The prices are pretty good too. For around $200–250, they offer DVD playing and a media extender, which is in the same price range of a media extender and an inexpensive DVD player.

Since this is a new development and it might open up DVDs to the home entertainment network you are building, it is being mentioned here to alert you that there is hope for DVDs on the network. Keep your eye on new models and learn if they can work with your media extenders or PCs in terms of sending DVD movies to them.

If you have a standard DVD player, keep it connected to your TV. Since there are limits to sharing DVD content in a home entertainment network, if you want to watch DVDs, you will need your trusty DVD players connected to your TVs.

Summary

Many home entertainment devices can connect to the Internet, and even require an Internet connection to operate, but it doesn't always enable them to fully integrate into your home entertainment network.

Except for a new media extender expansion unit for Xbox, most games need to connect to a TV and have access to the Internet for online game playing, but they are not designed to be played through a home entertainment network—you must play them using the game console connected to a TV and play other game consoles, even in your own home, through the Internet.

Digital video recorders are great for recording TV shows and have even begun to be capable of accessing photos and music from your PC, acting as a media extender, but they are still standalone devices. When thinking about digital video recording, a PC on a home entertainment network will be a better investment in the long run.

Programming Your Own Media Network

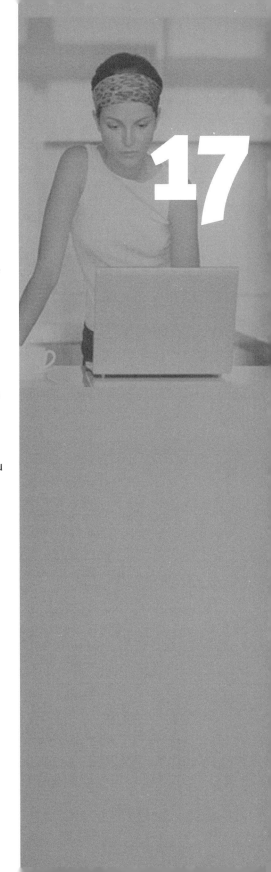

17

ow that you have used this book to think through all the devices you will be using in your home entertainment network and where to place them in your home, you have developed a true home entertainment network.

The whole purpose of your network is to bring multimedia to every room in your home. A home entertainment network truly enables you to put media content that used to be available on only one device or in one place in every place.

If you have made good use of media extenders, you should have a media client anywhere in your home where you have a TV or a stereo. Hooray for you!

With such a tremendous system in your home, after you get through the process of allowing each client to share the music, pictures, video, and TV shows from your server PC, you might want to stop and think about what you really have created: a media network.

That's what this chapter is about—how to take the technology of your home entertainment network, the amazing media content and media creation programs you have on your PCs, and begin to use it as a way of programming not only entertainment for your home, but also information, news, content, and messaging for your family.

Right now, you have many of the same tools that any major TV or radio broadcaster has:

- **A production studio:** Your main PC equipped with video and photo editing programs

- **A distribution network:** The wired or wireless network

- **Viewers:** All the people in your home using their TVs or PCs to view content from your network

- **Media Mogul:** You

Wow! And you thought you were just running wires, turning on file sharing, and running out to get those still hard-to-find media extenders. No, you were actually assembling a sophisticated media network in your home that is a micro version of any media network.

The following sections in this chapter are simple ideas of how you can create amazing, easy-to-produce, but very entertaining TV, text, and photographic content for the audience who lives in your home. Let's hope that your ratings are good, and they don't replace you with some upstart network programming whiz kid.

Planning Your Program Schedule

The first step in your media mogul career is the same step that the big-time media moguls worry about: the program schedule.

TV and radio programmers create 1-minute commercials and promotions and 30-minute, 1-hour, or 2-hour shows on a dedicated TV or radio channel for specific times of the day. The goal is to make your own content following those formats and, more than anything, create content that your audience will want to view.

Your possibilities are less about time slots and more about the way media extenders work: They display music, video, and pictures. The job for you is to create "network" spots and programs that take full advantage of that format. Here's how to think about the formats the media extenders dictate; then we'll take a look at how to create content for those formats.

- **Video:** You should start thinking that you can capture TV shows and add "clips" from them into your own shows, but mainly by using a Webcam or a digital camcorder (okay, an analog camcorder too), you can tape whatever you want, edit it together, and store it on the server as a file in the Video folder.

- **Music:** Think about it: A music file can be pure voice recordings. You can take a simple little microphone, hook it up to your PC, record messages, and save them as MP3 files. You can save those voice recordings in the Music folder.

- **Pictures:** Just as with the two preceding categories, who said picture files have to be pictures taken from a camera? If you create a text-based or graphic image in just about any photo editing or graphics program, you can save it as a JPEG file and it will show up like any snapshot JPEG in the Pictures file.

By changing the way you think about video, music, and pictures, you can use that ability to display each category with content you produce that doesn't look like video, music, or pictures. PCs and media extenders don't judge—they play media files. Let them play yours.

That's the larger concept. First, we'll take a look at how to create that type of original programming in each category. Then we'll take a look at how to organize it on your server PC so that it's easy to find, and finally we'll look at how to bring your own content together with TV shows, music, and other media you program for your own TV or radio network. Light up the big cigar, call for the Bentley, and stop taking calls from agents. Your career in network programming has begun.

Creating Your Own Video Programs

It's not expensive, or hard, to produce your own video programs. In fact, without spending any extra money, you already have the main tools you will need on your PC:

- A TV tuner card and a TV recording application
- Video capture application that came with your digital camcorder or Movie Maker 2.0 that comes with Windows XP to handle video capture and video editing

For a video capture device, if you don't have an analog or digital camcorder, for a very small amount of money (well under $100), you can purchase a Webcam that will do the job nicely.

Also great for creating short videos are digital cameras. If your digital camera has a "movie mode," it will create MPEG movies that will work great. That might be the best—and easiest—device to work with.

With all of those tools in hand, let's take a look at the process of creating a simple little newscast for your family to see each morning.

Producing the Video

The first thing you will need to do is write your script. You can "wing it," or improvise, but a short script or bullet list of items you want in your family newscast will help. If you want to do this every day, preparation makes it go a lot quicker.

Taping the Segment

After you have decided on what you want to say, take the following steps:

1. **Set up your camera:** Find a place to tape your news segment. Try the kitchen table or a desk in a home office. If you have a tripod, put your digital camera, camcorder, or Webcam on it. Tripods can be purchased for under $20 and are a good investment for this task.

2. **Get some help:** Your significant other, kids, or whoever is handy can get behind the camera, frame the shot, and press the start/stop button.

3. **Record your segment:** Keep it short and fun, and after you record it, review it on the camera or on your PC if you are using a Webcam. If you don't like it, do it again until you get it right. After a few days, you will become a pro and do these segments in one take.

Figure 17.1 shows a typical setup for a home news segment recording. It's just the kitchen table, a camera on a tripod, and you might notice a "green screen" in the background. That's for doing chromakey, where you can replace the "green" background with a video or picture just like weather people do on TV. Some programs allow you to do this; some don't. You might want to put up a simple background not for chromakeying, but just to make the background look nice.

FIGURE 17.1

A typical home TV studio is as simple as a table, chairs, and a camera on a tripod.

After producing your news segment, the next step is to get it on to your computer.

Transferring Files to the Movie Maker 2

For this example, we'll take a look at using Windows Movie Maker 2 to copy the video you created to your computer. You might want to create a file folder (anywhere on your hard drive) for working videos and put all the working files in one place.

Figure 17.2 shows the main screen of Movie Maker 2. On the left side, notice that there are options for capturing your movie from a camcorder or camera or importing a video. With your camcorder, digital camera, or Webcam connected, select this option.

As Windows Movie Maker 2 comes included with Windows XP Service Pack 2, let's take a look at how to capture a video from a digital camcorder, digital camera using the movie mode, or a Webcam.

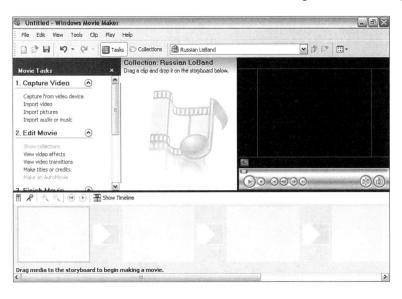

FIGURE 17.2

Using Windows Movie Maker 2, choose to capture video from your camera or camcorder.

- If you are using a digital camera with a movie mode, the MPEG file will be stored on the memory card of the camera. You can transfer the file directly from the camera, or the memory card to a file folder of your choice on your PC. In Movie Maker 2, choose Import Video from the menu choices on the Movie Tasks menu located on the left side of the screen, as shown in Figure 17.2. The video file will be added to your collection of video clips you can assemble and edit in Movie Maker 2.

- If you are using a Webcam or analog camcorder connected to your TV tuner card, use the Capture Video menu from the Movie Tasks menu, and select to capture the video from the live Webcam or analog camcorder. When you stop, it will be added as a file into your video collection for editing.

- If you are using a digital camcorder, choose Capture Video from the Movie Tasks menu. Be sure that your camcorder is connected to your PC using a FireWire/1394 cable and that the camcorder is on and in the record or play mode. MovieMaker will detect the digital camcorder, and you can either use the record mode to capture a live segment, or capture a recorded segment from the tape in your camcorder.

Using any of the preceding methods, you will be able to capture or create your own video segments. The segments can be introductions to TV shows or movies, or complete video segments—such as family news or highlights from a little league game.

After you have captured your video, it will be added to the list of files that you can use in the video collection area in the center of the Movie Maker 2 screen. Select the file and drag it on the timeline as shown in Figure 17.3.

If you have still pictures you would like to add, or even a music file, use the menu options on the left side of the screen to add them too. The menu options include importing pictures and adding music. This is simply a process of locating picture files (photos or even custom graphics you created and saved as JPEG files) and music files such as MP3 files or music captured from CDs. Figure 17.3 shows a mix of video, music, and video for a feature about a visit from a relative for a family news segment.

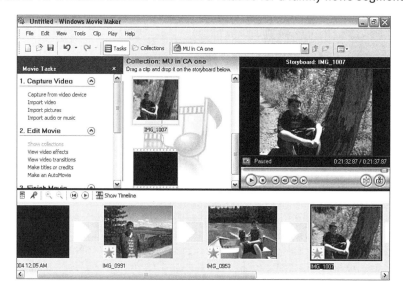

FIGURE 17.3

Drag video, pictures, and music files onto the Timeline in Movie Maker 2 so that you can start to edit them and add titles and effects.

Editing Your Video

With all of your captured videos and any other files you want to use, such as digital pictures and music, you can begin to use the timeline to put them in order, add transitions, and create the video you had in mind.

To create a simple movie in Movie Maker 2, you drag the video, music, or picture files one by one onto the timeline to create the order they will appear in your movie. You can view the movie being assembled either as a storyboard or as a timeline. The timeline view is the best when working with mixed media such as music and videos. You can switch to the timeline view from the View menu on the top of the screen, selecting Timeline if the current view is Storyboard.

By dragging files into the timeline, you will be assembling your video. You can preview it at any time in the movie preview window in the upper right corner of the screen by pressing Play. On the timeline, you can adjust the lengths of segments and make basic edits, even adding transitions and titles from the Edit Movie menu options in the Movie Tasks menu area of the screen.

You can also do a voice-over by hooking a microphone to the Mic port on your sound card. This process is shown in Figure 17.4. You connect your microphone, watch the movie, and add your narration in real time. The end result is a remarkably good TV newscast or TV show once you get good at it.

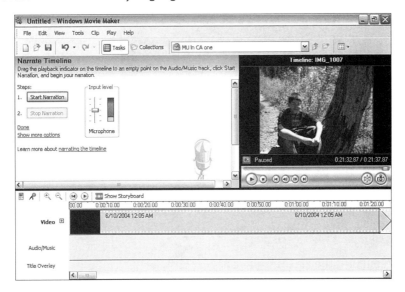

Figure 17.4

Once you have assembled all of your video content, if you want, you can add a voice-over narration and even background music.

Once you have your video segment produced, the finishing touch is a title slide to open and close the show. There are two ways you can do this. You can create a really nice title graphic in Photoshop Elements or any other graphics program, or you can simply use the title creation tools in Movie Maker 2, as shown in Figure 17.5.

As shown in Figure 17.5, Movie Maker 2 has a nice way of adding titles to a video. You can add titles

• At the beginning of the video

• Before a selected clip (such as a newscast in which you introduce the video of the visit from the relative, and the title is added at the beginning of the video clip)

FIGURE 17.5

The Titles menu in Movie Maker 2 does a great job of creating titles and placing them in the right location of your video.

- On the selected clip
- At the end of the selected clip
- As credits at the end of the movie

Those are pretty much the same title treatments you see on any TV show. As you get good at adding titles, you will find that your little video production will have a decidedly professional TV look and feel.

Save Your Video Production

Finally, with everything in place, and after you've reviewed the video and like it, you need to save it in a file format that will play on every device in your home entertainment network.

Figure 17.6 shows the Save Movie menu from Movie Maker 2. The menus will guide you through

- Where you want to save your movie (on your computer, on a CD or DVD, the Web, or other location).
- The actual directory where you will save the file.

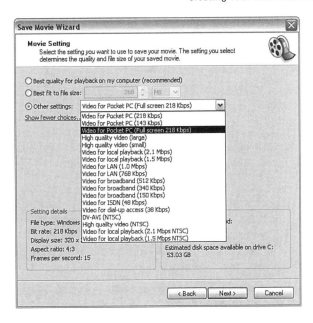

FIGURE 17.6

The final step in the process is finding the best video file format to save your video. Be sure to test and find the best quality file format that works on all of your network devices.

- The size or type of video file you want to save your movie as. You might want to experiment with a few of the various file formats and see which ones give you the best quality across your network. Remember, if you are using a wired network connection, your movie can be large. If you are using a wireless connection to media extenders, you will want to test some of the smaller file formats. A good starting point is to select the Save to My Computer option, identify where you want to save the file, and then from the different sizes and formats menu, choose the Video for LAN (1.0 Mbps) option.

Creating Your Own News Pages or Banners

Because your PCs and media extenders can all display picture files, such as JPEGs, this means that you can put together picture files and store them in a folder and place it in the Pictures folder that all of your network can access.

So, why limit your thinking of pictures to photographs? A picture is simply a file of any static visual image. This means that you can create JPEG files using a photo editing program depicting virtually any image. Some ideas for a home news page include creating JPEGs such as

- **Calendar pages:** Use rules and text or even calendar templates for printing calendars from popular programs such as Photoshop Elements and save them as a JPEG. You can play that calendar page on any PC or media extender, and it becomes your home activity calendar on the network.

- **Hot News pages:** Keep everyone up-to-date on family or work news with a simple page of text that you can produce in any photo editing program and save it as a JPEG file, as shown in Figure 17.7.

- **Phone Listing:** Who says that you can't put a phone list on your TV? Just as with Hot News pages, create a page of phone numbers in a photo editing program and save it as a JPEG file.

- **Fun Pages:** You can assemble all kinds of fun snippets with cartoons, kids drawings, awards, snapshots from some family event, or just about anything you want, and share it with everyone on the network. Use a photo editing program and mix pictures, scanned images, text, and other items you might have downloaded from websites and create your own theme pages.

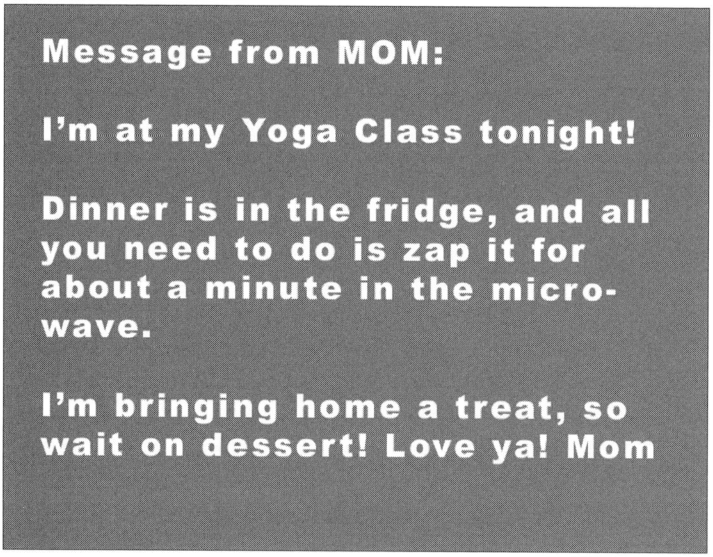

Message from MOM:

I'm at my Yoga Class tonight!

Dinner is in the fridge, and all you need to do is zap it for about a minute in the microwave.

I'm bringing home a treat, so wait on dessert! Love ya! Mom

FIGURE 17.7

Sample Hot News page from your picture-based news pages.

Those are just a few ideas for using picture-based JPEG pages to share all kinds of information throughout your home with everyone in it. The possibilities are endless. The nice thing is that you decide what news and items are important, not some media company!

To create the actual graphics, use any photo editing or graphics program that you are comfortable with. Windows XP Service Pack 2 comes with Windows Paint, which is very easy to use for this function. You can also use programs such as Adobe Photoshop Elements, which has lots of templates for creating text-based graphics such as calendars and picture books.

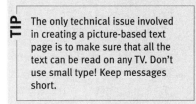

TIP

The only technical issue involved in creating a picture-based text page is to make sure that all the text can be read on any TV. Don't use small type! Keep messages short.

Here are some simple rules to use when creating graphics for display as news pages using the picture viewer of your media extender or PC connected to a TV:

1. Create your graphic at 640x480 pixels. This is the best size for working with TV screens. This size will completely fill your TV screen at the right quality, and is in the same 4:3 aspect ratio of TV.

2. Use soft colors, but keep contrast in mind. The main color to avoid for TV display is red. TVs have a hard time displaying pure red, and text tends to "bleed" when used on TV. Also avoid all white backgrounds. Blues work best on TVs, and black or white type is always a good choice.

3. When using type, go large—not small. Small type on TVs is very hard to read. A good rule is to have no more than four lines of type on a single screen, and only about 20 to 25 characters of type per line.

4. Avoid overly decorative type faces. Simple, block letters work best. Good choices for TV screens are Arial, Arial Narrow, or Times New Roman.

When you have created your collection of text-based JPEG pages, you will be able to store them in special folders inside your Pictures folder, which can be accessed by all PCs and media extenders on the home entertainment network.

Be sure to name the files in a way that make sense. For example, if the JPEG files are for a Monday morning message board slideshow, name them Monday 1, Noonday 2, and so on, so they will play in that order using the picture slideshow player on your PC or media extender.

Creating Audio Messages and Radio Stations

As you've seen, if you open your thinking to understand that files on computers are not limited to what you have always used them for (such as pictures for text messages), you can create all kinds of content.

When it comes to the Music Folder part of your home entertainment network menu, you can create all kinds of audio content. You can

- **Create Voice Messages:** Sometimes it's better to say something than to use text. If a relative is over and he wants to say hello to the family members he missed, or you just want to leave the equivalent of a voice mail, you can record a voice message, save it as an MP3 file, and put it in an audio message folder. Use Windows Recorder (from the Accessories menu) or Movie Maker 2 for this function.

- **Create a Radio Station:** If you have a bunch of favorite music that you want to share, you can either store the MP3 files in a folder or put shortcuts to them in the same folder. Label the folder "Dad's Mix" or "Hey, Check This Out!" and you've created your own mini-radio stations. While you're at it, why not add a voice file or two and become the DJ doing the intros to tracks! By numbering the files (put a number before the name of your voice track or each music track or shortcut), your files will play in that numerical order.

- **Create Playlists:** Because not all media extenders and even media players on PCs work the same regarding playlists, just as with the radio station ordering of music, you can create a folder of shortcuts to your favorite music and number the files so that your playlist will play in the same order regardless of what media extender or player you use on any device.

Working with playlists and existing MP3 files is simply a matter of "ordering" them in a folder. Recording your own voice narration or messages requires that you record your own audio files. You will need

- A simple PC microphone that connects to the "Mic" connection of your audio card.

- An audio program that can record from the Mic connection, or simply use the Sound Recorder application that comes with Windows XP Service Pack 2. This program is reached by going to the Start menu, selecting Programs, and then Accessories, the Entertainment. The Sound Recorder program is found in that folder.

Using your favorite audio program or Windows Sound Recorder, select Microphone as the audio source, click on the "record" button, and begin speaking into the microphone. At the end of the segment, click on the stop button. Press play to listen to your recording. If needed, repeat the recording and choose not to save the first recording. The file will be saved in the WAV format, which can be used by any media extender or most any media player program.

If you are using an audio program, you will also be able to edit audio clips together in the same way as you would a movie in Windows Movie Maker 2.

Organizing Your Media Network

By now, you can see that with a little creative thinking, and using the readily available programs that are already on your PC, you can indeed create a Media Network with all your own content.

The same rules apply to media content that you don't create. You can create folders in your Video folder of recorded TV shows such as "Kids Shows," "Action Programs," "Movies," or any other categories that you want. This really puts you in the position of programming your network with the content you want to see or the content you want your family to see.

After you begin to create your own content as described in this chapter, the next step is to simply create a folder strategy that helps everyone reach the content quickly and easily from any PC or media extender.

As shown in previous chapters, you will need to think of the "lowest common denominator," which will be the very simple user interface of media extenders. Figure 17.8 shows how a typical media extender divides content into video, music, and pictures (don't think of the radio button for your own radio station—that's for Internet radio connections).

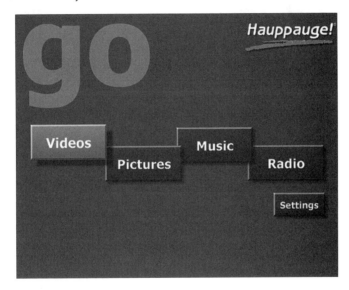

FIGURE 17.8

Start planning your home media network by thinking of how media extenders organize content: video, music, and pictures.

Begin storing the programs you create in easy-to-find folders, and then add the location of those folders to your media extenders' media server playlists. Each time you add a file to the folder, it will be made available to the media extender.

Put your custom "Morning News" show in a Family News folder, and use the same principle for any other custom produced shows. Also create folders that reside in the Video folder for TV shows, Kid Shows, or other folders of recorded TV shows.

At the end, you will turn on a TV connected to a media extender, choose video, and see the type of menu shown in Figure 17.9 listing all of your custom shows right along with recorded TV shows. This is the heart of your own TV network.

Next, do the exact same file organization process for picture files and audio files. It's simply a matter of organizing them and labeling them in an easy-to-understand and find format, and setting the media servers for the media extender to find them.

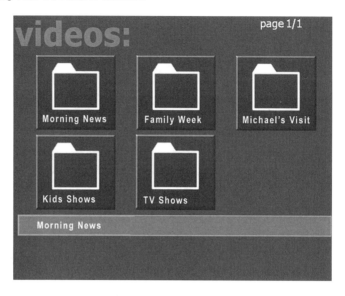

FIGURE 17.9

Organize your original content with recorded content such as recorded TV shows and put them all in the Video folder.

When you are done, you can keep updating, adding, or changing the files whenever you want.

This process is how you create a controlled media environment, and although you can simply use a home entertainment network to get at TV, music, and pictures from any room with a PC or media extender, this is what really makes all that effort of setting up the network fun and worthwhile.

Summary

By creating your own content for your home entertainment network, you expand the use of the investment to go beyond media access and present personalized media and content to your family.

The tools used to record TV and edit pictures and video are all available on your PC, so with a simple microphone, digital camera, camcorder, or Webcam, you can produce your own TV shows for distribution in your home.

You can also use the same tools to create news pages and text announcements, and even create your own radio station and audio messages.

When you organize your files into video, music, and picture folders, anyone using your home entertainment network will be able to access both commercial media content— and your own custom programming.

Resources

Building a digital home network is a complex activity involving a number of industry standards, protocols, and terms that you may encounter along the path of purchasing your networking equipment. The following resources will help you find additional products, content, and information to build your home entertainment network in the future.

Thoughts About the Digital Home

The following resources do a good job of making all of the highly complex industry-level terms—which is designed largely to get manufacturers to produce products that work with each other properly—easy for most people to understand.

Intel Digital Home website:

http://www.intel.com/personal/digital_home

Microsoft AT Home website:

http://www.microsoft.com/athome/default.mspx

Microsoft TV Shows about using media at home website:

http://www.microsoft.com/athome/tvshows/default.mspx

Thoughts About Wireless Networks and Network Security

Intel Go Wireless website:

http://www.intel.com/personal/wireless

Microsoft Network Security website:

http://www.microsoft.com/athome/security/default.mspx

TechSoup website:

http://www.techsoup.org/index.cfm

How Stuff Works website:

http://computer.howstuffworks.com/security-channel.htm

Practically Networked website:

http://www.practicallynetworked.com

Thoughts About Media-Centric PCs

Microsoft Windows XP Media Center Edition PC website:

http://www.microsoft.com/windowsxp/mediacenter/default.mspx

PC Magazine Opinion Page website:

http://www.pcmag.com/category2/0,1738,30,00.asp

Industry Standards for Wired and Wireless Networking

Intel website on Industry Standards Commitment:

http://www.intel.com/cd/ids/developer/asmo-na/eng/19335.htm

IEC: Wireless Standard website:

http://www.iec.org/online/tutorials/home_net/topic03.html

Wi-Fi website:

http://www.wi-fi.org/

Networking Hardware Resources

Although there are an incredible number of manufacturers of home networking hardware in the market, the following companies represent home networking equipment that is available at most retail outlets and online, and all conform to the latest industry standards described in this book.

Be sure to check the websites of the manufacturers you are interested in to make sure that the equipment you find from any retailer is the latest equipment being offered by the manufacturers.

Wired and Wireless Networking Hardware

Actiontec:

http://www.actiontec.com

Apple Computer:

http://www.apple.com/airportexpress

Belkin:

http://www.belkin.com/index.asp

D-Link:

http://www.dlink.com/

Linksys:

http://www.linksys.com/

Netgear:

http://www.netgear.com/

Media Extenders

Creative:

http://www.creative.com/

D-Link:

http://www.dlink.com/

Hauppauge:

http://www.hauppauge.com/

HP:

http://www.hp.com

Linksys:

http://www.linksys.com/

Pinnacle:

http://www.pinnaclesys.com/

Play@TV:

http://www.playattv.com/eng/

Sony:

http://www.sonystyle.com

Slim Devices:

http://www.slimdevices.com

Xbox Media Extender:

http://www.microsoft.com/windowsxp/mediacenter/evaluation/devices/
xboxextenderkit.mspx

> **NOTE**
> New media extenders are being released by more and more companies, and it is a new product category. Be sure to check for new entries by using any popular search engine before you make a purchase.

TV Tuner Cards

ATI:

http://www.ati.com/

nVidia:

http://www.nvidia.com/page/home

Plextor:

http://www.plextor.com/english/index.html

Hauppauge:

http://www.hauppauge.com/

Kworld:

http://www.kworld.com.tw/

Matrox:

http://www.matrox.com/video/home.cfm

MSI:

http://www.msicomputer.com/

Pinnacle:

http://www.pinnaclesys.com/

Networking Software

In addition to the security and networking utilities provided directly within Windows XP Service Pack 2, you might want to add additional network management utilities such as virus protection, file access management, and spyware programs.

The following is a list of some network software manufacturers that offer added networking resources.

Firewalls, AntiVirus, Spyware, and Spam Protection

The following companies all produce excellent firewall, antivirus, spyware, and spam protection products for home networks. Although hundreds of such products are on the market, start with these companies. If they do not have a product that meets your needs, a reference to a complete listing of companies appears at the bottom of the list.

Computer Associates:

http://www.ca.com/

McAfee:

http://www.mcafee.com/us/

PC-cillan:

http://www.trendmicro.com/en/products/us/personal.htm

Symantic:

http://www.symantec.com/product/

ZoneAlarm:

http://www.zonelabs.com/store/content/home.jsp

Freeware and Shareware:

And you will find a variety of freeware and shareware protection programs such as SpyBot Search & Destroy and AdAware at

http://www.download.com

For a comprehensive listing of most companies producing network security products, check the following:

Yahoo! listing of all firewall companies:

http://dir.yahoo.com/Business_and_Economy/Business_to_Business/Computers/
Security_and_Encryption/Software/Firewalls/

Network Entertainment Guide Software

Home entertainment networks are such a new category that not that much exists in the way of specific software for managing them. Most of the programs you will need will come with your media extender. The media extenders require that specific software and can't yet use other applications.

To help you find what programs are on TV, to schedule TV recordings, and to find content from the Internet that you can store as files on your PCs, the following products and websites are worth exploring.

Electronic Program Guides

Although your TV tuner card comes with an EPG (electronic program guide), it is not the only one that you have to use to schedule recordings. The following websites and products are great EPG products with very accurate TV listings.

TitanTV:

http://www.titantv.com/

TV Guide Online:

http://www.tvguide.com

Zap2it

http://www.zap2it.com

Of the above, TitanTV offers a feature that will allow you to schedule a recording using your TV tuner recording software directly from its EPG.

Each major TV network and most all local broadcasters have websites that list their TV schedule, and you should use those for even further details about a program or series you want to record or view.

Online Movie Rentals

You can rent movies from the following websites for download to your PC and unlimited viewing for a certain period of time.

CinemaNow:

http://www.cinemanow.com

Movielink:

http://www.movielink.com/

Online Music Sites

A large number of music stores exist online, but the following offer the ability to preview music and make direct purchases, and they have extremely large music libraries.

Apple iTunes:

http://www.apple.com/itunes

MusicMatch:

http://www.musicmatch.com

Napster:

http://www.napster.com

Real:

www.real.com

Internet Radio Station Portals

There are thousands of Internet radio stations. The following websites are "portals" that will help you find the stations you are looking for, and they are excellent for general music and radio information in addition to linking you to stations. Live365 has a TV-centric version of its site for Windows Media Center Edition users.

Apple iTunes:

www.apple.com

AOL Radio:

www.aol.com

Live365.com

http://www.live365.com/index.live

SHOUTcast:

http://www.shoutcast.com/index.phtml

INDEX

How can we make this index more useful? Email us at indexes@quepublishing.com

How can we make this index more useful? Email us at indexes@quepublishing.com

How can we make this index more useful? Email us at indexes@quepublishing.com

How can we make this index more useful? Email us at indexes@quepublishing.com

How can we make this index more useful? Email us at indexes@quepublishing.com

300

How can we make this index more useful? Email us at indexes@quepublishing.com

How can we make this index more useful? Email us at indexes@quepublishing.com

How can we make this index more useful? Email us at indexes@quepublishing.com

How can we make this index more useful? Email us at indexes@quepublishing.com

How can we make this index more useful? Email us at indexes@quepublishing.com

primary PC, locating (home entertainment network diagrams), 11

printers, portable device connections, 239-240

processors, PC networking requirements, 27

program schedules (media networks), planning, 274

Properties control panel (Windows), enabling drive sharing, 187

purchasing
music online, 218
RJ-45 CAT-5E Ethernet patch cables, 80

PVR (personal video recording) software, 32

Q - R

radio
Internet radio, 212-213
iTunes (Apple), 217
news/sports/weather media content, 222
SHOUTcast website, 216
websites, 293
TV/FM tuner cards, 32

radio stations, creating for media networks, 284

RAM, PC networking requirements, 27

RCA Lyra Audio/Video Jukebox portable media player, 231

RCA-type Audio In connectors (TV tuner cards), 140

RCA-type stereo-to-1/8" stereo mini-plug cable, 255

reading PC text on TV, 211

Real website, 292

receivers (satellite TV), 251. *See also* set top boxes

recording
DVR software, 32
PVR software, 32
TV shows
commercial skipping, 202
MPEG video file format, 201
multiple shows, recording, 204
nonlinear TV, 205
parental controls, 202, 206-207
pausing, 202
reasons for, 202
replaying, 202
scheduling, 32, 202-204
stopping, 202
time shifting, 202
watching shows while recording, 204-205
via TV tuner cards, 29
video segments (video production), 275-276

remote access attacks, 107

remote controls
cable/PC connections, 256-257
satellite/PC connections, 256-257
set top boxes, 252

remote sharing, firewall security, 97-100

remotes, TV tuner cards, 31

renaming computers via workgroups, 178

replaying TV recordings, 202

ReplayTV DVR (digital video recorders)
MyReplayTV website, 270
network connections, 269-271

resolution (TVs), 210

RJ-45 CAT-5E Ethernet patch cables, 79
length limitations, 81
purchasing, 80

RJ-45 wall jacks, 80

routers, 12, 52
broadband, 118-119
client/server networks, role in, 53
configuring, 86
firewalls, 106-107
changing settings, 109
configuring, 97-99
functions of, 100
functions of, 71, 81
installing
choosing Ethernet cables, 79-81
identifying PC Ethernet connections, 72
locating PC Ethernet ports, 72
NIC driver installation, 78-79
NIC installation, 73-77
PC requirements, 72
via installation wizard, 82-83
via web-based installation controls, 83-84
Internet connection, 87
dial-up connections, 89
dynamic connection settings, 88
PPPoE connection settings, 88
static connection settings, 88

How can we make this index more useful? Email us at indexes@quepublishing.com

How can we make this index more useful? Email us at indexes@quepublishing.com

How can we make this index more useful? Email us at indexes@quepublishing.com

U - V

How can we make this index more useful? Email us at indexes@quepublishing.com

How can we make this index more useful? Email us at indexes@quepublishing.com

How can we make this index more useful? Email us at indexes@quepublishing.com

How can we make this index more useful? Email us at indexes@quepublishing.com

X - Y - Z

How can we make this index more useful? Email us at indexes@quepublishing.com

More Great Titles from Que Publishing

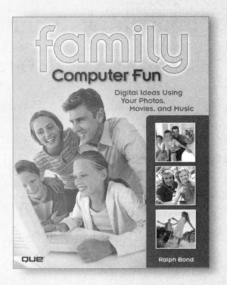

Family Computer Fun: Digital Ideas Using Your Photos, Music, and Movies

Ralph Bond

0-7897-3378-1

$24.99 USA / $34.99 CAN / £17.99 Net UK

Coming Summer 2005!

You Also Might Like

Absolute Beginner's Guide to WI-FI Wireless Networking

Harold Davis

0-7897-3115-0

$18.95 USA / $26.95 CAN / £13.99 Net UK

Absolute Beginner's Guide to Home Automation

Mark Soper

0-7897-3207-6

$21.99 USA / $29.99 CAN / £15.99 Net UK

Bad Pics Fixed Quick: How to Fix Lousy Digital Pictures

Michael Miller

0-7897-3209-2

$24.99 USA / $34.99 CAN / £17.99 Net UK